TODAY'S LIGHT™

FAQs
FREQUENTLY ASKED QUESTIONS

TODAY'S LIGHT™

FAQs

FREQUENTLY ASKED QUESTIONS

General Editors
Jane Fryar
James Galvin

Project Editor
Jonathan Farrar

SAINT LOUIS

Produced for Concordia by The Livingstone Corporation. Jonathan Farrar, project manager. James C. Galvin, editor. Greg Asimakoupoulos, Jeanette Dall, Cindy Kenney, Linda Joiner, writers. Paige Haley, Alan Sharrer, Rosalie Krusemark, project staff.
Interior design by Design Corps.
Cover design by Paetzold Design.
Scripture, unless otherwise indicated, is taken from the HOLY BIBLE, NEW INTERNATIONAL VERSION ®. NIV.® Copyright © 1973, 1978, 1984 by International Bible Society. Used by permission of Zondervan Publishing House. All rights reserved.

The "NIV" and "New International Version" trademarks are registered in the United States Patent and Trademark Office by International Bible Society. Use of either trademark requires the permission of International Bible Society.

Manufactured in the United States of America

ISBN 0-570-00534-5

Printed in the United States of America.
All rights reserved.
1 2 3 4 5 6 7 8 9   09 08 07 06 05 04 03 02 01 00 99

TABLE OF CONTENTS

WELCOME TO TODAY'S LIGHT FAQs

There is something exciting about reading through the Bible—especially when we're reading through the Bible with our church or our families. As you work your way through the Bible, you begin to see God's plan of salvation unfold—how He planned from the beginning to freely grant salvation to those who believe in His Son.

The Bible is God's Word—His truth in written form. It's exciting to spend time getting to know what God has in mind for His people. Yet, portions of Scripture can be difficult to understand. There are references to ancient customs of the Mideast. There are allusions that make more sense to ancient Israelites than to a believer in the twentieth century. That is why *Today's Light Frequently Asked Questions* was written. This book identifies the questions most people ask when they read through the Bible . . . and this book gives you succinct answers.

If you're leading a group—such as a Sunday school class, a small group, or even simply your family—this book is a valuable, timesaving resource for you. In it, you will find those questions that people ask the most and a short, straightforward answer. Some of the these questions and answers can serve as a springboard for thought-provoking discussions as well.

Those of us at Concordia Publishing House who have worked on the *Today's Light Bible and Today's Light Frequently Asked Questions* are praying that this book will help you learn what God's Word has to say and help you pass on God's truths to others.

Concordia Publishing House

YEAR ONE

DATE STARTED:

WEEK 1 • MONDAY
Genesis 1:1—2:25

What does it mean to be created in God's image?

God's creation of human beings was qualitatively different from His creation of the animals. God created man in His own image (Genesis 1). Clearly this does not mean that Adam and Eve looked like God; God is a spirit. Rather, Adam and Eve reflected God's nature. They were holy—sinless. They had the capacity to enjoy a loving relationship with God and with each other. They were creative, and they exercised stewardship over nature. Adam and Eve shattered all this when they fell into sin. Jesus came to make restoration possible. All who believe in Him will enjoy unblemished holiness, love, and creativity in heaven. Even now, our unique place in both the creation and redemption gives us a great sense of purpose and worth and a burning desire to reflect God's goodness.

WEEK 1 • TUESDAY
Genesis 3:1–24

How was Satan able to tempt Eve?

Satan tempted Eve by taking the form of one of God's creatures—the serpent. Satan asked Eve a seemingly harmless question that, nevertheless, made God appear arbitrary and oppressive: "Did God really say, 'You must not eat from any tree in the garden'?" (Genesis 3:1). Of course, this was a gross misstatement of what God had actually said in Genesis 2:17. He had said they could eat the fruit of any tree—except one. Next, Satan introduced the element of doubt. Eve had no reason to believe that God would mislead her, but she proved vulnerable to the lie that she knew better than God did what would be good for her. When she acted on this lie, she ceased to serve God and instead subjugated herself to the Deceiver. Still today Satan tries to deceive us by planting doubt and by appealing to our desires to be like God, to control our own destiny. Thank God for Jesus who obeyed and trusted the heavenly Father perfectly in our place! In His cross we have forgiveness and the power to trust and to obey.

WEEK 1 • WEDNESDAY   *Genesis 4:1—6:8*

How was Cain able to find a wife?

Up to this point in the biblical account, only four people are mentioned by name: Adam, Eve, Cain, and Abel. But Cain's wife is first mentioned in Genesis 4:17. Neither she nor her family origins are named. However, Genesis records that Adam and Eve had many children after their expulsion from the Garden. Cain's wife was probably one of his sisters or nieces. The human gene pool was just beginning; God saw to it that marrying a close relative was not yet a genetic risk.

WEEK 1 • THURSDAY   *Genesis 6:9—8:22*

How could there be enough water to cover the whole earth?

When God first created, He separated the waters of the sky and the waters below. Then, on the third day, He called back the waters to let dry ground appear (Genesis 1:9–10). So there is certainly enough water to cover all the earth. Even today, a large amount of water is stored in the ice caps at the North and South poles. In the account of the Flood, we read that God opened the deep springs and caused it to rain so that the dry land was covered over once again—just as it had been covered in the beginning (Genesis 7:18–20). All human and animal life was destroyed with the exception of those who took refuge with Noah in the ark.

WEEK 1 • FRIDAY   *Genesis 9:1—10:32*

Why was Ham punished so severely for telling his brothers about his father?

When someone makes a fool of himself, as Noah did by becoming drunk, true love for the person causes us to grieve, not to mock. Noah sinned by indulging to excess, but Ham's loveless words demonstrated a lack of respect for his father and for God (Genesis 9:22). Ham's brothers, on the other hand, sought to preserve their father's dignity. Jesus would later advise that we do the same to others as we would have them do to us (Matthew 7:12). Noah's curse against Ham was actually a prediction that

Ham's descendants would become increasingly wicked until they were finally driven from the land of Canaan by the Israelites. The fulfillment of this prediction is recorded in the book of Joshua.

WEEK 1 • SATURDAY   *Genesis 11:1—12:9*

Why did God confuse the languages of the world?

Sometimes a combination of two or more people with perverse ideas can multiply the evil that results. Obviously the people at Babel had the desire—first manifested in Adam and Eve—to exalt themselves rather than to obey God. The people who settled in the plain in Shinar sought to make a monument to their own greatness. They wanted to stay together as a people (Genesis 11:4). This goal stood in direct conflict with God's command to Noah to fill the earth (Genesis 9:1). God perceived their ambitions and saw the limitless wickedness and grief that would result (Genesis 11:6). In grace, God introduced various new languages so they could not carry out their plans (Genesis 11:7–8).

WEEK 2 • MONDAY
Genesis 12:10—13:18

Being a man of faith, why did Abram not tell the truth?

Abram, like all believers, was inconsistent when it came to trusting God. In simple terms, he was afraid. Having entered the land of Egypt as a refugee from the famine in Canaan, he could imagine a horrifying scenario: The Egyptians become impressed with Sarai's beauty and, then, try to kill him in order to take her into Pharaoh's harem. Instead of relying on God's supernatural protection, Abram devised a sinful plan. He used a half-truth (Sarai really was his half-sister as well as his wife) to insure that he would be given privileged treatment instead of being killed (Genesis 12:11–13). But despite Abram's faithlessness, God intervened on Sarai's behalf. He inflicted the Egyptians with diseases until they discovered the truth and released her and Abram. The Lord was faithful to His covenant promises even when His people proved unfaithful. What grace!

WEEK 2 • TUESDAY
Genesis 14:1—15:21

Who was Melchizedek?

Little is known about Melchizedek except that he was a priest-king of the city of Salem, later known as Jerusalem, and he was a "priest of God Most High" (Genesis 14:18). His name means "king of righteousness." By offering a tenth of all his spoils to this true priest, Abram acknowledged that the victory he had just experienced was God's alone. Melchizedek's priesthood is significant in the history of faith. The writer of the book of Hebrews sees Melchizedek as a picture, or type, of Christ in that He was a priest by divine appointment—not by birth into the lineage of Aaron.

WEEK 2 • WEDNESDAY
Genesis 16:1—17:27

What did circumcision represent?

Circumcision was an irreversible, physical sign of belonging to God. While many cultures in the ancient Mideast practiced it, from Abraham on, it came to signify membership in the community of God's people. In Genesis 17:10–11 God Himself established it as a sign of His covenant with Abraham and all his descendants. The act of circumcision itself was connected to the Word of God's promise and all the great benefits of adoption by the heavenly Father.

WEEK 2 • THURSDAY *Genesis 18:1—19:38*

Why did God allow Abraham to bargain with Him?

Our God is a God of relationship. In the discussion over the city of Sodom, God revealed Himself to Abraham as a God of both justice and mercy. In Genesis 18:17, God asked the rhetorical question, "Shall I hide from Abraham what I am about to do?" He concluded that the unique relationship He had initiated with Abraham was reason enough to discuss with Abraham the judgment He would rain down on Sodom. So with each question, "What if there are fifty righteous people in the city?" (Genesis 18:24)—then, forty-five, forty, thirty, twenty, and finally, ten— God showed Abraham that He did not delight in destroying the wicked. He confirmed for Abraham His patient and forbearing nature. Abraham's God—and ours—is both merciful and just.

WEEK 2 • FRIDAY *Genesis 20:1—21:34*

Why did Abraham lie about his wife again?

Apparently, fear of the powerful was a recurring problem for Abraham (Genesis 12:11–13). Just as he had done in Egypt, Abraham sought to save his own skin by lying, and asking Sarah to lie, about their true relationship (Genesis 20:2). Because both claimed to be brother and sister, Abimelech felt free to take Sarah into his harem. When he learned the truth, he appealed to the God of Abraham not to judge him harshly. He knew he had taken another man's wife. But he had done so in ignorance (Genesis 20:5). Once again, God intervened and returned Sarah to Abraham untouched. All this proves that the people of the Bible are flesh and blood characters, very much like us. Fear so enslaved Abraham that he failed to learn from God's first miraculous intervention. He repeated the same willful sins. Yet once again, God showed His mercy to Abraham—and to all whom would come to faith in the Savior descended from Abraham, our Lord Jesus.

WEEK 2 • SATURDAY   *Genesis 22:1–24*

Why was Abraham willing to sacrifice his son?

By God's grace Abraham had grown in knowing, understanding, and trusting the God who had made a covenant with him. Child sacrifice was a common, albeit abhorrent, practice of the pagan nations in the area. But apparently Abraham had learned from his previous interactions with the Lord that this command to sacrifice Isaac was not what it seemed to be on the surface. Abraham proceeded to follow the Lord's instructions to the letter, yet he fully expected God to intervene (see Genesis 22:3–8 and Hebrews 11:17–19). God did, indeed, intervene before Isaac could be killed.

WEEK 3 • MONDAY
Genesis 23:1—24:67

Why did Abraham's servant put his hand under his master's thigh?

The act of placing one's hand under the thigh of another was evidently an ancient custom for solemnizing a covenant between two people (see Genesis 24:2). In this case, it symbolized the close relationship and trust that would be required for Abraham to swear his servant to a task of great importance—finding a wife for his son Isaac among his relatives rather than the pagan Canaanites who lived nearby.

WEEK 3 • TUESDAY
Genesis 25:1—26:35

What was so important about Esau trading away his birthright?

The birthright, given to the eldest son in the ancient world, entitled Esau to certain privileges and responsibilities—including a greater share of the inheritance and the leadership of the family in the next generation. Esau showed disrespect for all the responsibilities and privileges he would inherit when he verbally deeded the birthright to Jacob in exchange for a bowl of stew (Genesis 25:32)!

WEEK 3 • WEDNESDAY
Genesis 27:1—28:22

Why couldn't Isaac have blessed both of his children?

Isaac's deathbed blessing bestowed on Jacob the privileges of the birthright and with it, the covenant promise of the Savior's family line (see Genesis 27:27–29, 34–35). In the culture of that day the blessing was a binding, legal action taken only once and never revoked. Jacob and Rebekah succeeded in tricking the blind and feeble Isaac into conferring the blessing on Jacob. Isaac could not take it back or bestow a second blessing on Esau after the fact. Isaac's words to his son Esau were the natural consequence of the exalted status Isaac had already conferred on Jacob—Esau would serve his brother (Genesis 27:36–40).

WEEK 3 • THURSDAY
Genesis 29:1—30:43

Why did Laban give Jacob the wrong daughter in marriage?

Laban proved to be a tricky, self-serving person—not unlike Jacob himself in this stage of Jacob's life. In the matter of the marriage of his daughters, however, Laban probably felt a responsibility to see that both of them were provided for in the future by having them marry well. It was apparently the custom of his tribe that the eldest daughter should marry first. Laban was also concerned that Leah, perhaps not as physically beautiful as her sister, would be left unmarried unless he took action. Rather than being straightforward about his intentions, he substituted Leah for Rachel on the wedding night when Jacob had drunk more than enough wine (Genesis 29:23, 25). When Jacob discovered the trick, Laban quickly offered excuses and placated his new son-in-law by allowing him to marry Rachel as well (Genesis 29:26–27). Yet, he shrewdly exacted the price of another seven years of service from Jacob.

WEEK 3 • FRIDAY
Genesis 31:1—33:20

Why did God change Jacob's name to Israel?

God sometimes changed the names of people as a way of showing the change that had taken place in their lives. Jacob had wrestled all night with the Angel of the Lord (see Genesis 32:24). Though the Angel dislocated his hip, Jacob did not give up and would not let the angel go without blessing him. Jacob's name means "He Grasps the Heel" because he was born holding on to his older brother's heel. Figuratively, this name could mean schemer or deceiver—a character trait Jacob lived out in relation to his brother Esau. God changed Jacob's name to Israel, meaning "He Wrestles with God and Prevails." This "Angel" was, in fact, God Himself. This new name showed what God was working in Jacob. By grace, Jacob was learning to live by faith rather than by advancing himself by his own schemes. God's people in future generations came to be known as Israel, named after this patriarch.

WEEK 3 • SATURDAY
Genesis 34:1—35:29

Why did Jacob's household own idols?

The problem of other gods beset God's people from the beginning (see Joshua 24:2). Clearly, Jacob's household harbored idols (Genesis 35:2). Rachel stole the household gods from her father, Laban, when Jacob packed up his family to leave (Genesis 31:19). It is likely that when Jacob's sons waged war against the Shechemites to avenge the taking of their sister Dinah, they took some statues as part of the booty (Genesis 34). In a sense, these gods were something Abraham's descendants accumulated along the way without giving thought to how these false gods afflicted their relationship with their covenant Lord. In Exodus 35:2–4 Jacob prepared to return to Bethel—the place where God had confirmed His covenant to Jacob in a dream. Jacob began to realize his responsibility as the spiritual head of his household. The Lord was the one and only true God. Jacob wanted his family to worship God alone, so he left the household idols behind in Shechem.

WEEK 4 • MONDAY
Genesis 36:1—37:36

Why were Joseph's brothers upset with him?

Joseph's brothers had plenty of reasons to hate him (Genesis 37:4). First of all, Jacob favored Joseph over the other eleven sons. Joseph was the first son of Rachel, the wife whom Jacob treasured most. Jacob had waited a long time for Rachel to bear children. When she finally did, her sons Joseph and Benjamin were born to Jacob in his old age. Moreover, Rachel had died giving birth to Benjamin. Jacob singled out Joseph—Rachel's eldest son—for honor by giving him a richly ornamented robe. Then on top of that, Joseph aggravated his half-brothers by bringing a negative report to Jacob about the elder brothers' stewardship of the flocks. Finally, Joseph added insult to injury by reporting two dreams, both of which predicted that the eleven brothers would bow down to Joseph sometime in the future (Genesis 37:2–11). Although the animosity of Joseph's brothers towards Joseph was founded on real grievances, their actions taken in anger were sinful.

WEEK 4 • TUESDAY
Genesis 38:1—39:23

Why did Tamar expect Judah to give her a husband?

In ancient Israel if a man died without leaving heirs, one of his brothers would marry his widow in order to give him offspring and keep his name alive for future generations. This custom protected women in a culture without social services and in which few women could support themselves. When Tamar's husband Er died, Judah gave her to his next son, Onan. But Onan did not want to fulfill his brotherly responsibilities, so God struck him down, leaving Tamar still not pregnant. Evidently, the third brother Shelah, was too young to marry at that point, so Judah sent Tamar back to her parents—perhaps hoping that everyone would forget about Shelah's duty to Tamar. When it became apparent to Tamar that Shelah had come of age, but still hadn't married her, she realized that Judah intended to circumvent his responsibility as head of the family to care for her (Genesis 38:11, 14). So she devised a trick. She posed as a prostitute to Judah and became pregnant with a son. When Judah realized what Tamar had done, even he himself admitted the justice of her case against him (Genesis 38:26).

WEEK 4 • WEDNESDAY
Genesis 40:1–23

How was Joseph able to interpret dreams?

In the case of his fellow prisoners in the Egyptian jail (Genesis 40:8) and later with Pharaoh himself (Genesis 41:16), Joseph clearly acknowledged that the interpretation of dreams was from God alone. He was simply the agent God used to reveal His plan. God had spoken to Joseph in dreams when he was a young man, but Joseph unwisely explained his dreams to his brothers (see Genesis 37). His words fueled their jealousy and contempt for him, and they sarcastically called him "the dreamer." But now Joseph seeks God for enlightenment and gives Him all the glory. Because of God's divine working, Joseph could do what no other wise man or magician in the kingdom could do: give accurate interpretations that later came to pass.

WEEK 4 • THURSDAY
Genesis 41:1–40

Why was Pharaoh so upset about a dream?

Egyptians believed that dreams were often prophecies or predictions of the future. So when Pharaoh dreamed of seven ugly, gaunt cows eating up seven sleek, fat ones, he expected the worst. Another dream compounded his distress that same night. It had similar subject matter—seven healthy grains swallowed by seven scorched ones! Finally, when none of his magicians or wise men could tell him what these dreams meant, Pharaoh became distraught (Genesis 41:8). Only then did the forgetful cupbearer remember Joseph, the man in prison who had correctly interpreted the dream that foretold his imminent freedom. By the power of God, Joseph provided both the interpretation of Pharaoh's troubling dreams and the wise counsel about how to prepare Egypt for the coming famine. In compassion God provided a very practical program that would save the Egyptians, and His own covenant people, from sure starvation.

WEEK 4 • FRIDAY
Genesis 41:41–57

Why was Joseph put in charge of Egypt?

Joseph was a virtual nobody in Egypt, coming directly into Pharaoh's presence from prison after being cleaned up to meet the standards of the royal court. Yet Joseph spoke with great authority, telling Pharaoh that God would give the interpretation of the dreams. He explained that both dreams signaled seven years of plenty to be followed by seven years of famine. This was a straightforward interpretation, yet none of Pharaoh's magicians or wise men had been able to decipher it. Without eyes of faith they were not able to see clearly. Joseph, still speaking under God's direction and with His wisdom, proposed a logical plan for preparing for the coming disaster. Joseph's plan made sense to Pharaoh and all his officials. Joseph's God-given ability to interpret dreams plainly and to suggest such a wise course of action impressed Pharaoh. He put Joseph in charge of the program that ultimately saved Pharaoh's people, and he made Joseph second in command (Genesis 41:37–40). Even pagan rulers who did not acknowledge the one, true God were used by God in His plan to rescue and save.

WEEK 4 • SATURDAY
Genesis 42:1—44:34

Why didn't Joseph tell his brothers who he was?

When 10 of Joseph's brothers came to buy grain in Egypt, they did not recognize him (Genesis 42:8). He had adopted the Egyptian manner of dress and speech, plus he was a ruler of great importance, second only to Pharaoh. They never expected to see again the brother they had despised and sold into slavery. This put Joseph in control of the situation. Initially, he took an antagonistic stance towards them—asking them about their family and pretending to suspect them as spies. In the process, Joseph learned that his father and youngest brother, Benjamin, were still alive. He also overheard conversations among the brothers that revealed their feelings of guilt for what they had done to Joseph (Genesis 42:13–23). Finally, withholding his identity gave the brothers opportunities to face the horror of their sin and to allow time for true repentance and change of heart. As this drama unfolded, Joseph was able to forgive his brothers as he himself had known forgiveness in his relationship with the Lord.

WEEK 5 • MONDAY
Genesis 45:1—46:34

Why did Joseph make Jacob move instead of sending him money and provisions?

Joseph truly wanted to see his elderly father before he died. Given Joseph's responsibilities in Egypt, it was unlikely he could visit his father. He also must have sensed that Jacob had given him up for dead. His father would not believe Joseph was truly alive unless he saw his son with his own eyes. Joseph could use the resources at his disposal to provide for his extended family (Genesis 45:9–11). Because his family kept flocks and herds, the region of Goshen in the Nile delta could provide adequate grazing land even during time of famine, which would continue for five more years. God provided for Jacob and his family as surely as He had provided for Jacob's father, Isaac, and his father, Abraham. The promise God had made to make Abraham a great nation would be fulfilled.

WEEK 5 • TUESDAY
Genesis 47:1—48:22

Why did the Egyptians not like shepherds?

Though we don't know why, the Egyptians had a particular prejudice against shepherds. It may have been a reaction to the shepherds' nomadic way of life and their close contact with animals. Shepherds wandered the countryside—living off the land—while the Egyptians had established a civilization on the fertile banks of the Nile River. Yet Pharaoh recognized their expertise and authorized Joseph to put some of his family in charge of his own livestock (Genesis 47:6). The Egyptian's prejudice made it possible for God's covenant people, now in a new land, to continue to live a familiar lifestyle and to maintain their unique identity as children of promise. Here we see the Lord using even the sins of the wicked to accomplish His plan to send a Savior through Abraham's descendants!

WEEK 5 • WEDNESDAY
Genesis 49:1—50:26

Why did Joseph want to be buried in Canaan?

Joseph had a strong sense of identity as a descendant of Abraham, Isaac, and Jacob. Despite the Egyptian language and customs he had adopted, the wives he had married there, and the power and prestige he had achieved in Egypt, his heart was in his homeland—the land God had promised to his ancestors. By asking his relatives to carry his bones back to Canaan when God would direct them there, he showed great faith that their stay in Egypt was only a temporary detour from the plan God had for His people (Genesis 50:25). Surely God would not waver from His promises. Joseph relied in confidence on those promises. When God led the Israelites out of Egypt more than 400 years later, Moses took Joseph's bones with him (Exodus 13:19).

WEEK 5 • THURSDAY
Exodus 1:1–22

Why did the Egyptians want to kill Hebrew infant boys?

Egyptian Pharaohs had long forgotten the legacy of Joseph. They watched with increasing alarm as the population of Israelites grew dramatically within Egyptian territory in the land of Goshen. God told Abraham that his descendants would be as countless as the stars and the sand, and this was coming to pass. The Egyptians turned to the Israelites as a logical source of slave labor and treated them ruthlessly. The Egyptians knew the Hebrews were surely unhappy with their lot as slaves and, as their numbers grew, rebellion became more and more probable. Furthermore, God had obviously blessed them in spite of their lower status with the greatest gift any ancient people could imagine—numerous children. By killing the male babies, the Egyptians could reduce the number of fighting men among the Hebrews, while still maintaining their source of slave labor (Exodus 1:20–22). But the Hebrew midwives feared God and defied Pharaoh's orders. In turn they received kindness from God.

WEEK 5 • FRIDAY
Exodus 2:1–25

Why did Pharaoh's daughter need someone to nurse Moses?

The only way to preserve an infant who had been separated from his mother was to find a wet nurse, a lactating woman who would nurse the child until he could eat solid food. Moses' mother hoped that the Egyptian princess would take pity on the tiny baby found in the papyrus basket along the Nile. Moses' sister Miriam stood by to watch. She then rushed forward and volunteered to find a nurse, whom Miriam did not identify as Moses' own birth mother. This deliverance pointed to an even more dramatic deliverance from fear and slavery which God would bring about through His servant Moses.

WEEK 5 • SATURDAY
Exodus 3:1—4:31

What is significant about God calling Himself "I am"?

When God spoke this name for Himself as the answer to Moses' question, He revealed the essence of His character. He used a play on words—probably because human language is ultimately insufficient to describe Him. The Hebrew is transliterated as *Yahweh*, a name that later came to be regarded as so sacred the Jews would not speak it. Though often translated in English as simply "Lord," the title actually connotes the One who always is (Exodus 3:14). The verb has a present active sense. God's being is wrapped up in Himself, and He needs nothing outside of Himself. He is forever living and active. Later God's own Son used this name to describe Himself and His oneness with the Father, a claim so bold that people sought to stone Him (John 8:58–59).

WEEK 6 • MONDAY
Exodus 5:1—6:30

What hardship did gathering straw create for the Israelite slaves?

For years the lot of the Israelite labor force in Egypt was to make the bricks used in major construction projects. Straw was mixed with clay to strengthen the bricks and make them more suitable for use in large structures. After Moses made his first request that Pharaoh allow the people to take a three-day journey into the wilderness to worship God (a directive from God Himself), Pharaoh increased their workload so that they would not listen to "lies" told by Moses and Aaron. He harshly required the Israelites to gather their own straw, rather than having it supplied by the Egyptian overseers, with no reduction in their daily quota. This made their tasks even harder. As Pharaoh and his slave masters hoped, the Israelites complained bitterly to Moses (Exodus 5:21).

WEEK 6 • TUESDAY
Exodus 7:1–25

What does it mean that God hardened Pharaoh's heart?

In Exodus 7:3–4, God gave Moses a preview of how He would free Israel from slavery in Egypt. God commanded Moses and Aaron to go to Pharaoh and ask him, in the name of the Lord, to let His people go. At the same time, He forewarned them that He would harden Pharaoh's heart so that His signs, wonders, and judgments would be multiplied in Egypt. As Moses offered signs and God brought plagues, Pharaoh demonstrated a hardened heart. In some instances, Scripture reports that Pharaoh himself hardened his heart. Later on the hardening appears to be God's activity. Certainly God knew Pharaoh's selfish and vindictive character, but He did not in advance condemn Pharaoh. Rather, God patiently worked through Moses' word and the plagues to bring Pharaoh to true faith and obedience. But Pharaoh would not listen. Finally, in love for His covenant people of every age, God confirmed Pharaoh's evil choice and used his stubbornness to deliver His people. It's worth noting that some Egyptians did believe and escape with Israel. (See Exodus 12:38.)

WEEK 6 • WEDNESDAY   *Exodus 8:1—9:35*

What was the significance of the plagues?

Each plague was a miraculous judgment of God on Pharaoh and idolatrous Egypt. Black magic and occult practices abounded, and the early plagues—turning the river to blood and causing frogs to overrun the land—were answered by the court magicians with similar feats. Soon, however, God was performing wonders that exceeded the magicians' powers. In addition, the plagues started and stopped at God's command and left the Israelites untouched. Eventually, the magicians advised Pharaoh to give in (Exodus 8:19). But Pharaoh himself held out against God, initially relenting only to revert to his stubborn defiance after each plague was lifted. Finally, God demonstrated His superiority over many of the specific idols the Egyptians worshiped—the gods of the Nile, light and darkness, the heavens, and so on. As the plagues progressed, the people of Egypt came to fear the Lord. Finally, God demonstrated His power over Pharaoh himself, who was also considered a god by the Egyptians. He took the life of Pharaoh's firstborn. In an astonishing demonstration of His power over life and death, God rendered Pharaoh helpless. Pharaoh couldn't even protect his own son. Once despised and enslaved, Israel finally left enriched, showered with gifts from their former masters. In all of this, God powerfully demonstrated His superiority over all other gods.

WEEK 6 • THURSDAY   *Exodus 10:1–29*

Why did the Lord harden Pharaoh's heart?

In Exodus 10:1–2, the Bible states that God hardened Pharaoh's heart so that He might perform His signs and wonders among the Egyptians. These numerous signs undoubtedly impressed the people of Egypt and caused some of them to fear the true God. Furthermore, if Pharaoh had relented right away, the people of Israel would not have seen the magnitude of God's intervention on their behalf or the depth of His love. By performing these signs, God wanted His own people to know that He was the Lord, the God of their fathers and the great I AM. Indeed, God's mighty deeds, by which He freed His people from slavery, are rehearsed by the Jewish people even to this day in the Passover, a festival fulfilled in Christ.

WEEK 6 • FRIDAY

Exodus 11:1—12:51

What was the significance of the blood on the doorposts?

God gave detailed instructions to the people of Israel. At a specific time on a specific day they were to mark their doorposts with the blood of a newly sacrificed lamb or kid goat. God was about to send the most horrible of all the plagues on the Egyptians. The angel of death would kill the firstborn son in each household. But the Lord would pass over those homes on which the blood of the unblemished lamb was found. The lambs slaughtered that night are a picture, or type, of the perfect Passover Lamb of God, Jesus Christ, whose blood likewise covers and cleanses us from sin. Death and destruction pass over all who are marked by the blood of this perfect Sacrifice, foreshadowed already here and fulfilled on Calvary.

WEEK 6 • SATURDAY

Exodus 13:1–22

Why were only the firstborn children consecrated to God?

The firstborn children of the Israelites were the ones spared by the angel of death when God struck down the firstborn of all the Egyptian households (Exodus 12:29–30). To consecrate means to set apart for a holy purpose. In future generations, animal sacrifices were made to consecrate the firstborn, signifying that they rightfully belonged to God. This was to be an integral part of remembering God's deliverance of His people from Egypt—one of the foundational events in His relationship with them. Those who had experienced God's saving act were to recount it to their children and their children's children. God ultimately sacrificed His firstborn, only Son for the sins of the world.

WEEK 7 • MONDAY   *Exodus 14:1–31*

What was the significance of crossing the Red Sea?

After Pharaoh let the people of Israel go, he regretted the loss of slave labor and set out with his armies to pursue them (Exodus 14:5–7). The Egyptians caught up to the Israelites between the mountains and the Red Sea. The Israelites had not left Egypt as a mighty fighting force—they had come with their families, possessions, and livestock. By all appearances, they were doomed against the powerful enemy. Only God's miraculous intervention could save them. He divided the waters and dried up the sea so they could cross on dry ground. Then God closed the waters over the pursuing chariots and horsemen, drowning them in a dramatic display of His saving love and awesome power. As a result, the people feared the Lord and put their trust in Him and in Moses as His spokesperson (Exodus 14:31). The crossing of the Red Sea, one dramatic act of deliverance, foreshadows how God would later deliver His people, through Christ, out of sin and into new life. And this "baptism" also stands as a reminder of our own baptismal "exodus" from sin's power into life and salvation in Christ. (See 1 Corinthians 10:1–2.)

WEEK 7 • TUESDAY   *Exodus 15:1–27*

Why does Moses call Miriam a prophetess?

Miriam was a prophetess because she received revelations from God (see also Numbers 12). Along with her brothers, Moses and Aaron, Miriam was a leader of God's people (see Micah 6:4). A prophet, or a prophetess, proclaimed the words and deeds of God. Miriam did this in a beautiful song of celebration and victory, leading the women as they played tambourines, sang, and danced. Some of Scripture's most important teachings were recorded in psalms and spiritual songs (Colossians 3:16–17).

WEEK 7 • WEDNESDAY
Exodus 16:1—17:16

Why did some people collect extra manna when they were told not to?

As they traveled through the desert, the people complained and grumbled about their food. Some even wished to return to Egypt, where they had all the food they wanted. God once again made miraculous provision for them by raining down manna from heaven. This waferlike bread appeared each morning with the dew and melted away after the people gathered what they needed. God told them to gather just enough for one day, except what was to be saved each Friday for the Sabbath. Some of the people did not trust God fully, and they hoarded manna. It rotted (Exodus 16:20).

WEEK 7 • THURSDAY
Exodus 18:1–27

Why were judges needed?

Jethro, Moses' father-in-law, observed how his son-in-law was spending almost all of his time seeking God's will and then judging disputes between individuals. The people waited from "morning till evening," while Moses himself was becoming exhausted. Jethro proposed a wise solution: Moses should choose a sufficient number of capable and honest men. He was to teach them God's decrees, and then let them judge the simpler cases. This freed Moses to concentrate on the more complicated matters and on his calling as God's spokesman to the people (Exodus 18:17–23).

WEEK 7 • FRIDAY
Exodus 19:1—20:26

Why wasn't anyone else allowed on Mount Sinai?

God took seriously His revelation of Himself. Thus, God told Moses that He would come down to Mount Sinai and speak to him while the people heard Him. God wanted the people to continue to trust Moses as His appointed spokesman (Exodus 19:5–8). When the day came, God descended with fire and smoke, an earthquake, and the loud sound of a trumpet. Through Moses God had warned the people not to come too close to the mountain. If anyone did go "up the mountain or touch the foot of it," that person would be killed. Only because God had called him could Moses "go up the mountain" without harm. Moses was to serve not only as a spokesman but also as a mediator, just as Jesus, the Second Moses, serves as our Mediator before God.

.

WEEK 7 • SATURDAY   *Exodus 21:1—22:31*

Why were the Hebrews allowed to buy and sell slaves?

In civil law given by God through Moses, slavery was permitted. Even though it violated the Lord's perfect will, He allowed it while placing strict boundaries around the slaveowners' behavior. Israel had spent years in slavery to the Egyptians, but now the people under specific circumstances could purchase a fellow Hebrew. This slavery (really a kind of indentured servitude) helped provide economic security. A person in debt could sell his services for a period of six years in order to pay off the debt. In the seventh year, he was to be set free (Exodus 21:2); no Israelite was to be a perpetual slave. Secondary wives or concubines in a household were technically viewed as servants. The laws governing slavery protected them from an owner's abuse of power. For instance, an owner could never sell a woman to a foreigner because of the abuse she might suffer under foreigners. Also, if the owner didn't fulfill his obligations to provide for her, she could leave her master and go free (Exodus 21:8–11). Down through the ages, slavery would point to the bondage to sin and death that shackles all of humanity. The seventh year, in which freedom was given, would also point to the freedom from sin and death that Christ has won for us with His death and resurrection. (See Matt. 19:1–9 for a similar example; see also Gal. 5:14.)

WEEK 8 • MONDAY

Exodus 23:1—24:18

Why did Moses sprinkle blood on the people?

Blood was integral in the making of a covenant. According to Leviticus (17:11), the life of any creature is in the blood. Sprinkling sacrificial blood on an object indicated that God had made that object clean and holy. The blood on the altar pointed to God's forgiveness and His acceptance of the offering. The blood sprinkled on the people indicated that they were holy, forgiven, and set apart as God's covenant people. This covenant remained in effect until the day Jesus instituted the Lord's Supper. There He said, "This is My blood of the covenant, which is poured out for many for the forgiveness of sins" (Matthew 26:28). As Pontius Pilate washed his hands of innocent blood, the people responded that Jesus' blood should be on them and their children. They actually spoke more than they knew. While they meant that they would assume responsibility for Jesus' death, God's intent was that Jesus' blood poured out in His death on the cross would cover them and all humanity with His forgiveness.

WEEK 8 • TUESDAY

Exodus 25:1—27:21

Why did God want the Israelites to make a tabernacle?

In commanding the people to construct the tabernacle, God was establishing a dwelling place for Himself among His people (Exodus 25:8). God gave the Israelites a very detailed design, including materials and furnishings, for His sanctuary or dwelling place. The people gave the best of their earthly treasures to thank God, who had brought them out of slavery. The tabernacle was a sign of God's presence with His people. Evangelist John referred back to the tabernacle when he wrote: "The Word became flesh and made His dwelling among us" (John 1:14). The Greek verb for "dwell" can be translated "pitched His tent" or "tabernacled among us." Immanuel, "God with us," tabernacled among us to live, die, and rise from death for the forgiveness of our sins.

WEEK 8 • WEDNESDAY   *Exodus 28:1—29:46*

What is an ephod?

An ephod, made of richly dyed yarns and finely twisted linen, was a sleeveless garment worn by the priest while he served in the tabernacle. Two stones were set in gold filigree on the shoulders of the garment. Each stone was engraved with six names of the sons of Jacob, or the names of the tribes of Israel. These were called memorial stones. A priest wore the ephod when he entered God's presence, thus symbolically carrying God's people into His presence.

WEEK 8 • THURSDAY   *Exodus 30:1—31:18*

What was the purpose of the Sabbath?

The Sabbath, the seventh day of each week, was observed as a day of rest. It was a gift from God. The Sabbath looked back to the beginning of the world as God rested after finishing His work of creation. The Sabbath would remind the Israelites that the Lord had made them holy, had set them apart to be His own (Exodus 31:13). The Sabbath belonged to the Lord as the Ten Commandments indicate. Jesus proclaimed that He is Lord of the Sabbath (Mark 2:28). He is the one who invites us into the Sabbath-rest He Himself has prepared by His own death and resurrection for the forgiveness of our sins (Hebrews 4). We rest in Him, confident that He has made us His own holy people. In Christ, we need no longer labor and struggle to be good enough to please God. Righteousness is God's gift to us.

WEEK 8 • FRIDAY   *Exodus 32:1–35*

Why did the Israelites make a golden calf?

God called Moses to come up Mount Sinai. A cloud covered the mountain and the glory of the Lord looked like a consuming fire. The people waited below at a safe distance. On the mountain God gave Moses the Law. While Moses was on the mountain for 40 days and nights, the people became restless. Instead of trusting the God who had delivered them, the Israelites demanded that Aaron make them gods they could see (Exodus

32:1). These gods would be similar to those of the Egyptians—made with human hands and easily manageable. Yet these gods would not deliver and help them as the Lord had. The human heart without Christ always wants to trust something it can see and manage. Such a god cannot help us. Only the God who made Himself known in Christ Jesus and His life, death, and resurrection can deliver us from sin and death.

WEEK 8 • SATURDAY   *Exodus 33:1–23*

Why wouldn't God show Moses His face?

God told Moses that no one could see His face and live. God did however er reveal Himself to Moses on Mt. Sinai. God Himself put Moses in a cleft of the rock and covered him with His hand while He passed by in all His glory. In doing this, God revealed His goodness and proclaimed His name, His covenant name—the LORD. Later in history God revealed Himself in His Son, Jesus Christ. John (1:14, 18) reminds us that we have seen God's glory in Jesus Christ, who came from the Father. On the Mount of Transfiguration (Luke 9:30–32) Moses, along with Elijah and three of Jesus' disciples, did briefly see God's glory revealed in Jesus. In a sense, we see God's glory in His Word and Sacrament. Through these, God will sustain us until that day when we shall see Him face-to-face.

WEEK 9 • MONDAY
Exodus 34:1–35

Why did Moses wear a veil?

After the incident with the golden calf, Moses went up Mount Sinai a second time—again for 40 days and nights. During this time God spoke with Moses and gave him a second set of tablets inscribed with the Ten Commandments. When Moses came down, his face shone with so much radiance that Aaron and the people were afraid to come near him. After Moses delivered God's message to the people, he then covered his face with a veil. He remained veiled until the next time he went into the Lord's presence. Moses continued to veil his face to hide the fact that his radiance was fading. In his second letter to the Corinthians (3:7–18), the apostle Paul said that the veil of Moses kept the people from seeing the temporary character of the Old Covenant. Only Christ was able to remove that veil and reveal the New Covenant of God's love.

WEEK 9 • TUESDAY
Exodus 35:1—36:38

Where did former slaves get so much jewelry?

When the Israelites finally left Egypt, God made the Egyptians favorably disposed toward them. God told His people to ask for gifts, and the Egyptians loaded them down with gold, silver, precious stones, and rich cloth (see Exodus 12:31–36). This was undoubtedly the source of the gifts offered by the people for the construction of the tabernacle (Exodus 35:4–9).

WEEK 9 • WEDNESDAY
Exodus 37:1—38:31

Why were poles needed for the ark and the table?

Because Israel was still a nomadic people—not yet settled in the land God had promised—the tabernacle and all of its furnishings were designed to be packed up and carried. The ark of the covenant, which had been made at Sinai by Bezalel according to the pattern given to Moses, was the sign of God's presence among His people. By carrying the ark on poles inserted through gold rings on each side, the Levites could carry it without actually touching it (Exodus 37:5, 13). Because the ark represented the presence of the Holy God among His people, anyone who touched it was immediately struck dead (see 2 Samuel 6:6–7). This was one way among many that the Lord taught His people the difference between the holy and the unholy, the holy and the sinful. This helped them—and us—understand the disastrous effects of sin and our need for the Savior.

WEEK 9 • THURSDAY   *Exodus 39:1—40:38*

Why did God show Himself as a pillar of fire and of a cloud?

Throughout, the Book of Exodus describes the pillar of fire and the pillar of cloud. God also used these two pillars as signs of His presence with His people as He led them out of Egypt (Exodus 13:21–22). Day or night, God was with them. God used the pillars of fire and cloud to protect the Israelites from the pursuing Egyptian armies. The last verses of Exodus describe how the cloud of the Lord's glory filled the tabernacle, again a sign of God's presence and protection.

WEEK 9 • FRIDAY   *Leviticus 1:1–17*

Why did the Israelites sacrifice animals to God?

A holy God cannot ignore sin nor let it go unpunished. In His mercy, God did accept the life and blood of an animal as a temporary substitute for the sinner, who was deserving of death. The sights, sounds, smells, and rituals of the sacrifice were vivid reminders that God's people would be reconciled to Him through a sacrifice. Yet the animal sacrifices were never finished; the priests repeated them year by year. But when Jesus Christ, the sinless Son of God, willingly gave up His life for sinners, that sacrifice ended the need for repeated animal sacrifices. God's holiness was satisfied by Christ's perfect sacrifice (see Romans 3:21–26; Hebrews 10:11–14).

WEEK 9 • SATURDAY   *Leviticus 2:1—3:17*

Why were there so many different types of offerings?

The Lord's salvation in Christ was so enormous, it took many offerings to picture it adequately. For instance, the burnt offering showed Christ's total dedication to God as our substitute. By laying his hands on the head of the animal, the sinner symbolically transferred his sins. This foreshadowed Jesus' death in our place. With the grain offerings, the people offered the first and best of their produce to God. Bread made from the grain was given to the priests. The fellowship or peace offerings culminated in a festival meal eaten in the presence of God, signifying that the broken relationship between God and humankind had been healed and peace with God restored. Other sacrifices carried other meanings, all related to Jesus' life and work.

WEEK 10 • MONDAY   *Leviticus 4:1—6:30*

Why did unintentional sins need forgiveness?

We have a saying, "Ignorance of the law is no excuse." In a similar way, to God, sin is sin. It falls short of His holiness and ruins our relationship with Him and with other people. The same damage and offense occurs whether the sin is committed knowingly or unintentionally. The guilt offerings were God's provision for restoring people to fellowship with Him as soon as they became aware of the transgression (Leviticus 4:13–14). These, of course, pointed to Jesus, the Lamb of God, who would be sacrificed to pay for all sin.

WEEK 10 • TUESDAY   *Leviticus 7:1—9:24*

Why couldn't the Israelites eat blood?

Blood, whether of an animal or a person, symbolized God's gift of life. In their sacrifices, the Israelites returned the blood to God by draining it off on the altar and not using any of it in their preparations to eat the meat. To eat blood would be to show disrespect for the life God had given (Leviticus 7:22–27).

WEEK 10 • WEDNESDAY   *Leviticus 10:1—11:47*

Why didn't God accept the fire offered by Nadab and Abihu?

Nadab and Abihu, Aaron's sons, offered unauthorized or unholy fire before the Lord. The text does not say exactly what made it unholy or unauthorized. It could be that they took upon themselves responsibilities and authority reserved for their father, Aaron. The instructions God gave Aaron immediately following the incident give us another clue (Leviticus 10:8–11). Perhaps Nadab and Abihu entered God's holy presence while intoxicated. In this state they may have disregarded God's specific directions about offering sacrifices. In any case, the severity of God's punishment made it clear that God was not to be mocked.

WEEK 10 • THURSDAY *Leviticus 12:1—15:33*

Why were new mothers of daughters unclean longer than mothers of sons?

The designation of a person as unclean was not the equivalent of calling that person dirty or sinful. Any bodily emission disqualified a person from entering the place of worship for a specified length of time. The birth of a child was regarded as a blessed event, attended with much celebration. Because of their bleeding after childbirth, however, women were barred from the sanctuary (Leviticus 12:1–5). We do not know for sure the exact reason for the difference between the birth of male and female children. One possibility: perhaps mothers of daughters were isolated twice as long as a symbol of the baby girl's future status as a bearer of children—one term of 33 days was served for the mother herself and the second for her baby daughter.

WEEK 10 • FRIDAY *Leviticus 16:1—17:16*

What did the scapegoat represent?

The scapegoat was a living sacrifice to atone for sin. First the priest was to lay both his hands on the goat's head and confess aloud all the sins of the people. Then the live goat was led off into the desert to perish, symbolically carrying the sins of the people far away from them also and from the Lord's sight (Leviticus 16:20–22). This yearly ritual was abolished when Christ offered Himself as the perfect sacrifice to forgive all sin and to remove all guilt.

WEEK 10 • SATURDAY *Leviticus 18:1—19:37*

Why did God give so many laws concerning sexual sins?

Israel's life in all its aspects was to reflect the holiness of God, who called and treated Israel as His bride. Sexual acts were a regular part of pagan worship in surrounding cultures, where ritual prostitution took place in the temples. God wanted those who worshiped Him to be significantly different. All of the acts proscribed in Leviticus 18:6–28 directly contradicted God's purpose when He created human beings and placed them in families (Genesis 2). Loving God and loving one's neighbor as oneself did not leave room for the violence and pain sexual sin caused as it defiled the individual and, by extension, the whole of God's people. Indeed, as God saw it, sexual sin defiled the land (Leviticus 18:27–28). God's laws concerning sexual relations were designed to help Israel live in God-pleasing family and community relationships as His called, chosen, and set apart people. (See also Leviticus 19.)

WEEK 11 • MONDAY
Leviticus 20:1—22:33

Why didn't God accept imperfect animals for sacrifices?

An offering of a defective animal was not acceptable to God for two reasons. First and foremost, it did not correspond to His own perfection (Leviticus 22:17–25). It was an offense to His holiness and could not foreshadow the perfect sacrifice of Christ, the spotless Lamb of God. Second, a blemished animal would not cost the owner as much as a healthy one. If the owner could offer an imperfect animal to God and sell the prize one, he would gain in a material way. But in doing so, the person showed a profound lack of respect for God—an unwillingness to give the first and the best to the Lord. (See 2 Samuel 24:24.)

WEEK 11 • TUESDAY
Leviticus 23:1—25:55

Why were blasphemers punished so harshly?

God established the law against blasphemy (see Exodus 22:28), but no penalty for the sin until a violation came before Moses (Leviticus 24:10–16). All Israel knew that God would not count the person guiltless who blasphemed His name (Exodus 20:7). To disrespect or revile the I AM who had revealed Himself to Moses, would surely have grave consequences. It did. God decreed that the blasphemer must be put to death. In an unusual addition, the community was to participate in his stoning. Those who heard his wicked use of the Lord's name were to first lay their hands on his head, attesting to the truth of their testimony, and showing that the blasphemer alone, not the nation, bore the guilt of this sin.

WEEK 11 • WEDNESDAY
Leviticus 26:1—27:34

What did it mean to redeem something dedicated to God?

God required the Israelites to dedicate certain things to Him, including their firstborn children and animals, the firstfruits of their crops, and so on. This showed that God held first place in their lives, that they owed Him everything they were and all they had. Some of the people went beyond this to voluntarily offer other persons, animals, houses, or land to God. Ever since the night of the first Passover, God had provided for a substitute in some of these cases, particularly in the case of sons, since God abhorred human sacrifice of the sorts practiced by the pagan peoples of Canaan. Leviticus 27:1–15 spells out acceptable values for redeeming persons and animals with money, usually by adding a fifth of its monetary value to the offering. Thus God's people fulfilled their vows by giving specific amounts of money to God rather than actually killing a person or animal.

WEEK 11 • THURSDAY   *Numbers 1:1—3:51*

Why did God want Moses to take a census?

The census that God instructed Moses to take had multiple uses. First, it showed the Israelites how many fighting men they had available for the conquest of Canaan. It served as a military roster. Second, it would be useful for future generations in tracing genealogy and in determining the amount of land each tribe would need once the land was conquered and parceled out (Joshua 13–21). Finally, the census demonstrated to the people of that day and to those who came later how richly God had blessed the family of Jacob during their 400-year stay in Egypt. They entered Egypt as an extended family of 70 people (Genesis 46:27) and left there as a huge nation blessed by an almighty God, just as He had promised (Genesis 12:3).

WEEK 11 • FRIDAY   *Numbers 4:1—6:27*

What did the Nazirite vow mean?

The Nazirite vow involved separation from the community and consecration to God's service for as short a time as 30 days or for an entire lifetime. The requirements of this vow, as set forth by God, were as follows: The person taking the vow was to abstain from all wine and any other food or drink that came from the grape. He was not to cut his hair for the duration of the vow. He was not to come into contact with a dead body (Numbers 6:1–21). By setting himself apart in this way and making these sacrifices of common pleasures and duties, the Nazirite demonstrated his desire to belong to God in a unique way. Some of the best-known Nazirites of the Bible were Samson, Samuel, and John the Baptizer.

WEEK 11 • SATURDAY *Numbers 7:1—8:26*

Why were the Levites set apart for God?

Along with the priestly descendants of Aaron, the Levites were chosen by God to serve in the tabernacle. Among other duties the Levites carried the Tent of Meeting and all of the other items used in worship when Israel packed up and moved from one place to another. It was a life of both honor and service. When Moses initially consecrated the Levites for this work, he presented them as a wave offering before the Lord (Numbers 8:13–14). In the same sense that the Hebrews gave the first and best of their crops and flocks to God, they gave an entire tribe (one out of 12) exclusively for His service. The Levites belonged to God in a way that no other tribe did, set apart in place of all the firstborn sons of Israel.

WEEK 12 • MONDAY   *Numbers 9:1—10:36*

Why did God require unleavened bread for celebrating the Passover?

The Passover was a memorial of God's great intervention in bringing His people out of slavery in Egypt (Numbers 9:4–5, 11). At the original Passover, they took their bread fresh from kneading, before it had time to rise, because they had to leave quickly when Pharaoh finally relented and told them to go. Yeast is also symbolic of sin as it grows and spreads throughout a person or community. Thus, unleavened bread not only reminded the people of God's deliverance from slavery in Egypt, but it also symbolized God's will that His people remain distinct and unpolluted, set apart by Him from the world around them.

WEEK 12 • TUESDAY   *Numbers 11:1—12:16*

Why did God punish Miriam so harshly?

Miriam and Aaron chafed at the way God had chosen to deal with them. They both criticized Moses for his choice of a wife and asserted their equal position as leaders in Israel. In fact, Miriam and Aaron did hear from God. But God had chosen Moses to lead the nation in a unique way. The insubordination of Miriam and Aaron showed a disregard and disrespect for the Lord's will. The account mentions Miriam first, perhaps because she started the rebellion (Numbers 12:1). This could account for her leprosy and exclusion from the community. Aaron repented of their sin, and Moses himself prayed for mercy for Miriam (Numbers 12:1–13). God heard the prayer of His servant Moses and showed mercy on Miriam and Aaron. He still delights in showing mercy to sinners in Jesus.

WEEK 12 • WEDNESDAY   *Numbers 13:1—15:41*

Who were the Nephilim?

Moses sent 12 leaders of the Israelites as spies into the land of Canaan to assess the situation. Ten of these men fixated on a group of people, the descendants of Anak, whom they compared to the Nephilim. The

Nephilim were legendary giants from the time preceding the flood (Genesis 6:3–4). That analogy struck fear in the hearts of the Hebrew people. Indeed, the descendants of Anak who lived in the land of Canaan were of exceptional stature and strength. But Joshua and Caleb, the other two spies, saw the potential dangers of the Promised Land through eyes of faith, their vision made clear by their trust in the all-powerful Lord who loved them. He would be faithful to His promises. The same Lord who had led them out of one land would surely lead them safely into another.

WEEK 12 • THURSDAY   *Numbers 16:1—18:32*

Why did Moses place the staffs before God?

God commanded Moses to place one staff from each of the 12 tribes before the Lord in the Tent of the Testimony. God would then use these to make known once more His choice of the tribe that would serve Him as priests. Earlier, three men and a large group of followers had rebelled against Moses and Aaron, contending that since all Israelites belonged to God, none were more special than any other in terms of serving Him and speaking for Him. However, God answered these people decisively and in severe judgment when He opened the earth to swallow them! Despite that lesson, the people complained again, and a plague began, killing 14,700 people. God stopped the plague when Aaron interceded on their behalf. After all this rebellion, God wanted to make His will perfectly clear so that the grumbling would end and the lives of His people preserved (Numbers 17:10). God caused Aaron's staff, representing the tribe of Levi, not only to sprout but also to produce almonds, a remarkable miracle. Even more remarkable is the Lord's patience and mercy in dealing with His people despite their on-going disobedience. This mercy comes to us, too, in Jesus.

WEEK 12 • FRIDAY   *Numbers 19:1—20:29*

How did Moses dishonor God?

The people of Israel complained once again about the lack of water in the desert. God had repeatedly met their needs in spite of their unbelief and grumbling. According to Numbers 20:6–8, Moses and Aaron brought the complaint before God. God instructed them to go out and speak to the rock, and it would gush forth water. Previously, Moses had been told to take the staff through which God had done so many mighty works and strike the rock. This time God's instructions were different. Moses was angry about the Israelites' continual lack of trust. Rather than doing what God said, Moses struck the rock in self-indulgent anger. God brought forth water anyway, but Moses and Aaron were not allowed to enter the Promised Land of Canaan.

WEEK 12 • SATURDAY   *Numbers 21:1–35*

How did looking at the bronze snake heal people?

The Israelites continued to complain about God's provision for them. Their blasphemy led God to send a plague of poisonous snakes among the people. Many people suffered and died from the bites of these snakes. The people realized their sin had brought this judgment on them, and they pleaded with Moses to pray for them. God answered by having Moses make a bronze serpent and place it high on a pole. Whoever had been bitten could look up at this snake and live. The snake itself possessed no magic healing powers. Rather, God mercifully provided a way of escape through His promise attached to the snake: Look and live! (Numbers 21:8–9). This rescue, one of pure grace, pointed to an even more significant rescue. God's own Son would be lifted up on the tree of the cross, and all who looked on Him in faith would be saved from eternal death (John 3:14–15).

WEEK 13 • MONDAY
Numbers 22:1—25:18

Why did God choose to use a donkey to speak to Balaam?

Balaam was a sorcerer and a pagan priest. He knew something of the God of Israel and, indeed, the Lord had spoken to him. The pagan kings had already chosen to listen to Balaam, and the Lord therefore used Balaam to communicate His will to them. Balaam remained his own man, however, obeying the Lord and delivering His messages only when it benefited him in some way. King Balak offered Balaam great rewards to curse Israel. Lest Balaam be further tempted to pursue his own agenda, the Lord revealed Himself in a way that evoked Balaam's respectful fear. By appearing first to Balaam's donkey and then having that donkey speak to Balaam, God humbled him. A simple donkey knew more about Israel's God and His ways than Balaam—a professional priest and sorcerer—knew (Numbers 22:21–35). The Lord opened both the donkey's mouth and pagan prophet's eyes—both miraculously!

WEEK 13 • TUESDAY
Numbers 26:1—27:23

Why were Zelophehad's daughters concerned about their inheritance?

Codified in the laws of Israel was the tradition that a family's oldest son inherited the property. If there was no male heir, a servant from the household could inherit whatever a man had accumulated. Zelophehad belonged to the generation of Israelites who had died in the desert. His five daughters were concerned that their family name not disappear. No doubt they also worried about their own economic security, since without land they would be without any means of support. The sisters went to Moses with their problem. God directed Moses to add to the law of inheritance, making it clear that, in the absence of sons, daughters could inherit property. When there were no sons or daughters, a dead man's property would go to his own brothers, next to his father's brothers, and finally to the nearest relative in his clan (Numbers 27:5–11). In this way, property would remain in the family. The laws of inheritance made it difficult or even impossible for any one individual or tribe to amass wealth in the form of property at the expense of other tribes or families. It helped to prevent poverty and thus the need for massive welfare programs in Israel.

WEEK 13 • WEDNESDAY *Numbers 28:1—30:16*

What was so important about breaking a vow?

God commanded certain sacrifices in ancient Israel. If someone wanted to show devotion to God beyond that, he or she might make a vow, promising to do something for God. Others might make a pledge to abstain from something for a certain period of time, again as an act of worship. To break such a vow lightly, because of inconvenience, lack of patience, or peer pressure, for instance, would convey that human words don't matter or, conversely, that God doesn't mind broken promises. The Lord faithfully keeps His Word. His people imitate Him in their own faithfulness. Jesus makes this point in Matthew 5:33–37. He obeyed this command of God in our place, thus giving us His own right standing with God and making it possible for us also to obey in His strength.

WEEK 13 • THURSDAY *Numbers 31:1–54*

Why did God want to punish the Midianites?

The Midianites had ancestral connections to Israel as descendants of Abraham and Keturah. Moses had taken refuge from Egypt in the land of Midian, where he married a Midianite woman. Despite this, the Midianites had been enemies of Israel for generations. The women of Midian had seduced some of the men of Israel into Baal worship as Balaam had suggested (Numbers 25:1–4; 31:16). Left to intermingle with their Israelite cousins, they would surely corrupt the nation with their paganism and thus disrupt the Lord's plan to send the Savior through the Seed of Abraham, Isaac, and Jacob. They had abandoned the worship of the Lord long before. Thus, He enabled the Israelites to defeat Midian in battle. He also required that all of the males and all of the females of child-bearing age be put to death (Numbers 31:1–17). Virgins were exempt from this judgment. This minimized the corrupting effect Midian's idol worship could have in Israel.

WEEK 13 • FRIDAY   *Numbers 32:1—34:29*

Why was Moses upset that two tribes wanted the land east of the Jordan River?

When the tribes of Reuben, Gad, and the half-tribe of Manasseh asked to be granted their inheritance east of the Jordan, Moses assumed that they were trying to escape the hardships and risks of battles on the other side of the Jordan. These battles were necessary before all of the tribes took ownership of the Promised Land. In this case, Moses had jumped to the wrong conclusion. These tribes, primarily shepherds, were attracted to the eastern lands because the area was suitable for raising livestock. They knew they had a duty to help their fellow Israelites and were willing to fulfill it. They proposed leaving their families and animals in the fortified cities east of the Jordan and crossing ahead of the rest of the people. They would take the lead in helping the other tribes conquer their land before returning to their own allotments (Numbers 32:16–19).

WEEK 13 • SATURDAY   *Numbers 35:1—36:13*

Why did God set up cities of refuge?

The ancient tradition of justice provided that a close relative could take revenge on anyone who killed a loved one. When the murder was intentional, God sanctioned this punishment. Yet God made provision for those times when someone was killed through the fault, but not the intention, of another person. In such a case, justice required that the accused be given a chance to defend himself before an impartial group of judges. If the killing was deemed an accident, that person could live in one of the cities God had set aside as cities of refuge. The person could live there and be legally protected from the relative who sought revenge. He had to stay within that city until the death of the current high priest, at which time there was a general amnesty. If he ventured out before that time, he gave up his protection (Numbers 35:9–28). These cities are a picture, or type, of Jesus who is our refuge from the wrath of God, which we have incurred by our sin.

WEEK 14 • MONDAY   *Deuteronomy 1:1–46*

Why were the Israelites so afraid to enter the Promised Land?

The Israelites had been wandering in the wilderness, but now the Lord intended to take them into the Promised Land. Moses reminded them of what had happened nearly 40 years earlier. The Israelites weren't willing to enter Canaan, and they rebelled against the Lord's command (Deuteronomy 1:26). Why were they so afraid? The spies sent into Canaan brought back reports of giants and imposing city walls. These "giants" were descendants of Anak, and may have been seven to nine feet tall! In addition, many of the land's fortified cities had walls as high as 30 feet. These reports so terrified the people that they became discouraged and fearful. The mighty, covenant-making Lord had led them out of slavery, fed them for four decades, guided them by cloud and by fire, and multiplied their numbers. While God had made promises and fulfilled them, His people had disobeyed. While God had shown mercy, His people had grumbled. But the Lord would fulfill His promise to take them into Canaan despite their history of doubt.

WEEK 14 • TUESDAY   *Deuteronomy 2:1–37*

Why were some nations completely destroyed by the Israelites and others left alone?

Before the Israelites could settle in the land that the Lord had promised them, He told them how to treat the various people-groups in the region. The Lord spared some nations, including Edom, Moab, and Ammon, because He had given these lands to these people as an inheritance, and He keeps His word—even to the heathen! The Lord commanded the Israelites to destroy some nations completely (e.g., the Amorites) for two reasons. First, God was using the Israelites as His tool to bring His judgment on people who, century after century, had rebelled against Him. Second, the Lord knew that if these pagan neighbors survived, they would tempt the Israelites to turn away from the true God. The Lord had promised Abraham, Isaac, and Jacob that the Savior would come from their descendants. Thus it was important that Israel retain its distinct identity as the people of the covenant so that the Lord could fulfill His promise to send the world's Savior.

WEEK 14 • WEDNESDAY   *Deuteronomy 3:1–29*

Why wouldn't the Lord allow Moses to enter the Promised Land?

Moses pleaded with the Lord that he be permitted to cross over the Jordan River to see the land of promise. But the Lord would not grant that request (Deuteronomy 3:25–26). Moses had disobeyed God's command at Meribah (Numbers 20:12). His actions had dishonored the Lord. As a consequence, Moses would not be allowed to enter Canaan with Israel. Nonetheless, the Lord did in grace allow Moses to see the Promised Land from the top of Mount Nebo. Then He took Moses to the true Land of Promise—the heavenly home. Moses was 120 years old when he died, but his physical strength and his eyesight were unaffected by his age (Deuteronomy 34:5–7).

WEEK 14 • THURSDAY   *Deuteronomy 4:1–49*

How can God be jealous?

In his farewell speech to the Israelites, Moses admonished the people to obey the Law of God. Moses especially warned them against worshiping any other gods, because the Lord is a consuming fire—a jealous God (Deuteronomy 4:24). We usually think of jealousy in negative terms, because human beings are usually jealous of what doesn't belong to us. But the Lord's jealousy is a righteous jealousy. The Lord is zealous to retain and protect what belongs to Him alone; in this case, He was jealous for His people. He had made Israel a nation, had protected and blessed them. He had initiated His covenant with Israel in His infinite love. He wanted them to live as His consecrated, obedient, joyful people. After all He had done, He surely had a right to claim them as His own! The Lord today continues to claim His people—the church. He has given His Son into death to make His relationship of love with us possible. How wonderful this relationship is! How much we need to rely on His grace so as not to forfeit it by rebellion or unbelief.

WEEK 14 • FRIDAY   *Deuteronomy 5:1–33*

Why was it important for Moses to review the Ten Commandments?

The Lord had given the Ten Commandments to the Israelites on Mount Sinai 40 years earlier, but now Moses called the people—a new generation—together to review the Law of God. (Deuteronomy takes its name from this reiteration, this "second law.") Knowing he was about to die, Moses wanted to encourage Israel to obey the Lord (Deuteronomy 5:1). God had given His Law to them, just as He had given it to their parents. The Lord's covenant belonged to them, too, as it had belonged to their parents before them. Moses' sermon reminded the people that the Lord had promised to shower blessings on those who obeyed the Law, but had also promised judgment on all who disobeyed. Since all of us fail to obey God's Law perfectly, we all fall under this judgment. But the good news is that in Christ we escape God's coming judgment. Jesus endured that judgment for us and in exchange has given us His very own righteousness. What grace!

WEEK 14 • SATURDAY   *Deuteronomy 6:1–25*

What does it mean to test God?

Moses warned the Israelites not to test the Lord as they had done at Massah (Deuteronomy 6:16), where the Israelites murmured and quarreled with Moses. They put the Lord to the test by complaining about what God had given them. Instead of trusting the Lord and believing His promises, they voiced doubts about whether He cared about them. God wanted all Israel to turn to Him to meet their every need. Instead, they complained. Thus we see that to "test" the Lord is an act of unbelief. In testing God, we place ourselves and our wisdom (mere creatures, though we are) above the Creator and His wisdom. What arrogance! Jesus quoted Deuteronomy 6:16 when Satan tempted Him: "Do not put the Lord your God to the test" (Matthew 4:7).

WEEK 15 • MONDAY   *Deuteronomy 7:1–26*

Why was it so dangerous for the Israelites to intermarry with the people of Canaan?

The Lord forbade Israel's intermarriage with the people of Canaan (Deuteronomy 7:3). Racial prejudice did not motivate this command. Rather, the Lord wanted to prevent the Israelites from drifting in their devotion to Him alone. Marriage to an unbelieving Canaanite would inevitably weaken an Israelite's commitment to the Lord. God had chosen these people to be His treasured possession. The Canaanite partner would, no doubt, import pagan ideals and possibly even pagan idols into the family. Thus, such intermarriage would lead, at best, to tolerance of false gods. The holy nation, the nation from whom the Savior would one day come, could ill afford such spiritual contamination.

WEEK 15 • TUESDAY   *Deuteronomy 8:1–20*

What was so bad about forgetting the Lord?

Moses told the Israelites to remember the many ways the Lord had met their every need on their journey from Egypt to Canaan. Then he admonished the people not to forget the Lord (Deuteronomy 8:11). Moses knew that the Lord would bless the Israelites in the land of Canaan. Moses also knew that in times of plenty, human beings easily forget the Giver of all good gifts. This temptation appeals to our sense of independence and self-importance. How easily we take credit for our own prosperity. Forgetting the Lord isn't a symptom of a bad memory. Rather, it provides evidence that one has turned to other gods, has displaced the true God with gods of one's own making. Again and again in Deuteronomy, Moses reminds his hearers to remember the Lord who, despite our sins, never forgets us.

WEEK 15 • WEDNESDAY   *Deuteronomy 9:1—10:22*

Why did the Israelites worship a golden calf?

The Canaanites worshiped Baal as a fertility god, a deity who determined the quality and quantity of their crops and livestock. As the Israelites worshiped the golden calf, they may well have been imitating some of the pagan customs of the people around them. The sins of Israel had angered the Lord many times during their wilderness wanderings; this time, the Lord threatened to destroy the nation and make a nation from the line of Moses. Moses prayed for the people, reminding the Lord of His covenant promises. God, in mercy, forgave. The bull-gods of many Canaanite cultures represented power and sex. (It's not so hard to think of a culture today whose members worships power or sex, is it?)

WEEK 15 • THURSDAY   *Deuteronomy 11:1—12:32*

Why were the Israelites restricted to worshiping God in only one place?

The Lord had told Israel how He wanted them to worship. Deuteronomy 12:5 specifies that they do so in the place He would choose. The Canaanites worshiped their nature gods wherever they *thought* (or guessed!) these gods resided. Usually, they worshiped these gods on high hills or under trees. God wanted to set His people apart in every aspect of their lives. In particular, He wanted their worship to focus on Him alone. He wanted them to avoid mixing their worship of Him with worship of Canaanite deities. A central place of worship would accent three truths:

• The fact that the Lord alone was the true God. The Canaanite "gods" were mere idols.

• The fact that the Lord had consecrated Israel as His own holy, unique people; He would not share their worship with anything or anyone else.

• The fact that God had given Israel political and spiritual unity; they gathered together with one another to worship Him.

The "central sanctuary" moved with the people during the time of Moses (the Tabernacle). It stood in Jerusalem at the time of Solomon and the kings who followed him (the Temple). Jesus Himself was the sign of God's presence among His people when He lived here on earth. Since His ascension into heaven, all believers are themselves "temples of God" (1 Corinthians 3:16–17), the sign of His presence as we live and work among those who don't know our Savior.

WEEK 15 • FRIDAY   *Deuteronomy 13:1–18*

Why would God test the Israelites with a false prophet?

After warning the Israelites against pagan worship, Moses discussed ways in which the temptation would likely come. He warned them about false prophets, who would perform miraculous signs or wonders and then invite the people to worship other gods. Moses explained that when that occurred, the Lord was testing them (Deuteronomy 13:1–3). The nation could prove its faithfulness to the Lord by rejecting such false prophets. In such a test, the Lord was giving the Israelites an opportunity to worship by demonstrating their unwavering commitment to the one, true God. He Himself would help them pass such a "test" as they relied on Him and on His Word. Just as iron is "tested" (strengthened) by heating and sudden cooling, so the people would grow stronger in their confident trust in the Lord as they rejected the false prophets Moses describes here.

WEEK 15 • SATURDAY   *Deuteronomy 14:1—15:23*

Why did God command the Israelites to tithe?

In returning to God 10 percent of their income each year (Deuteronomy 14:22), the Israelites had an opportunity to worship. By giving a tithe, the first and the best of their material blessings, they demonstrated their thankfulness for all His blessings. They also testified to their trust in His promises to provide for them. Finally, the tithe would function as a reminder that all they had came from the Lord and belonged to Him— even as the Israelites themselves did.

WEEK 16 • MONDAY
Deuteronomy 16:1—17:20

Why did the Lord specify the month of Abib for celebrating the Passover?

The Israelites observed several annual religious feasts, but the most important was Passover. The Passover was celebrated in the month of Abib (Deuteronomy 16:1), which corresponds to late March/early April, because that was the anniversary of the Lord's deliverance of His people. The Passover commemorated the night the Lord "passed over" the blood-marked houses of the Israelites, sparing the lives of His people's firstborn sons. In contrast, all the firstborn of the Egyptians died. In this dramatic demonstration of power, the Lord showed His determination to take His people out of the clay pits of Egypt in which they slaved. The unblemished lamb (or kid goat) sacrificed at Passover foreshadowed the one, final, perfect Sacrifice for all human sin—Jesus Christ.

WEEK 16 • TUESDAY
Deuteronomy 18:1—19:21

What were the "cities of refuge"?

Ancient custom allowed the close relatives of a murder victim to track down the killer and take revenge. Such "justice" was usually swift, but sometimes led to blood feuds in which many people died. It sometimes also resulted in the death of someone who had killed another person unintentionally—a killing that courts today might rule accidental or judge to be involuntary manslaughter. Moses gave explicit directions for setting aside three cities as cities of refuge (Deuteronomy 19:1–3). Bezer, Ramoth, and Golan (Deuteronomy 4:43) were centrally located and were accessible by roads. Any killer could flee to one of these cities to receive a fair trial. If he was found innocent, he could remain in that city to live and work under the watchful eyes of the Levites, safe from any "avenger of blood." When the Lord enlarged the Israelites' territory, three cities west of the Jordan River would be designated as additional cities of refuge. (See Joshua 20:7.)

WEEK 16 • WEDNESDAY   *Deuteronomy 20:1—21:23*

Why did Israel destroy the children in conquered cities along with everyone else?

God promised to protect the Israelites when they went to war and to give them victory. He also gave definite orders on how to deal with the people of captured cities—they were to be put to death. Nothing that breathed was to be left alive (Deuteronomy 20:16). God had waited patiently for the Canaanites to repent of their evil ways. They had not. Now He had determined to call a halt to their wickedness. The day of judgment had come, and the Lord appointed the Israelites to punish these wicked and rebellious people. Secondly, God knew that left to share the territory with Israel, the Canaanites would draw Israel into idolatry. We don't know exactly why the Lord included infants in His command to destroy these pagan cultures. But we do know that the Lord is just. His ways are always right, though far above our understanding at times. While His wrath can spill over from one generation to the next, He also shows abundant mercy to a "thousand generations" (Exodus 20:5–6) of those who love Him. In Jesus, He has provided a way for all human beings to escape the wrath of His coming, final judgment.

WEEK 16 • THURSDAY   *Deuteronomy 22:1—23:25*

Why were people who committed adultery condemned to death?

God gave the Israelites numerous laws about sexual matters because these sins had the power to disrupt families, destroy individual lives, and turn the hearts of God's people away from Him. So strong is God's love that some sexual sins were punishable by death (Deuteronomy 22:20–27). The Lord intended the marriage relationship to reflect Israel's relationship of love and loyalty to the Lord. Just as the Lord expected Israel to be faithful to Him, so He expected husbands and wives to be faithful to each other. Just as God had given marriage to His people as a gift, so also in His wisdom He gave laws to protect the sanctity of marriage. All this He did in a culture in which sexual purity was rare and sexual sins pervasive. Israel never lived up to God's ideal. Neither do we. Thus, our need for a Savior, the One who earned forgiveness for us and who makes it possible for us to confront and forgive those who sin against us in our most intimate relationships.

WEEK 16 • FRIDAY   *Deuteronomy 24:1–22*

Why did God's law allow a man to divorce his wife?

Even though divorce was widespread in the ancient Mid East, the Old Testament always regarded divorce as a tragedy. Deuteronomy 24:1 allowed a man who found something indecent about his wife to write a certificate of divorce and send her away. This law regulated and restricted an existing practice—one that the Lord did not condone. Jesus addressed a misunderstanding of this law in Matthew 19. The Pharisees asked Him why Moses had commanded that a man divorce his wife and send her away. Jesus corrected them, saying Moses permitted—not commanded—it because "your hearts were hard" (Matthew 19:7–8). God's plan for marriage was this: "No longer two, but one" (Matthew 19:6), a union meant to last a lifetime. In the Lord's eyes, divorce was permanent and final; once divorced, they could never remarry.

WEEK 16 • SATURDAY   *Deuteronomy 25:1—26:19*

Why was offering firstfruits important?

The Feast of the Firstfruits reminded Israel of all that the Lord had provided for them. When the Israelites had settled in the Promised Land, they were to take some of the firstfruits of all that they produced and give them to the Lord (Deuteronomy 26:1–4). The offering described here occurred only once and must not be confused with the annual offering of firstfruits. This firstfruits offering was to take place after Israel's first harvest in Canaan. It was a celebration of Israel's transition from being a nation of nomads to becoming an agricultural society. The people offered the first of their harvest to the Lord to thank Him for blessing them. In this way they both worshiped and testified to others about the Lord's provision.

WEEK 17 • MONDAY   *Deuteronomy 27:1–26*

Why couldn't the Israelites use tools to fashion an altar?

The Israelites were to set up an altar on Mount Ebal when they crossed the Jordan River into the Promised Land. This altar, made of uncut stones (Deuteronomy 27:5), would honor the Lord, Israel's deliverer. In this way, Israel would be reminded that nothing they did made their worship acceptable to the Lord. Only His grace invited them into His presence. Also, this law would discourage Israel from carving images on their altars, images that might eventually become idols, just as the golden calf had. Thus we can see that the Lord gave no arbitrary rules simply to see His people jump through hoops. Rather, each law came to Israel as a gift, designed to protect them from their own sinful desires and the selfish violence of other people.

WEEK 17 • TUESDAY   *Deuteronomy 28:1–68*

Why would God pronounce curses on anyone?

God told the Israelites that obedience to Him and His commands would bring abundant blessings on the nation. However, disobedience would draw down curses (Deuteronomy 28:15). This chapter then delivers, in rapid-fire progression, curse after curse that awaited those who persisted in disobedience. None of this misfortune would bring God delight. In fact, each curse had essentially one goal: to bring God's people to true repentance so that they would return to the Lord and worship Him alone. (This is the work of God's Law.) While the blessings and curses of Deuteronomy 28 belong to the covenant God made with Israel at Sinai (the "Old Covenant"), they remind us today of the serious penalty earned by those who disobey God's Law. That penalty is death, a penalty that rightly belonged to us! But in Jesus the blessing of God is now ours; in the cross, we are set free from the curse of the Law (Galatians 3:13–14). That's good news, that's the Gospel!

WEEK 17 • WEDNESDAY   *Deuteronomy 29:1–29*

What was the importance of God's covenant with Israel at Sinai?

The Lord delivered Israel from slavery in Egypt and, in grace, took them as His "bride." He promised to love and care for them, to hear their prayers and bless them. But this covenant was conditional. It required Israel to remain faithful to the Lord, to worship Him alone, to honor His name, and to live as His holy people. If the Israelites obeyed the laws connected to the Lord's covenant, the Lord promised to bless them abundantly. If they disobeyed, God warned them of coming judgment. Of course, ancient Israel could not keep up their end. They broke the covenant again and again—not because the covenant was flawed, but because they were. And so are we. Our sinful nature makes it impossible for human beings to keep God's law. That made a "new covenant" necessary. Our Lord Jesus instituted this new covenant and sealed it in the blood of His cross. (See Matthew 26:26–28.) In this new covenant, the Lord once again shows Himself to be a God of mercy and rescue, sending His Son, whose blood was shed to cover our sins and to grant life forever.

WEEK 17 • THURSDAY   *Deuteronomy 30:1–20*

What does it mean for God to circumcise a person's heart?

This circumcision was an inward gift. In this "circumcision" the Lord would graciously grant the nation a new will to obey Him in place of their former sinfulness. The people would learn to love and serve the Lord from within—a process described figuratively as circumcision of the heart. Hearts are still changed by God's Spirit. The love we have for God comes from God Himself.

WEEK 17 • FRIDAY   *Deuteronomy 31:1–30*

How did God prepare Joshua to lead Israel?

God Himself chose Joshua as Moses' successor. Joshua, son of Nun, had been Moses' assistant for many years. As one of the 12 spies first to enter Canaan, only he and Caleb believed that Israel could conquer the land.

His confidence rested not in Israel's might but in the Lord's promise to march with them and to grant victory. God gave Joshua strength and courage based on His promises to His people. Mentored by Moses, Joshua willingly assumed his new role. As he did so, God filled Joshua with the spirit of wisdom (Deuteronomy 34:9).

WEEK 17 • SATURDAY   *Deuteronomy 32:1–52*

Why did Moses write a song about what God had done for Israel?

Moses preached three farewell sermons to Israel. Then he recited an entire song (Deuteronomy 31:30). This song gave a brief history of Israel. It reminded the people of their nation's past failures to trust the Lord. Then it warned them to avoid repeating these sins. Finally, the song offered hope that was found only in trusting the Lord. Israel would sing Moses' song in their covenant-renewal ceremonies.

WEEK 18 • MONDAY   *Deuteronomy 33:1–29*

What is the significance of Moses blessing the people?

In ancient cultures, it was customary for a father to pronounce blessings on his sons before he died. (See Genesis 49, where Jacob blessed his sons.) Now Moses blesses the descendants of these sons—the nation Israel. For 40 years, Moses had led this nation, caring for them like a father. In his final words of blessing, Moses glorified the one, true God and reminded Israel once gain of their special status as His blessed and chosen people. Even after Moses' death, Israel's God would continue to lead, protect, and strengthen His people.

WEEK 18 • TUESDAY   *Deuteronomy 34:1–12*

Why didn't God allow the Israelites to know where Moses was buried?

From the top of Mount Nebo, the Lord in His kindness gave Moses a panoramic view of the Promised Land. Then Moses died, just as the Lord said. God Himself buried Moses in Moab, in the valley opposite Beth Peor. The grave may have been hidden to keep the Israelites from making it into a shrine.

WEEK 18 • WEDNESDAY   *Joshua 1:1–18*

Why did God command Joshua to meditate on the Law day and night?

As the new leader of God's people, Joshua shouldered heavy responsibilities. But he did not need to carry these himself. He could trust the Lord's promises to protect His people and to bring them into the Promised Land. The Lord encouraged Joshua to think continually about these promises. Moses had written them down in the five books we know as the Pentateuch (Genesis, Exodus, Leviticus, Numbers, Deuteronomy). By reading and meditating on this "Law"—the entirety of the written Scriptures at that time, Joshua would retain the strength and courage he would need for the tasks the Lord had given him. Our strength and our courage come from this same source, our gracious God who has revealed Himself in His Word and in His Son, our Savior.

WEEK 18 • THURSDAY   *Joshua 2:1—3:17*

Was it right for Rahab to lie?

Scripture does not condemn Rahab's lie in this account. The Bible doesn't try to hide the weaknesses of its subjects. God forbids lying (Proverbs 12:22; Ephesians 4:25). Yet, the New Testament writers applaud Rahab for her heroic faith in the God of Israel (see Hebrews 11:31; James 2:25). Rahab was counted righteous because of that faith. The worst that can be said is that Rahab chose between the lesser of two evils—betray the spies or mislead the soldiers of Jericho. The Lord kept Rahab and her family safe. Even more significantly, the Lord bestowed on Rahab the honor of being an ancestor of the Savior (Matthew 1:5).

WEEK 18 • FRIDAY   *Joshua 4:1—5:12*

Why did God want the Israelites to build a memorial at this site?

After God's people safely crossed the Jordan River, God asked them to build a memorial in His name (Joshua 4:2–3). One man from each of the 12 tribes carried a large stone from the middle of the Jordan River, which was still dry due to the Lord's miraculous intervention. Coming as they did from the river bed, these stones would have been extraordinarily smooth. The memorial Israel made from them would remind future generations of the Lord's power in stopping the flow of the Jordan River so that His people could cross safely into the Promised Land. Inspiring faith in the hearts of God's people, the memorial had another purpose too. All the Canaanite kings heard about the miracle at Jordon and they "no longer had the courage to face the Israelites" (Joshua 5:1).

WEEK 18 • SATURDAY   *Joshua 5:13—7:26*

Why did God want the Israelites to march around the city for seven days?

The "commander of the Lord's army" told Joshua to "march around the city once with all the armed men." Israel repeated this for six days. On the seventh day, they marched around the city seven times (Joshua 6:3–4).

This tactic did two things. First and foremost, the Lord wanted His people to understand that the power to defeat the enemy came from Him alone, not from their own strategy or military might. Second, the tactic gave Israel's army a chance to demonstrate their faith and obedience, even in the face of the enemy. The sevens in the account underscore the sacred significance of this event—seven priests, seven trumpets, seven days, seven encirclements on the seventh day. Surely the anticipation mounted as the Lord's people march in confidence, awaiting His victory over Jericho. As they march, the ark symbolizes the Lord's presence with them. On the other side of the city walls, the people of Jericho waited also, but in fear.

WEEK 19 • MONDAY   *Joshua 8:1—9:27*

Why did the Israelites keep their promise to the Gibeonites even though they had been deceived?

Without asking for the Lord's guidance, Israel's leaders swore an oath in the Lord's name that they would let the Gibeonites live. Three days later they found out the Gibeonites had tricked them; Gibeon stood within the territory the Lord had given Israel. Nevertheless, the Israelites kept the promise. The agreement, ratified by an oath in the name of the Lord was sacred. The Gibeonites' lies and trickery could not nullify it. God had commanded that the Israelites keep their oaths; later on, He Himself would honor the treaty (2 Samuel 21). Though Israel's leaders should not have agreed to a treaty without consulting the Lord, He remained faithful to His people.

WEEK 19 • TUESDAY   *Joshua 10:1–43*

How is it possible for the sun to stand still?

Actually, we could say that the sun always stands still—the earth rotates around it. Joshua addressed the sun rather than the earth because of what he observed. Some think an unusual refraction of the sun's rays gave additional hours of light. But the best explanation seems to be that in answer to Joshua's prayer, the Lord slowed the rotation of the earth. Regardless of how it happened, the Lord worked a miracle to help His people. The God who created the universe, rules the universe—for the good of His children.

WEEK 19 • WEDNESDAY   *Joshua 11:1—12:24*

Why did God want the horses crippled and the chariots burned?

The kings of northern Canaan heard of Joshua's victories over the kings in the south. They decided to join forces to fight Israel. Though this resulted in a huge army, the Lord told Joshua not to be afraid. He Himself would continue to fight for His people and fulfill His promise to give the land of Canaan to the descendants of Abraham. God's command that

Israel hamstring the horses and burn the chariots (Joshua 11:6) may seem wasteful, cruel, or unnecessary. However, the Canaanites used horses in their pagan worship. Then, too, destroying these weapons of war would prevent Israel's enemies from using them against the nation again. Finally, it would keep Israel from adding these new weapons of war to their arsenal, trusting in them rather than relying on the Lord alone. Psalm 33:16–17 reflects well the situation: "No king is saved by the size of his army. . . . A horse is a vain hope for deliverance." Rather, "our help is in the name of the LORD" (Psalm 124:8).

WEEK 19 • THURSDAY *Joshua 13:1—15:63*

Why were other nations still living in the Promised Land?

The Lord had given Joshua and the Israelite army victory over the major military powers in Canaan. But pockets of resistance remained. The people of Geshur and Maacah continued to live among the Israelites (Joshua 13:13). While the Scripture does not cite specific reasons for this, it seems that the Israelites simply failed to finish the task the Lord had assigned. This disobedience and its consequences would present countless difficulties for the Israelites. Remember, Israel would one day welcome the world's Savior. Any pagan influence on their worship or their way of life threatened God's plan to redeem the world through Christ's cross. That fact makes Canaan's geography critically important, even to us today!

WEEK 19 • FRIDAY *Joshua 16:1—17:18*

Why were the Israelites drawing lots for their inheritance?

After centuries of slavery in Egypt, years of wandering in the desert, and bloody years of conquest in Canaan, the tribes of Israel would finally receive their "inheritance"—their allotment of land. They drew lots to determine their assigned territory because the Lord wanted to impress on them a fact they were prone to forget! This land was not theirs by virtue of what they had done in conquering it. Rather, it came to them by inheritance, as an unmerited reward given freely to them by the Lord. While they did draw lots, no element of chance was involved. The Lord guided the process, giving each tribe the territory He wanted them to receive.

WEEK 19 • SATURDAY
Joshua 18:1—19:51

What was the Tent of Meeting?

Israel came together at Shiloh to cast the lots that determined each tribe's land allotment. Shiloh remained the center of Israel's worship for almost 400 years. The Tent of Meeting, known earlier as the tabernacle, was set up at Shiloh. Moses supervised the initial construction of the tabernacle (see Exodus 26 and 27 for a full description). Israel worshiped there during their wilderness wanderings. Inside the Tent of Meeting stood the ark of the covenant, the tabernacle's most important furnishing. The ark served as the visible sign of God's presence among His people; it would remain in the tabernacle at Shiloh until the Philistines captured it in the days of Samuel the prophet (1 Samuel 4:1–11). Shiloh's central location made the Tent of Meeting accessible to all 12 tribes.

WEEK 20 • MONDAY
Joshua 20:1—21:45

Why were Levites given towns instead of land?

Years before Moses, Jacob had cursed his son Levi's fierce anger and cruelty. The curse said that Levi's descendants would be scattered throughout Israel. The Lord turned this curse into a blessing in giving the Levites 48 towns scattered throughout Israel. Joshua tells us that the Levites inherited, not land, but their service to the Lord (18:7). God had promised through Moses (Numbers 35:1–8) that the Levites would receive cities and pasturelands, no discreet territory. In effect, this emphasized that the Lord Himself and Israel's offerings were the true inheritance of the Levites. This arrangement demonstrated the Lord's care for all His people. Scattered throughout Israel, the Levites became teachers, instructing Israelites in the Lord's covenant. Like the Levites, we too are "aliens and strangers on earth" (Hebrews 11:13). We have no "enduring city" (Hebrews 13:14). Rather, the Lord and the salvation He gives are our lasting inheritance (1 Peter 1:3–5).

WEEK 20 • TUESDAY
Joshua 22:1–34

Why were the Israelites upset about the altar built by the eastern tribes?

The eastern tribes of Reuben, Gad, and Manasseh had helped the other tribes conquer Canaan. With this task complete, the eastern tribes headed home, back across the Jordan River. But on the way, they stopped beside the Jordan to build an imposing altar. The western tribes were shocked! This altar meant that the eastern tribes were breaking the covenant of the Lord. This new altar implied other gods, a breaking of the First Commandment, and a mocking of the altar at Shiloh. Shiloh was the only place God had provided for burnt offerings and sacrifices. Furthermore, their unity as one nation, as "a kingdom of priests" (Exodus 19:6) was threatened by this disobedience. The eastern tribes, however, explained that the altar was built only as a memorial. It would not be used for sacrifice. Instead, it reminded the eastern tribes that they belonged to the Lord, too. The memorial altar was to be a sign of solidarity with the tribes west of Jordan. It would remind future generations to worship the true God. That clarification restored unity.

WEEK 20 • WEDNESDAY
Joshua 23:1–16

Why was it important for the Israelites not to associate with the nations around them?

Before Joshua died, he gathered all the leaders of Israel to give them words of encouragement and warning from God. The warnings concerned Israel's relationships with the pagans still living in Canaan (Joshua 23:6–7). These pagan peoples worshiped false gods. Even so, Israel would find these idolatrous ways tempting. But falling for these temptations would amount to faithlessness in the Lord and in His promise. It would also jeopardize God's plan to bring the Savior from the descendants of Abraham, Isaac, and Jacob. For all these reasons, Israel was to avoid associating with the surrounding nations.

WEEK 20 • THURSDAY
Joshua 24:1–33

Why did the Israelites have Joseph's bones?

On his deathbed Joseph gave instructions concerning his burial (Genesis 50:25–26). These instructions were based on God's promises. Hebrews 11:22 brings this out: "By faith Joseph, when his end was near, spoke about the exodus of the Israelites from Egypt and gave instructions about his bones." In faith Israel preserved Joseph's bones for 400 years in Egypt. Moses took the bones from Egypt at the exodus (Exodus 13:19). Now that the Lord's promise to bring Israel back to Canaan had been fulfilled, Joseph could finally be buried at Shechem. Jacob had purchased this plot of land (Genesis 33:19). Joseph's bones rest at the center of the land allotted to his sons, Ephraim and Manasseh, just as Shechem was to be the central city of those two tribes.

WEEK 20 • FRIDAY
Judges 1:1–36

Why were the Israelites unable to drive out the people who had iron chariots?

The Lord had promised to drive out the remaining Canaanites (Joshua 13:6), even though they had iron chariots and "though they [were] strong"

(17:18). Now, after Joshua's death, it seemed that God had reneged on His promise. Judah led the fight against the remaining Canaanites. At first Israel defeated the Canaanites in the hill country, but they failed to conquer those living on the plains. The list of the defeats suffered by the Israelites closes this chapter. Iron chariots had nothing to do with these defeats. Such chariots had not been a problem before (Joshua 11:1–9). Rather, the problem lay in Israel's disobedience, in the people's unwillingness to trust the covenant God who had promised them help and victory (Judges 2:1–3).

WEEK 20 • SATURDAY   *Judges 2:1–23*

What were the Baals?

The second generation of Israelites after Joshua's death did not follow the Lord. They did evil in the eyes of the Lord and served the Baals (Judges 2:11). Baal, a common noun meaning "owner," "lord," or "husband," was the Canaanite name for the Syrian god Hadad, the god of storms and wars. Baal is pictured as standing on a bull, a common Canaanite symbol of fertility and strength. The Canaanites regarded every locality as the possession of a particular Baal, a local deity. In serving these Baals, Israel broke the First Commandment. No longer did Israel rely on God's promises. Instead, the people joined the Canaanites in trying to manipulate nature-gods (really demons—1 Corinthians 10:20!) to amass wealth and power.

WEEK 21 • MONDAY   *Judges 3:1–30*

Why did the people of Israel turn from their faith in God?

God had warned Israel time and again about the dangers of associating with pagans. He explicitly forbade intermarriage with the Canaanites. Despite these warnings, the Israelites lived among the pagan people of Canaan, they let their sons marry Canaanite women, and they gave their own daughters into marriage with Canaanite men. Before long, Israel began to worship the gods of the Canaanites (Judges 3:6). At the same time, they failed to teach their children about the Lord and about all He had done for Israel. The nation's fall into the grossest idolatry was, at that point, inevitable.

WEEK 21 • TUESDAY   *Judges 3:31—5:31*

Why did Barak want Deborah to join him in the battle?

After Joshua's death, judges ruled Israel for more than 300 years. These judges were able to save Israel from its oppressors only because the Lord gave the enemy into their hands. Only one of these judges was a woman. Deborah, a prophetess, resolved disputes that arose in Israel at the time (Judges 4:4–5). Deborah commissioned Barak to gather 10,000 men to fight the army of Sisera. Barak insisted that Deborah go with him into battle. He was apparently reluctant to undertake what seemed to be a suicidal mission without the reassuring presence of the prophetess. Deborah agreed and this gave Barak the courage to lead the attack. Because of his timidity in trusting God's promise, Barak would share the glory of his victory with Jael, the woman who actually killed Sisera (Judges 4:17–22).

WEEK 21 • WEDNESDAY   *Judges 6:1–8:35*

Why did Gideon twice put out a fleece?

God, in the guise of an angel, called Gideon to lead the Israelites against the Midianites. The Lord promised to be with Gideon to accomplish this. Even so, Gideon asked for a sign. He would put a wool fleece on the ground. The next morning, if the fleece was wet and the ground dry,

Gideon would know he had spoken with the Lord and could trust His promised presence. It happened just that way. Gideon then asked for a second sign, but this time in reverse, dry fleece and wet ground. That also happened (Judges 6:36–39). Gideon knew he was no hero. Doubts and uncertainties attacked his faith. Perhaps he regretted his first "sign"—the fleece might naturally have accumulated dew because of the conditions of the ground around it. That would account for his second request for a special sign. God, in grace, granted it. This gave Gideon the courage to take his next step.

WEEK 21 • THURSDAY   Judges 9:1—10:18

Why did the curse of Jotham come true?

After Gideon's death, one of his 71 sons, Abimelech, wanted to be the leader of Israel. To achieve this, Abimelech killed all of his brothers except Jotham, the youngest, who had escaped. When Jotham heard that the people of Shechem had made Abimelech king, Jotham cursed both Abimelech and the people (Judges 9:20). Like many curses in the Old Testament, Jotham's curse aligned with God's judgment on wickedness. The curse itself did not bring disaster upon Abimelech. Rather, the Lord used Jotham to speak His judgment on Abimelech and the people.

WEEK 21 • FRIDAY   Judges 11:1—12:15

Why would Jephthah make such a foolish vow?

Jephthah the "judge" (or "deliverer") led the Israelites in battle against the Ammonites. Jephthah vowed that if the Lord gave him victory, he would sacrifice to the Lord the first thing that came out the door of his house (Judges 11:30–31). In making such a vow, Jephthah betrayed a flawed knowledge of the Lord. He calculated Israel's relationship with God to be one of exchange—"if we do this for God, He will do this for us." Such a vow showed a lack of faith in the Lord's promise of help and victory. Jephthah attempted to strike a deal with God, the very God who acts out of love, mercy, and grace. This same God would later give His only Son into death so that all who believe in Him would be delivered from death. It's possible that Jephthah did not sacrifice his daughter as a burnt offering. Perhaps he redeemed her using the provision the Lord had made in Leviticus 27:1–15. Some have suggested that she remained a virgin all her life. Given the corruption in Israel at the time, though, Jephthah may have followed through with his foolish oath.

WEEK 21 • SATURDAY *Judges 13:1—16:31*

How could Samson destroy a whole temple?

God blessed Samson, one of the "judges" (or "deliverers") of Israel, with extraordinary strength. While his uncut hair served as a sign of his strength, Samson's uncut hair was also an outward sign of an inner dedication to God. This was part of his vow as a Nazirite. When he violated that covenant with the Lord, the source of his strength, God's Spirit, who had previously come upon Samson in power (Judges 14:6), now left him. Samson's strength left with the Spirit (Judges 16:20). The Philistines easily captured and blinded him. Put on display before thousands of Philistines during a thanksgiving feast in the temple of their god, Dagon, Samson asked to be tied between two pillars where he could rest. Then he prayed that the Lord would strengthen him one last time and give him revenge on the Philistines. Samson then pushed against the pillars, and the whole temple collapsed (Judges 16:28–30). Archaeologists have discovered a Philistine temple constructed in a way that may explain Samson's victory. This temple was constructed around two closely spaced wooden pillars which apparently provided support for the roof. This suggests that Samson might have loosened the central pillars of the temple and pushed them from their marble bases to collapse the whole roof and bring down the interior walls as well. In any case, Samson exerted extraordinary—supernatural—strength.

WEEK 22 • MONDAY
Judges 17:1—18:31

What was wrong with Micah hiring his own priest?

Not long after the death of Joshua, evil ran rampant throughout Israel. That "everyone did as he saw fit" (Judges 17:6) was demonstrated by the ways Israel ignored God's laws and broke His covenant by open, rebellious wickedness and idolatry. One example is Micah. (This was not the prophet who would later pen one book of the Old Testament.) A thief, Micah used stolen money to build some idols and place them in a shrine in his house. However, he knew that only a Levite could perform priestly functions. Though his devotion to just this one provision of God's law and his disobedience to the rest of that law is hard to understand, Micah employed a wandering Levite from Bethlehem as his personal priest (Judges 17:10). In doing so, Micah hoped to receive God's stamp of approval and the blessing of the Canaanite gods—thus getting the "best of both worlds." The Lord, of course, took a dim view of all this. The account serves to illustrate the depravity in Israel during the era of the judges.

WEEK 22 • TUESDAY
Judges 19:1—20:48

Why did the Levite cut up his concubine's body?

This account relates closely to the story of Micah and his idols in Judges 17 and 18. Both demonstrate the great evil infecting Israel at the time of the judges. The Levite introduced in Judges 19 stopped to spend the night in the city of Gibeah. The Levite had a travelling companion—a concubine. (This affront to the laws of chastity by a Levite, a servant of the Lord, is in itself scandalous.) Some wicked men of the city began attacking the house where the Levite was staying, demanding to perform homosexual acts with the newly arrived visitor. To appease them, the Levite sent his concubine out to them. They gang raped her all night, and in the morning she lay dead on the threshold. Her murder outraged the Levite. In response, he hacked the concubine's body into 12 pieces and sent one part to each of the 12 tribes of Israel (Judges 19:29). Apparently unaware of his own contribution to the murder, the Levite's actions did awaken Israel from its moral lethargy. Most of Israel assembled before the Lord to deal with the evil done by the men of Gibeah. The Israelites marched on the vile offenders and eventually defeated them. But the story didn't end there. (See Judges 21.)

WEEK 22 • WEDNESDAY

Judges 21:1–25

Why were the Israelites worried about one tribe disappearing?

Eleven of Israel's 12 tribes attacked the tribe of Benjamin because of the rape and murder of the concubine in Gibeah (Judges 18—20; Gibeah was a city in Benjamin's territory). When the battle ended, all but 600 Benjamite men lay dead. Because Benjamite women and children had died, too, it appeared that the tribe of Benjamin would disappear. This posed a problem: in their anger, the 11 tribes had taken a vow that none of them would give their daughters in marriage to a Benjamite. Mosaic law prohibited the 600 Benjamite men from marrying non-Israelites. Rather that asking the Lord's forgiveness for their foolish vow, the 11 tribes concocted a scheme to get around the letter of the law. Judges 21 describes it. This whole sequence of events testifies to how far Israel had removed itself from the will and Word of God. Further, it illustrates the human depravity that made our need for a Savior so great.

WEEK 22 • THURSDAY

Ruth 1:1—2:23

Why did Boaz allow strangers to harvest his fields after his workers had finished?

The law of Moses (Leviticus 19:9; Deuteronomy 24:19) instructed landowners to leave what the harvesters missed. That way, the poor, the alien, the widow, and the fatherless could glean the remaining grain to meet their family's needs. For the same reason, the Lord directed that the corners of each field be left for the poor to reap. Some generous landowners were known to leave as much as one-fourth of their crop for the needy and for foreigners living in the land. Boaz's generosity and his kindness to Ruth stands in sharp contrast to the greed, depravity, and lovelessness that characterized this era in Israelite history. One could hardly guess that Boaz's obedience to the Law of Moses took place during the same time frame as the wickedness reported in the book of Judges.

WEEK 22 • FRIDAY

Ruth 3:1—4:22

What is a kinsman-redeemer?

A kinsman-redeemer was a close relative to whom needy members of the extended family could turn for help. The Law of Moses required such a relative to marry his brother's widow to provide an heir for a brother who had died. It also required that relative to redeem land that his close relatives had sold outside the family during a time of economic need. Finally, a kinsman-redeemer was obligated to redeem a relative who had been sold into slavery and to avenge the murder of a relative. "Redemption" of a family name and property provided social stability in the covenant nation. Through that same covenant nation the Lord promised to raise up a kinsman of all humankind, one who would "redeem Israel from all their sins" (Psalm 130:8). Jesus the Christ is that Kinsman-Redeemer through whom "we have redemption through His blood, the forgiveness of sins" (Ephesians 1:7).

WEEK 22 • SATURDAY

1 Samuel 1:1–28

Why was Hannah so upset about not having a son?

Elkanah, a man of faith, took seriously his spiritual responsibilities. He had two wives. (The Lord allowed, but did not condone, polygamy during this time in Israel's history.) Elkanah's wife Peninnah gave birth to several sons and daughters, but Hannah was not able to conceive (1 Samuel 1:5). In the culture of the day, children were a sign of God's blessing. For a woman to be barren was viewed as a disgrace, perhaps even a curse from God. Even though Elkanah deeply loved Hannah and attempted to convince her that her inability to have a baby meant nothing to him, she longed to have a child. To make matters worse, Peninnah continually flaunted her fertility in front of barren Hannah.

WEEK 23 • MONDAY
1 Samuel 2:1–36

What were Eli's sons doing that was so wrong?

Although Eli was a godly high priest, he was an indulgent father who pampered his sons. They grew up believing that they could disregard the Lord's commands, doing whatever they pleased. Their lives serve as examples of the refrain in the Book of Judges (21:25): "Everyone did as he saw fit." Eli's sons apparently received the sacrifices as the people brought them to Shiloh. As members of the priestly family, these sons had a right to a share of this meat after it had been offered to the Lord (Leviticus 3:3–5). But instead of waiting until after the sacrifice, Eli's sons demanded that the worshipers give them a disproportional share of the raw offering. Adding sin to sin, they also ate the meat before the fat had been burned off (1 Samuel 2:13–17). The attitude this disobedience shows and the sexual sins they committed in addition all showed the contempt they had for the Lord. Little wonder, then, that their actions and attitudes brought down God's judgment.

WEEK 23 • TUESDAY
1 Samuel 3:1–21

Why was Samuel allowed to sleep in the tabernacle?

Remembering her promise to the Lord, Hannah sent her son, Samuel, to be raised by the high priest in Shiloh at the tabernacle compound. As one who assisted the priests in the work of the tabernacle, Samuel slept where Eli, his sons, and the other priests slept (1 Samuel 3:3–4). The tabernacle was arranged in such a way that the ark of the covenant was sheltered behind a curtain in the Most Holy Place, removed from the altar of sacrifice, the bread of presence, and the rest of the tabernacle rooms. Only the high priest was allowed to go behind the curtain, and then only once a year, on the Day of Atonement. The rooms where Samuel and the others slept were probably only a few yards removed from the ark that represented God's dwelling place on earth.

WEEK 23 • WEDNESDAY   *1 Samuel 4:1–22*

What is significant about the ark being captured by the Philistines?

When Israel went to battle against the Philistines, they were soundly defeated. The elders of the Israelites were dumbfounded that the Lord would allow their enemy to be victorious over them. In trying to answer their question "Why this defeat?" the elders of Israel did not look very deeply. Instead of considering that they themselves might be the problem, they blamed the Lord. Thus they took the ark of the covenant from the tabernacle in Shiloh onto the battlefield. The ark was the sign of the Lord's presence with His people. The Israelites probably remembered the presence of the ark at previous victories in their history. They presumed that having the ark present would magically produce their desired victory. But the Lord would not be manipulated. In the next battle, the Philistines won again, and the ark of God was captured (1 Samuel 4:11). Perhaps the best commentary on this whole situation comes from Eli's daughter-in-law. When she heard not only of her husband's death but also of the loss of the ark, she went into premature labor and gave birth to a son. As she lay dying, she named her son Ichabod, meaning "No glory" and uttered, "The glory has departed from Israel" (1 Samuel 4:21).

WEEK 23 • THURSDAY   *1 Samuel 5:1—6:21*

Why did the Philistine priests suggest using cows that had never been yoked to return the ark?

After the Philistines captured the ark of the covenant, havoc broke out in the Philistines' land. The destruction and sickness proved unbearable. Suspecting the Israelite's God was responsible, the pagan priests devised a plan to find out. They built a new cart on which they placed the ark. They yoked two milk cows to it. These cows had never been used in this way—apparently they had recently given birth to their first calves. Their biological urge would be to return to their nursing calves—not to pull a cart. So if the unbroken cows successfully transported the ark back to Israel, it would prove the Lord's involvement to the Philistines. With the ark back in Israel, perhaps the Lord would remove the curse from Philistia.

WEEK 23 • FRIDAY

1 Samuel 7:1–17

What was the significance of Samuel pouring out water before the Lord?

As the last of Israel's judges, Samuel was concerned that his nation give up its evil ways and return to the Lord. They were to give up every substitute for the Lord and separate themselves from the pagan gods. Samuel issued a nationwide call for repentance and rededication to the Lord. With penitent hearts the people gathered at Mizpah, drew water, and poured it out on the ground before the Lord. This outpouring expressed their sorrow over their sins and their need for cleansing (1 Samuel 7:6).

WEEK 23 • SATURDAY

1 Samuel 8:1–22

Why was Samuel upset that the Israelites were asking for a king?

With Samuel aging and his sons growing even more corrupt, the people saw their need for better leadership. They came to Samuel with the demand that he appoint a king for them. Their real motives soon became apparent—they wanted to be like other nations who had a king. This demand and the motives behind it upset Samuel. He saw it as a rejection of his own leadership. The Lord, however, told Samuel the truth. The people's demand betrayed their rejection of the Lord Himself. Through Samuel God warned the people about the consequences of their demand. Their kings would tax them, draft their sons, and make many demands on them. This, in contrast to the "great King over all the earth" (Psalm 47:2) who had defended them in the past. Still, this argument got Samuel nowhere. The people repeated their demand, and the Lord relented.

WEEK 24 • MONDAY   *1 Samuel 9:1—10:27*

Why did Samuel pour oil over Saul's head?

The Lord revealed to Samuel that He had chosen Saul, a man from the land of Benjamin, to serve as the first king of Israel. Samuel was to anoint him (1 Samuel 10:1). Samuel did so. Other nations around Israel used similar ceremonies. But Samuel's involvement showed that the office of king had divine sanction; the Lord had placed Saul in this office. Even though Saul and the kings that followed him could only achieve imperfectly what the Lord wanted done, they would point to another one, the Anointed One, the Messiah, Jesus the Christ who would accomplish God's will perfectly. Jesus would live a perfect life in our place, then die to win the battle over sin, Satan, and death for us.

WEEK 24 • TUESDAY   *1 Samuel 11:1–15*

Why did Saul have to be confirmed as king?

Samuel had anointed Saul in private (1 Samuel 10:1). Then Saul was selected as the king-designate at Mizpah (1 Samuel 10:17–27). Now Saul was confirmed "as king in the presence of the LORD" (1 Samuel 11:15) with a formal worship service including sacrificial rites. At this inaugural or coronation, Saul assumed the responsibilities and privileges of his office. The fellowship or peace offerings were offered to God to invoke His blessings on the new ruler.

WEEK 24 • WEDNESDAY   *1 Samuel 12:1–25*

Why were the Israelites afraid for having asked for a king?

In his farewell sermon Samuel stressed the faithfulness of the Lord despite the unfaithfulness of His people. After reviewing God's past dealings with His people, Samuel used the people's request for a king as an example of their unfaithfulness. While this request wickedly rejected the Lord's gracious rule and the theocracy He had given them, nevertheless the Lord would in grace use Israel's future monarchs to carry out His saving purpose for His people. To confirm his words, Samuel called for a thunderstorm. This time of year—during the wheat harvest—Israel is usually dry and hot. But in response to Samuel's prayer, a thunderstorm blew in. The terrified people, in awe of the Lord's power, confessed their sin and asked Samuel to intercede for them. Samuel responds with words of mercy from the Lord. Despite Israel's sins, the Lord will not forsake His people. They need not fear. Here Samuel the intercessor is a "type," or picture, of Christ—the great High Priest who continually intercedes for us.

WEEK 24 • THURSDAY   1 Samuel 13:1–22

Why did God reject Saul for making the offering?

Saul anxiously awaited Samuel's arrival while he and his troops waited in fear as the Philistines advanced. When Samuel did not arrive as promised, Saul's men began to scatter. Saul decided to take matters into his own hands. Saul's impatience showed only his unwillingness to trust the Lord. It betrayed a disrespectful attitude toward Samuel, God's prophet. It also demonstrated a sinful lust for power. The Lord had already given Saul political power; now Saul took priestly authority upon himself. (Only the Levitical priests were to offer sacrifices.)

This incident brought Saul's rebellion to a head. While Saul had begun his reign in humility and with a servant's heart, his position apparently led him to arrogance and irreverence. Angered by Saul's sin, the Lord announced through Samuel that his kingdom would not endure (1 Samuel 13:14). Even then, Saul did not repent.

WEEK 24 • FRIDAY   1 Samuel 14:1–52

What did it mean when Saul asked the priest to withdraw his hand?

Jonathan and his armor-bearer successfully attacked a small group of the Philistine troops. This caused a panic among the Philistines, making them easy targets. But yet again Saul showed his impatience. In order to seek God's will before entering the battle, Saul sent for the ark of the covenant (or perhaps more accurately, the ephod). The priest apparently began the process of discerning God's will with the Urim and Thummim, but Saul interrupted. Wanting to seize the military advantage of the moment, the king commanded the priest to withdraw his hand (1 Samuel 14:18–19), thus putting a stop to drawing of the sacred lots. Saul had decided to enter into battle based on his own assessment of the situation. Here again we see Saul's arrogant commitment to his own insight rather than a humble dependence on the Lord and a commitment to obey Him.

WEEK 24 • SATURDAY   1 Samuel 15:1–35

Why did Samuel refuse to forgive Saul?

Through Samuel the Lord gave Saul specific instructions regarding how to punish the Amalekites for crimes against Israel. Israel's army was to destroy everyone and burn their possessions. But Saul thought he had a better idea. He spared the Amalek king and saved the best sheep and cattle. When Samuel confronted Saul, the king concocted an excuse about wanting to sacrifice the animals to the Lord. Yet again we see Saul's arrogant, disobedient, impenitent heart. With this deliberate rebellion, Saul sealed his own fate. No son of Saul would take Israel's throne after him.

WEEK 25 • MONDAY
1 Samuel 16:1–23

Why didn't Jesse bring David before Samuel?

The Lord sent Samuel to Jesse in Bethlehem to find and anoint the next king of Israel. Seven of Jesse's sons passed before Samuel—any one of them a good candidate to succeed Saul as Israel's king. But the Lord had selected someone else—Jesse's youngest son who was out in the pasture tending the family's sheep. Perhaps Jesse thought David too young to meet this important visitor. In any case, God held David in high regard. Samuel anointed David in a clandestine ceremony, thus designating David Israel's heir-apparent. Saul would remain the legal king of Israel until his death. But the Lord would soon replace the rebellious Saul with a "man after His own heart"—David, the shepherd boy.

WEEK 25 • TUESDAY
1 Samuel 17:1–58

Why did Saul allow David to fight Goliath alone?

The Philistines and Israelites camped on opposite sides of the Valley of Elah. The Philistine champion fighter Goliath challenged the Israelites to choose a man to meet him in battle. The man who won could declare victory for his army in the battle. Battles were sometimes fought in this manner, one man against another, in order to save a great deal of bloodshed.

David appeared to walk onto the battlefield alone. However, he was not alone in his fight against Goliath, for God was with him. He knew the Lord would fight for him—a "son of the covenant." We, too, can trust God's presence and power at work for us as we rely on the covenant He established with us in our Baptism.

WEEK 25 • WEDNESDAY
1 Samuel 18:1—19:24

Why were Saul and his soldiers prophesying?

David successfully completed everything Saul sent him to do. As David earned more and more praise from the people, David's success inflamed Saul's jealousy. Saul tried several times to have David killed. One day, King Saul received word that David had gone to visit the prophet Samuel at Ramah. Saul dispatched several groups of soldiers to capture David and kill him. But the Spirit of God came upon each squad. They were unhurt, but they began to prophesy; in this context, we can probably assume this involved an enthusiastic praising of God. This continued until Saul himself came to Ramah to look for David (1 Samuel 19:20–23). But the Lord caused Saul also to "prophesy," thus thwarting Saul's evil plan and saving David's life.

WEEK 25 • THURSDAY   1 Samuel 20:1—21:15

Why did David pretend to be insane?

David fled from Saul to the Philistine city of Gath, which he thought would be a safe place to hide. But Gath was Goliath's hometown, and before long someone there recognized David, the "giant-slayer." Brought before King Achish, David feared for his life. Thus he feigned insanity as a way to protect himself. It worked. Believing David posed no threat, the king and people of Gath let him go.

WEEK 25 • FRIDAY   1 Samuel 22:1–23

Why were the king's officials afraid to kill the priests?

Doeg told King Saul that the priest Ahimelech had given David and his men food. Ahimelech had also returned Goliath's sword to David. After all, David had certainly earned it! But Saul felt betrayed. Playing the coward, Saul ordered his officers to kill Ahimelech. They refused. Ahimelech was the Lord's priest (1 Samuel 22:17). They may have feared the king, but they feared the Lord more. The foreigner Doeg, however, more than eager to win Saul's favor, carried out Saul's command.

WEEK 25 • SATURDAY   1 Samuel 23:1–29

Why did David ask for the ephod?

The "ephod" was an article of clothing worn by the High Priest as he carried out his official duties. This garment apparently had a pouch or pocket sewn into it. The Urim and Thummim were kept there. No one knows for sure what these looked like or exactly how they were used, but somehow they provided guidance about God's will. After David's victory over the Philistines in Keilah, Saul decided to pursue him to this gated town. When David learned of this, he asked for the ephod (1 Samuel 23:9). Through it and the High Priest who performed the rite associated with it, the Lord told David that Saul would come to Keilah and that the citizens of Keilah would surrender David and his men to Saul. Changing his plan to stay in the city, David fled before Saul's army could arrive.

WEEK 26 • MONDAY   *1 Samuel 24:1–22*

Why did David spare Saul's life?

As Saul pursued David in the Desert of En Gedi, the king by chance entered a cave to relieve himself. Unbeknownst to Saul, David and his soldiers had hidden in the back of the cave. To David's men, this seemed the perfect opportunity for David to be rid of Saul's persecution. How easily David could kill Saul at a vulnerable moment. But instead, David cut off a corner of Saul's robe. Later, David waved it, showing it to Saul from a safe distance. He explained his reasoning to the king. Saul was the "Lord's anointed servant." Such respect David had for God's will that he refused to use his "common sense" to resolve the danger and hardship Saul's murderous rage had caused him. We, too, can trust our Lord. Even when ignoring His commands seem to make "common sense," the Holy Spirit will empower us to obey our Lord. In Him, we find true peace despite our outward circumstances.

WEEK 26 • TUESDAY   *1 Samuel 25:1–44*

Why was David so angry at Nabal?

For months while they camped in the Desert of Maon, David and his men had protected the sheep and shepherds of Nabal. They had done a great service, and they expected that at shearing time Nabal would repay David. However, Nabal scoffed at David's request that Nabal share a meal to celebrate the shearing (1 Samuel 25:7–11). In Israelite society common courtesy demanded that residents feed travelers who passed their home. In addition, David and his men had proven their worth to Nabal, and Nabal's shepherds had testified to their help. Perhaps, too, David saw the incident with Nabal as a kind of "last straw." Living on the run as he had for many months would exhaust anyone. Concerned for his men, worried about the safety of his family, wondering where the next meal would come from—David's plate was full. The incident with Nabal set off a spark near what would naturally have been dry kindling in David's heart.

WEEK 26 • WEDNESDAY   *1 Samuel 26:1–25*

Why does David call Saul "the Lord's anointed" even though Samuel had anointed David himself to be king?

Once again Saul pursued David, this time in the Desert of Ziph. David's scouts had reported this to David. To get a close-up view of Saul's encampment, David and his nephew Abishai silently crept into the camp late that night. Finding Saul asleep, Abishai offered to kill him. Again, David forbade it. Again, David reminded Abishai of Saul's position as "the Lord's anointed." The Lord would one day hand the kingdom over to David, but King Saul was still its rightful ruler (1 Samuel 26:9). Again we see the contrast between Saul's willful impatience and David's Spirit-led reliance on the Lord's will and word. As a "type" or picture of Christ, David demonstrates the kind of whole-hearted loyalty to the Lord that Christ Himself would some day show. David obeyed imperfectly; Jesus obeyed perfectly in our place.

WEEK 26 • THURSDAY   *1 Samuel 27:1—29:11*

Why would Saul consult a medium?

The Lord had strictly forbidden witchcraft of any kind. Early in his reign, Saul himself had executed all the mediums he could find. But now desperation settled on Saul like a shroud. The Philistines had attacked Israel once again. Saul called upon the Lord, asking for help, for a plan. But God would not answer. So once more Saul took matters into his own hands; he found a witch and asked for her help. Did Samuel really appear to Saul? We don't know. The witch may have conjured up a demon. On the other hand, the Lord may have sent Samuel to Saul with a final message of Law. In either case, Saul still refused to fall on his face in repentance. Instead, he pulled himself together and went off to face the Philistines alone.

WEEK 26 • FRIDAY   *1 Samuel 30:1–31*

Why did David give some of the plunder to the elders of Judah?

The Amalekites had raided Negev and Ziklag and taken all their women as booty. David asked God if he should pursue his enemy and if he would overtake them. The Lord affirmed David's plan. David found the Amalekites, fought them, and recovered everything they had taken. When he returned to Ziklag, David sent some of the plunder to the elders in Judah (1 Samuel 30:26) in gratitude for their help to him as Saul pursued him.

WEEK 26 • SATURDAY   *1 Samuel 31:1–13*

Why did Saul and his armor-bearer take their own lives?

The Philistines overpowered the Israelites in battle. Saul's sons had already died on Mount Gilboa, and Saul knew that his enemies would soon overtake him. The Philistines were known to torture prisoners taken alive, and Saul wanted to avoid this fate. Instead of seeking God's forgiveness, guidance, and help, Saul took matters into his own hands one last time. Saul asked his armor-bearer to kill him, but the young man refused. So Saul fell on his own sword (1 Samuel 31:4–5). When Saul's armor-bearer saw what Saul had done, he too committed suicide. Without condoning suicide, the Scripture merely reports the incident. Here we see the outcome of a life lived in disobedience and self-will.

WEEK 27 • MONDAY
2 Samuel 1:1—2:32

Why did David execute the Amalekite?

An Amalekite came to David with the news that he had killed Saul at Saul's request. Saul had made this request—but to his armor-bearer. The boy refused, and Saul killed himself (1 Samuel 31:4). The Amalekite may have lied, hoping for a reward and certain that David would be glad to hear of Saul's death. David, however, was enraged by the man's account of how he had murdered the king—the Lord's anointed. David decreed the Amalekite's execution. David gave a loving and heartfelt tribute to the fallen king and his son Jonathan, his greatest friend. To the end, David respected and honored Saul because David honored the Lord, the One who had anointed them both.

WEEK 27 • TUESDAY
2 Samuel 3:1—4:12

Why did David so greatly mourn Abner's death?

Abner had headed Saul's army. But after Saul's death, Abner made peace with David and supported David's claim to the throne. Joab, who commanded David's army, killed Abner to avenge his brother's death (2 Samuel 3:27, 30). Abner had killed Joab's brother Asahel in an earlier conflict. The loss of Abner, a loyal and skilled military officer, angered and saddened David. King David showed great respect for Abner by giving him an honorable burial and proclaiming a day of public mourning. David's compassion and forgiving spirit is evident here, traits made possible by David's trust in the Lord. David's genuine grief proved to all Israel once again that he took no delight in the downfall of the house of Saul. David wanted his ascension to the throne to unify Israel—not divide it.

WEEK 27 • WEDNESDAY   *2 Samuel 5:1–25*

Why did David want to make Jerusalem, a city occupied by Jebusites, his capital?

The Jebusites, a Canaanite people, inhabited the area in and around Jerusalem. Jerusalem was a natural fortress because of its location on a long hill flanked by deep ravines. The Jebusites felt confident that no one could breach their walls; even the "blind and lame" could defend the city, they bragged. But David captured the stronghold and made it his capital (2 Samuel 5:8–9). He fortified the city even further and moved his family there. Establishing Jerusalem as the royal city was one of the most significant accomplishments of David's reign. Because Jerusalem had remained in Jebusite control since the days of Joshua, the 12 tribes of Israel considered it a neutral location. By locating his royal city in a newly conquered town on the border of two tribes (Judah and Benjamin), David showed he didn't favor any one tribe and, thus, united the kingdom under his rule. Furthermore, Jerusalem's location gave David a strategic military advantage. This city gives us a glimpse of the heavenly Jerusalem and the peace that awaits us there. God Himself is the Fortress and the sure defense that keeps His chosen ones safe within the walls of His power and grace.

WEEK 27 • THURSDAY   *2 Samuel 6:1–23*

Why did God put Uzzah to death?

The ark of the covenant had apparently been kept in Abinadab's home for some 20 years before David decided to move it to Jerusalem (1 Samuel 7:2). David wanted to restore worship to the center of Israel's life, to emphasize his people's covenant relationship with the Lord. The ark of the covenant, considered God's "throne" on earth, symbolized that relationship in a greater way than any other artifact. But David overlooked God's rules for moving and handling the ark. According to Numbers 4:5–15, the ark was to be moved only by the Levites, who were to carry it using the carrying poles. No one was ever to touch the ark itself. Uzzah did, however, reach out to touch it in an attempt to keep the ark from falling to the ground. He violated the Lord's clear command, literally taking the matter into his own hands. When Uzzah touched the ark, God acted swiftly and dramatically to protect His holiness before the people. Uzzah's death served as a shocking and vivid reminder to David and Israel that those who claim to serve the Lord must obey His commands. God's holy nature demands that those who approach Him be holy. How, then, do we dare come into His presence? By faith we stand before Him in Christ's own righteousness. We have been made holy through the death and resurrection of the perfect Son. Connected to that holiness in our Baptism, we enjoy the Father's favor. He gladly welcomes us into His presence.

WEEK 27 • FRIDAY
2 Samuel 7:1–29

How could David's throne be established forever?

David wanted to build a temple for the Lord. But God had other plans. Through His prophet Nathan, God told David he would not build the temple, the house of the Lord. Instead, the Lord would build David a "house"—a dynasty of kings (2 Samuel 7:11–16). God promised to continue the dynasty of David forever. All the kings who ruled in Jerusalem after David (20 in all) were his descendants. David's earthly dynasty lasted 400 years. And from this house of David came Jesus, the Son of David and the King who reigns forever and ever in a kingdom that never ends. All believers enjoy citizenship in that eternal kingdom.

WEEK 27 • SATURDAY
2 Samuel 8:1—10:19

Why would cutting someone's beard and clothes start a war?

When the king of the Ammonites died, his son Hanun succeeded him as king. David sent ambassadors to the new king to express his sympathy. But Hanun's officers convinced him that the men were spies. Hanun then seized the men, shaved off half of each one's beard, cut off the lower half of their robes, and sent them away (2 Samuel 10:3–4). By doing this, the Ammonites insulted and humiliated David's emissaries, and by implication, David and his people. Beards symbolized dignity, maturity, and manhood. Cutting off a man's robe at the buttocks was a customary way of humiliating prisoners of war. David had sent the men to Hanun in an act of kindness and good faith, and his kindness was met with contempt and insults. These actions were, in effect, a declaration of war.

WEEK 28 • MONDAY

2 Samuel 11:1—12:31

Why was Bathsheba bathing outside?

David had sent Joab, his commander-in-chief, out with the Israelite army to fight the Ammonites. But David remained in Jerusalem. One evening David became restless and walked around on the roof of the palace. From there, David could see the entire city. From this vantage point, he could see Bathsheba, wife of Uriah, bathing (2 Samuel 11:2). Why was Bathsheba bathing outside? This was probably a ritual bath, prescribed by law after the seven-day period of monthly impurity due to menstruation. (See Leviticus 15:19–33.) Apparently Bathsheba thought she would be alone; she probably did not count on observers from the neighboring palace roof! The adulterous affair that resulted shows David, the mighty king, at his absolute worst. By his sin, David broke his relationship with the Lord. But in grace the Lord sent Nathan the prophet to confront David. Then the Lord worked in David His gift of repentance. In mercy, the Lord forgave David and restored him.

WEEK 28 • TUESDAY

2 Samuel 13:1—14:24

Why did Tamar not want to leave Amnon?

David had numerous wives and children. This led to many family troubles and much grief. David's own sin against God's plan for marriage had tragic consequences in his family. Amnon was David's firstborn son, and Tamar was Amnon's half sister, David's daughter by his wife Maacah. Amnon fell in love with Tamar, but when she refused him, he raped her then cruelly rejected her (2 Samuel 13:1, 10–15). Tamar wanted to stay with Amnon because he could spare her humiliation if he acknowledged what he had done to her. No longer a virgin, Tamar could not be offered by her father to any other potential husband and would be forced to remain unmarried for the rest of her life. Therefore, though it sounds unthinkable in our culture, Tamar wanted to be married to Amnon. Because of his sexual assault, marriage to him was her right (Deuteronomy 22:28–29).

WEEK 28 • WEDNESDAY   2 Samuel 14:25—16:23

Why did David choose to flee instead of stay in Jerusalem and fight?

With cunning charm and deceit, Absalom had been wooing the people away from David, his father. When he felt the time was ripe for revolution, Absalom declared himself king. Absalom's conspiracy gained strength, and his following kept growing (2 Samuel 15:12). David saw the hopelessness of fighting Absalom without the proper number of troops assembled. Uncertain of the extent of Absalom's support, David feared being trapped in Jerusalem. If that were to happen, it would mean the loss of both his support and the capital in one blow. Also, he wanted to spare the city from destruction. In addition to all this, David loved his son and perhaps believed that a delayed confrontation might give Absalom time to change his mind. So he left Jerusalem and headed east to the Transjordan. Interestingly, as David fled Jerusalem, he crossed the Kidron Valley and headed up the Mount of Olives. Many years later the Son of David, the Messiah, would walk this way, going toward Jerusalem instead of fleeing it. There He would face His enemies. For both David and Jesus, it was a way of sorrow.

WEEK 28 • THURSDAY   2 Samuel 17:1—18:33

Why did Ahithophel kill himself?

Ahithophel was Bathsheba's grandfather and had been at one time a wise and respected counselor to David. But now he had aligned himself with Absalom and rebels who followed him. Everyone knew that Ahithophel gave advice with uncommon wisdom, almost as though it came directly from God (2 Samuel 16:23). So Absalom asked for Ahithophel's advice, but he also sought counsel from Hushai, David's close friend, who pretended to be part of Absalom's rebellion. Through Hushai the Lord answered David's prayer (2 Samuel 15:31). Hushai came up with a plan that appealed to Absalom's vanity. Absalom followed it, rejecting Ahithophel. Ahithophel hanged himself in frustration and bitterness. Undoubtedly, too, Ahitophel sensed that Absalom's rebellion would fail; then Ahitophel would face charges of treason.

WEEK 28 • FRIDAY 2 Samuel 19:1—20:26

Why did Joab kill Amasa?

Amasa was a nephew of David and cousin of both Absalom and Joab. Absalom had appointed Amasa to head his army in place of Joab. After Absalom's defeat, David made Amasa his new commander and ordered him to reorganize the army of Judah and quell a rebellion that arose shortly after Absalom's treason. Joab's men went to fight under the command of Abishai. When Joab and Amasa met, Joab took hold of Amasa's beard as if to greet him with a kiss. But instead, Joab stabbed Amasa (2 Samuel 20:4–10); most likely Joab killed Amasa to regain his position as commander of David's army. Years earlier, Joab had murdered Abner in this same way and for similar reasons. It may also be that Amasa was secretly working against the king. Amasa had, after all, served as Absalom's general (2 Samuel 17:25).

WEEK 28 • SATURDAY 2 Samuel 21:1—22:51

Why were Saul's sons and grandsons killed for the murders Saul had committed?

During the reign of David, Israel suffered a three-year drought and widespread famine. David asked God about the cause of the drought. The Lord said it had come about because Saul had waged war against the Gibeonites, breaking Israel's covenant with them (see Joshua 9:3–16; 2 Samuel 21:1). When David asked the Gibeonites what he should do to make amends, they asked that seven of Saul's male descendants be given over to them for execution. In a sense, the death of Saul's two sons and five grandsons may be regarded as a judgment of God against Saul for his cruelty, following the principles of the blood avenger (Numbers 35:19). These men may very well have carried out Saul's orders. In any case, justice was executed by David on behalf of the Gibeonites.

WEEK 29 • MONDAY   2 Samuel 23:1–39

Why did David pour out the water after his soldiers risked their lives for it?

The stories of David's mighty men serve as a literary flashback and give a more complete picture of David's reign. The deed recorded in 2 Samuel 23:13–17 took place as David hid out from Saul in the wilderness and during the early days of David's reign while he was fighting the Philistines. David made an off-hand remark about his thirst; and his soldiers risked their lives to bring him water. But then David poured out the water on the ground as an offering to God, because he was so moved by the sacrifice it represented. When Hebrews offered sacrifices, they never consumed the blood. It represented life and was poured out before God. David would not drink this water, which represented the lives of his soldiers. Instead, he offered it to God in gratitude for his loyal followers.

WEEK 29 • TUESDAY   2 Samuel 24:1–25

What is the significance of the threshing floor David bought?

David took a census during peacetime. Apparently, he wanted to glory in the size and power of Israel and its army. By doing this, David gave the impression that Israel's impressive victories had come because of his superior forces rather than the grace of Israel's covenant Lord. Because of David's vanity, God sent a plague on Israel, and 70,000 people died. This seems unjust unless we consider that it's highly likely these people shared in King David's arrogance concerning Israel's military might. God stopped the angel who was afflicting the people at the threshing floor of Araunah (2 Samuel 24:15–16). Araunah offered everything necessary for David to build an altar there. But David insisted on paying for the threshing floor, and then he used it to sacrifice for his sin of focusing on military power. After David's death, God chose this site as the location of Solomon's temple. This gave the people a new focus for national unity: a place where together they could worship the living God. Centuries later, near that temple site, God allowed His Son to die on Calvary's cross as the perfect, once-for-all sacrifice for the sins of the world. David paid the price for the threshing floor, yet God paid a much dearer price for our salvation.

WEEK 29 • WEDNESDAY   *1 Kings 1:1—2:46*

Why was Solomon so upset when Adonijah asked that Abishag be his wife?

When David was old, his servants found a young, beautiful virgin named Abishag to lie with him and keep him warm. She also served as David's nurse but had no sexual relations with him (1 Kings 1:3–4). Adonijah was David's fourth son and the oldest surviving son. Therefore, he was the logical choice to succeed his father as king. But the Lord had not chosen Adonijah. Led by the Lord, David named Solomon as his successor, and the priest anointed Solomon as the new king. When Bathsheba, Solomon's mother, passed on Adonijah's request that Abishag be given to him in marriage, Solomon became angry and vowed that Adonijah's request would cost him his life. Solomon understood the request as an attempt to usurp the throne. Though Abishag had had no sexual relations with David, she technically belonged to his royal harem. Possession of the royal harem in that ancient world signified the right of succession. Marriage to Abishag would strengthen Adonijah's treasonous claim to the throne.

WEEK 29 • THURSDAY   *1 Kings 3:1—4:34*

Why did Solomon marry a foreigner?

As Solomon became king, he swiftly eliminated those who opposed him and replaced them with new men loyal to him. Soon his kingdom was firmly established and secure (1 Kings 2:46). One might wonder then why the king married a foreigner. Solomon made a peace treaty with the king of Egypt and sealed it by marrying his daughter. The motivation for this marriage was obviously political. Marriage between royal families was common in the ancient Near East because it helped to secure peace. Most of Solomon's 700 marriages were political in nature. These marriages built friendships with surrounding nations, but they also proved to be the beginning of Solomon's eventual downfall.

WEEK 29 • FRIDAY   *1 Kings 5:1—7:51*

What was the significance of not using any iron tools at the temple site?

God gave Solomon wisdom and also chose Solomon as the one to build His temple. As the building progressed, the workers used no iron tools at the building site. Solomon commanded that his workers not use tools because he didn't want to disobey God's law concerning altars. Altars dedicated to God were to be made of uncut stones—stones on which no iron tool was used (see Deuteronomy 27:5). God didn't want the people to be tempted to carve images in the altars dedicated to Him, as they did when they created a calf to worship (see Exodus 32:4). He wanted them to worship Him—not any images. Yet tools were forbidden only at the construction site, not at the quarry. Using pre-fitted stones made the construction of the temple go much faster.

WEEK 29 • SATURDAY   *1 Kings 8:1–66*

Why did Solomon offer so many sacrifices?

When the construction of the temple was complete, Solomon brought in all the furnishings. Just reading about their beauty takes one's breath away. On the day of dedication, the priests brought the ark of the covenant into the temple. This great day of dedication stands beside the day of the exodus from Egypt in importance. God would dwell in this magnificent temple. Here He would receive His people's offerings, hear their prayers, grant them pardon. Today we are the Lord's temple. The holy Christian church is still filled with precious things—His people, "living stones" built on the sure foundation of the apostles and the prophets with Christ Himself as the chief cornerstone. On the day of dedication King Solomon and the people of Israel sacrificed countless sheep and cattle (1 Kings 8:5). These reflected the nation's thankfulness to the Lord for giving them a central and permanent place of worship. Solomon and Israel gave in abundance to God, who had given (and still gives) even more abundantly.

WEEK 30 • MONDAY   *1 Kings 9:1—10:29*

What is the significance of Solomon accumulating chariots and horses?

Under God's blessing, King Solomon became the richest and wisest of all the kings on earth. Year after year, rulers from all over the world came to hear Solomon's wisdom. Everyone who came brought a gift (1 Kings 10:25). The accumulation of horses and chariots was forbidden by Mosaic law (Deuteronomy 17:16), but Solomon had 1,400 chariots and 12,000 horses. The Lord prohibited this, because He wanted His people to depend on Him for their protection and victories, not on their own power. The presence of strong physical defenses in Israel turned the hearts of Solomon and of the people away from trust in the Lord.

WEEK 30 • TUESDAY   *1 Kings 11:1–43*

If Solomon was so wise, how could he turn to other gods?

Solomon had many foreign wives besides Pharaoh's daughter: 700 wives and 300 concubines (1 Kings 11:3). The size of the harem reflects his wealth and his court's splendor. These wives and concubines led Solomon astray spiritually. For all his wisdom, Solomon was a sinner, as are all human beings. Apparently, Solomon could not say no to compromise or to lustful desires. Though Solomon's multiple marriages were primarily political in nature, as time went on, he became quite attached to these women—and eventually to their gods. The atmosphere of paganism and idolatry introduced into Solomon's court by his foreign wives gradually led Solomon himself into idolatry. Solomon did not totally abandon the true God, but he worshiped other gods as well. This is called syncretism; the Lord expressly forbade it. Solomon possessed great wisdom, but he did not apply that wisdom in his own life. Because Solomon did not keep God's commands, the Lord said his empire would disintegrate and eventually divide into two hostile camps.

WEEK 30 • WEDNESDAY

1 Kings 12:1–33

Why did Jeroboam set up two golden calves?

The kingdom of Israel split apart after Solomon's death. His son Rehoboam became king in Judah (ruling over the southern tribes of Judah and Benjamin), and Jeroboam became king in Israel (ruling the remaining 10 tribes in the north). Through a prophet, God told the two opposing kings not to fight each other (1 Kings 12:24). Jeroboam did not trust his people's commitment to him, so he devised a plan to secure his people's loyalty—he set up two golden calves. One calf was located in Dan in the far north of Israel, and the other was located in Bethel close to the southern border of Judah. If the people went to Dan or Bethel to worship, it would keep them from returning to the magnificent temple in Jerusalem, which was not part of Jeroboam's territory. Jeroboam feared that if people returned to Jerusalem they would then shift their allegiance back to Rehoboam, Solomon's son. Jeroboam not only tried to redirect the people's worship but also he broke other commands of God. He ordained priests outside the tribe of Israel and changed the date on which his people would celebrate.

WEEK 30 • THURSDAY

1 Kings 13:1—14:31

Why did the man of God die for trusting what a prophet said?

An unnamed prophet brought an unsettling message to Jeroboam. Eventually Jeroboam realized this messenger had come from God, and the king offered the prophet hospitality and gifts. The prophet refused because God had told him not to eat or drink and not to go home the way he came (1 Kings 13:9). On his way home, the messenger met an old prophet who seduced him to come to his home to eat and drink. After leaving the old prophet's house, the messenger was killed by a lion. The prophet died because he listened to the elderly prophet's claim to have a different message from God. The messenger ignored God's clear instructions and followed those of another human being, even though that human being had prophet credentials. Following false prophets always leads to death and destruction. A true prophet never contradicts God's Word.

WEEK 30 • FRIDAY   *1 Kings 15:1—16:34*

What is an Asherah pole?

Many of the kings of Judah dishonored God by praying to idols. Included in this idol worship by both the kings and the people were the Asherah poles. 1 Kings 15:13 calls these repulsive. Asherah was the consort of El, the chief Canaanite god. She was the beautiful goddess of war and fertility. Wooden poles, perhaps carved in her image, were often set up in her honor and placed near other pagan objects of worship to encourage worship of Asherah. This worship involved the worshiper in cultic prostitution with pagan priests and, more commonly, priestesses. Even before Israel entered the Promised Land, the Lord told His people to cut down these poles (Exodus 34:13) and burn them (Deuteronomy 12:3). But the kings ignored God's Word. A later king of Judah, Asa, "did what was right in the eyes of the LORD" (1 Kings 15:11, 13) when he cut down one of these poles and burned it in the Kidron Valley.

WEEK 30 • SATURDAY   *1 Kings 17:1—18:46*

Why did the prophets of Baal slash themselves with swords?

Elijah, prophet of the true God, called for a showdown between the prophets of Baal and himself. In reality this amounted to a showdown between his God and theirs. Elijah told the people to make up their minds to follow either the Lord or Baal, not both (1 Kings 18:21). The test was to see whether Elijah's God or Baal would send fire to burn the sacrifice. The 450 prophets of Baal called on Baal from morning to noon with no response. Then they slashed themselves with swords. Self-inflicted wounds were symbolic of self-sacrifice. By this desperate act the priests hoped to convince Baal of the fervor of their devotion and to move him to reward them by doing what they had asked. These prophets served a false god, one who could neither hear nor help. Elijah called on the Lord in a simple prayer, and the Lord showed His mighty power in dramatic fashion. The people who watched exclaimed, "The LORD—He is God!" (1 Kings 18:39).

WEEK 31 • MONDAY
                                          1 Kings 19:1–21

What was the significance of Elijah throwing his cloak around Elisha?

Elijah had served as the Lord's faithful prophet in Judah for many years. After Elijah's victory over Baal on Mount Carmel, the Lord told Elijah to anoint Elisha to succeed him as prophet (1 Kings 19:16). Elijah's cloak symbolized his prophetic office. When he put it around Elisha's shoulders, Elisha understood that he would serve as Elijah's successor. God gave Elisha a new identity and set him apart for a prophetic mission. Just as God gave Joshua ("The LORD saves") to Moses to complete the work Moses had begun, now God gave Elisha ("God saves") to Elijah.

WEEK 31 • TUESDAY
                                          1 Kings 20:1–43

Why did the man die for refusing to injure a prophet?

So-called "schools of prophets" in Israel taught the law of Moses and the Word of the Lord. A young prophet from one of these "schools" received a message from God to have one of the other prophets strike him with a weapon (1 Kings 20:35). When the man refused, a lion attacked and killed him. This may seem like harsh punishment for refusing to injure a prophet, but in reality the man had refused to obey the Lord's clear—though admittedly unusual—command. His fate was a clear message to Ahab showing the seriousness of disobeying God's Word.

WEEK 31 • WEDNESDAY
                                          1 Kings 21:1—22:53

Why was a vineyard so valuable?

Naboth was a neighbor of King Ahab and owned a vineyard close to the palace. Ahab wanted the land for a vegetable garden. Ahab offered to buy the vineyard from Naboth or to give him a better vineyard in exchange (1 Kings 21:2). However, Naboth refused the king's offer. Naboth was a God-fearing Israelite. In obedience to the Mosaic law, Naboth refused to sell his inheritance, because he rightly regarded it as a trust. The land itself was the Lord's; Naboth and his family were only stewards. To sell the vineyard would violate the land laws of Leviticus 25. Ahab's covetousness of another man's land reminds us of an earlier king, David, who coveted another man's wife. Both kings paid a high price for their sin.

WEEK 31 • THURSDAY   2 Kings 1:1—2:25

What did Elisha mean when he asked Elijah for a double portion of his spirit?

The Lord was about to take Elijah up into heaven visibly in a whirlwind. Elisha stayed with Elijah to the very end. When Elijah asked what he could do for Elisha before he went to heaven, Elisha asked for a double portion of Elijah's spirit (2 Kings 2:9). What exactly did Elisha want? Elisha was asking for a double share of Elijah's prophetic power. According to custom, the firstborn son received a double share of his father's inheritance. Elisha asked for that share that belonged to him as Elijah's successor, a practical gift that would help in his work as spiritual leader of the nation. But the gift wasn't Elijah's to give; only the Lord could grant Elisha's request. In mercy He did, and still today the Lord continues to pass the enabling Spirit to prophets of every generation who serve as His spokesmen.

WEEK 31 • FRIDAY   2 Kings 3:1—4:44

Was the child truly dead or merely unconscious?

A Shunammite woman had befriended Elisha by providing a room for him to use whenever he was in the area. She and her husband had only one child, a son. One day he died quite suddenly (2 Kings 4:18–21). The woman went to Elisha for help. The prophet returned with her, prayed earnestly for the boy, and God restored the young boy to life. Was the child really dead? Yes! The Bible emphatically states three times that the boy was dead. Elisha's staff, laid on the boy, hadn't wakened him (2 Kings 4:31). And as Elisha prayed and lay on the boy's body, the body became warm, indicating that the body had been cold in death. God truly brought the boy back to life, thereby demonstrating His power over death itself. This miracle worked through Elisha pointed toward Jesus' own ministry centuries later when he raised Lazarus from the dead (see John 11). The

Lord rules over all of life. Life itself comes to us as His gift at His direction. Jesus is the resurrection and the life, and those who put their hope in Him will live forever.

WEEK 31 • SATURDAY   *2 Kings 5:1–27*

How could Elisha say Naaman would be forgiven for bowing before an idol?

Naaman commanded the army of the king of Aram. Naaman had leprosy, a horrible skin disorder. Naaman went to Elisha looking for a cure. When Naaman followed Elisha's simple direction to wash seven times in the Jordan River, he was healed. Afterward, Naaman came to faith in the true God. But Naaman also said that at times he would have to bow down to an idol when he was with the king (2 Kings 5:18), and he asked for forgiveness. Naaman was not asking for permission to worship the god Rimmon, but rather for permission to do his civic duty, helping the king get down and up as he bowed before Rimmon. His bowing alongside would no longer be an act of worship. Elisha didn't directly address the issue but simply told Naaman, "Go in peace." This new believer was in God's grace and would be led and guided by the Lord.

WEEK 32 • MONDAY   *2 Kings 6:1—7:20*

What happens during a siege of a fortified city?

When the king of Aram laid siege to Samaria, the people in that city suffered greatly. King Joram wrongfully blamed Elisha for this suffering. Before the development of modern artillery that could simply batter down walls, a siege was an important military tactic. Like a naval blockade on the water, a siege cut off all traffic in and out of a city. Supplies, especially food and water, were kept from the people in an attempt to starve them into surrendering. Any siege, successful or not, meant terrible suffering for the common people.

WEEK 32 • TUESDAY   *2 Kings 8:1–29*

Why did King Ben-Hadad offer a gift to Elisha?

Ben-Hadad, king of Aram, was ill. When he heard Elisha was in Damascus, the king told his servant to meet Elisha and ask whether he would recover. Experiences in battle had shown Ben-Hadad that Elisha's God was mighty, and so he sought his counsel. The gift for Elisha included 40 camel-loads of the finest wares of Damascus (2 Kings 8:8–9). Why did the king offer a gift to Elisha? In fact, the caravan may not have carried as much wealth as one might suppose. It was customary in the ancient Near East to make a great show of giving gifts, and it was fairly common to have one camel carry only one gift. Regardless, the gift was generous, and Ben-Hadad evidently thought such a gift would buy God's favor and favorably influence Elisha's answer. People still seek to buy God's favor, whether it be with gifts of money or good deeds. In truth, we have nothing to give; He needs nothing from us. How much better to wait humbly on the Lord and then give thanks for His kindness toward us, especially for His mercy in Jesus our Savior.

WEEK 32 • WEDNESDAY   *2 Kings 9:1—10:36*

Why did the bystanders allow dogs to eat Jezebel's body?

Jehu, anointed king of Israel by Elisha, destroyed all of Ahab's family at the Lord's command. He had Jezebel, Ahab's wife and the mother of King Joram, thrown out a window and killed as well. Jehu ordered that she be buried. But when his men went to bury her, they found nothing except her skull, feet, and hands. Dogs had eaten Jezebel's body. In ancient Israel, dogs were not household pets; they were wild scavengers that ran in packs. The Israelites considered it a horrible disgrace if their dead did not receive a proper burial. But no one bothered to protect Jezebel's corpse because she was so despised. See Elijah's prophecy concerning Jezebel's death in 1 Kings 21:23. Her name has been preserved as a symbol of wickedness and idolatry. Jezebel died a horrible death because of her sin.

WEEK 32 • THURSDAY   *2 Kings 11:1—12:21*

Why was the temple in disrepair?

Once a magnificent place of worship, the temple had fallen into disrepair. Joash ordered the priests to repair the damage (2 Kings 12:5). But 16 years later the work had not begun! Since the temple was now 140 years old, some of the disrepair was due to age. But most of the damage and neglect had occurred during the reign of Judah's previous evil leaders, especially Queen Athaliah. Dirt and filth had accumulated, the gold and bronze had gone unpolished, and heathen idols had been set up inside the temple itself. All this shows how far the people had strayed from the Lord, the God who had made His presence known among them in that temple. Because Judah had turned from the Lord, it is no surprise that they had turned also from His dwelling place.

WEEK 32 • FRIDAY

2 Kings 13:1—14:29

What were the high places and why were the kings reluctant to remove them?

Located on the tops of hills, the so-called high places were used for religious rites. But the Lord had chosen the temple in Jerusalem as the place where He should be worshiped. The Israelites could only offer sacrifices to God at the place He chose, not just anywhere (Deuteronomy 12:13–14). The Israelites did worship the Lord, the God of Israel at some of these high places. Perhaps Judah's kings saw this as a justification for not destroying them. These places were, however, the first places where worship of pagan gods appeared. They were far from harmless.

WEEK 32 • SATURDAY

2 Kings 15:1—16:20

Why would anyone sacrifice their children?

Ahaz, king of Judah, didn't follow the ways of the Lord. Instead he followed the example of the wicked kings of Israel. He even sacrificed his own son in fire (2 Kings 16:3). Child sacrifice was a common practice of the pagan Canaanite nations. The reasoning was this: if a god would give assistance for the sacrifice of a goat or bull, a human life would buy a much stronger favor. The Lord strictly forbade this practice (Leviticus 18:21; Deuteronomy 18:10). His prophet Jeremiah would later repeat God's position on the practice, calling it detestable (Jeremiah 32:35). Children were a gift and a blessing, a very obvious way by which the Lord showed His love to Israel. Firstborn sons were to be consecrated to God, not sacrificed. Someday God would sacrifice His Son, but He did not ask that of His people.

WEEK 33 • MONDAY

2 Kings 17:1–41

Who were the Samaritans and where did they come from?

Just as God had warned through the prophets, the Assyrians conquered Israel, and the 10 tribes were taken into exile. The king of Assyria then brought people from other countries and settled them in Samaria. They took over Samaria—the entire northern kingdom of Israel—and lived in its towns (2 Kings 17:24). The policy of Assyria toward conquered lands was to deport the inhabitants in order to wipe out their ethnic and national identities, thus making rebellion virtually impossible. Then, many prominent Assyrians were imported to the region to replace these exiles. These Assyrians took leadership positions in the conquered country. Once again, Gentiles lived in this land, the land the Lord had promised to Abraham and given to his descendants. Israel's continuous rebellion against God provoked Him to anger until finally, God delivered them to the enemy. But despite Israel's sin, the Lord would keep His promise to Judah, that from this tribe would come a new and faithful King, the Savior who would reign forever.

WEEK 33 • TUESDAY

2 Kings 18:1—19:37

Why did the Assyrian commander hurl insults at the people of Jerusalem?

The land of Judah was caught between two powers, Egypt and Assyria. Both wanted to overtake Judah. The Assyrian commander came to bait Hezekiah prior to battle (2 Kings 18:17). His blasphemous and arrogant remarks were intended to divide the king and his people. His comments were not only demoralizing but also an all-out effort to destroy the belief system King Hezekiah had fought so hard to restore in Judah. The scheme backfired. Instead of surrendering, Hezekiah turned to the Lord in prayer, and the Lord won a great victory for His people.

WEEK 33 • WEDNESDAY   *2 Kings 20:1–21*

Why was it so bad for Hezekiah to show the Babylonians his wealth?

Judah's kings faced continual temptations to trust human alliances rather than relying on the Lord and on His word of promise. In 2 Kings, we read that Hezekiah became ill to the point of death, but he asked for mercy and the Lord healed him. On hearing this, Merodach-Baladan, son of the king of Babylon, sent messengers bearing letters and gifts, hoping to win Hezekiah's alliance against Assyria. When the messengers arrived, Hezekiah proudly showed them all of his wealth and possessions (2 Kings 20:13). Evidently Hezekiah wanted an alliance with the Babylonians as much or more than they did. But in boasting of his wealth and power, Hezekiah robbed God of the glory and honor and thanks that rightly belonged to Him. One day soon everything in Hezekiah's palace, including some of Hezekiah's own descendants, would be taken into captivity by the very Babylonians Hezekiah saw as potential allies.

WEEK 33 • THURSDAY   *2 Kings 21:1–26*

How could a young boy like Manasseh rule Judah?

Manasseh, Hezekiah's son, became king when he was 12 years old (2 Kings 21:1). His birth took place after King Hezekiah had become ill. Manasseh served as co-regent with his father for 10 years. He also had the help of his mother together with other advisors and priests. Even so Manasseh's reign was like that of his evil grandfather, Ahaz. Manasseh rebuilt the altars and idols that Hezekiah had destroyed and did many other evils in the eyes of the Lord.

WEEK 33 • FRIDAY   *2 Kings 22:1—23:37*

How could the Scriptures be lost?

When Josiah became king, he reigned in honor and did what was right in the eyes of God. During his reign, Josiah sent his secretary Shaphan to the temple to have it repaired. In doing so, Shaphan found the Book of the Law (2 Kings 22:8). When King Josiah heard the words from this book, he tore his robes in sorrow for all the evil that kings of the past had committed and tolerated. It was this corrupt behavior that had caused the books of the Scriptures to become lost and forgotten in the first place. The people had worshiped false gods and thus showed that they thought they didn't need God's Word. Because they considered it useless, they eventually lost it in the rubble of the neglected temple.

WEEK 33 • SATURDAY   *2 Kings 24:1—25:30*

What did it mean for the Judeans to go into captivity?

On three separate occasions, the Babylonians attacked Judah. Each time, Babylon deported large numbers of people to Babylon. During the second attack, most of Judah's leaders, including its king (2 Kings 24:10), found themselves leaving the land that the Lord had promised to Abraham. This left only the poorest and weakest people. By placing these people in positions of leadership, the Babylonians won their allegiance. The leaders who had been taken captive, however, were integrated into Babylonian society and government. Despite those who absorbed and were absorbed by the Babylonian culture, God preserved a remnant who would later return to Judah.

WEEK 34 • MONDAY
1 Chronicles 1:1—4:43

Why was this genealogical list so important to the Israelites?

The genealogical list in 1 Chronicles 1:1—4:43 was created for a people who had barely survived exile in Babylon and who now once again walked the soil of their fathers. The multitude of names in these chapters shows the link of the exiles with their past and especially with the covenant the Lord had made with Abraham. Appearances to the contrary, they were the people through whom the Creator of all had chosen to bless all the families of the earth (Genesis 12:1–3). These genealogies pointed to the promise that from these people would come salvation "through the one man, Jesus Christ" (Romans 5:17).

WEEK 34 • TUESDAY
1 Chronicles 5:1—8:40

Why is Manasseh called a half-tribe?

The Reubenites, the Gadites, and the half-tribe of Manasseh waged a war and won because the Lord fought for them (1 Chronicles 5:18–20). The tribe of Manasseh came from seven different families, one from Machir and the others from Gilead, thus creating two halves. They occupied land on both sides of the Jordan. One half of the tribe resided to the west of the Jordan, finding land north of Ephraim. The other half of the tribe resided to the east of the Jordan, occupying Bashan and part of Gilead.

WEEK 34 • WEDNESDAY
1 Chronicles 9:1—12:40

Why did so many fighting men join David?

David was anointed king by the Lord's prophet Samuel. David captured the city of Jerusalem (1 Chronicles 11:1–9). Because the Lord Almighty blessed him, David's strength and authority increased. More and more warriors were drawn to him as these warriors confessed their faith in God's Word and aligned themselves with the Lord's anointed. With their support, David eventually became king over all the tribes of Israel.

WEEK 34 • THURSDAY   *1 Chronicles 13:1—14:17*

How did David get an answer when he inquired of God?

When the Philistines heard that David had been anointed king over Israel, they prepared for battle and went to search for him. As David went out to meet them, he asked God if he should attack the Philistines (1 Chronicles 14:10). In seeking his answer, David turned, as was his usual practice, to the priest who used the Urim and Thummim to discern the Lord's will. Possibly used something like dice, these stones somehow communicated God's answer. The Lord told David He would hand the Philistines over to David. On the strength of that promise, David attacked and won a great victory.

WEEK 34 • FRIDAY   *1 Chronicles 15:1—16:43*

Why was the ark in Jerusalem while the tabernacle was still at Gibeon?

David prepared a place for the ark of the covenant by pitching a tent for it. In keeping with God's instructions, David commanded that only the Levites could move the ark to its new location (1 Chronicles 15:1–2). The tabernacle at that time was located at Gibeon, where offerings and sacrifices were still being made. The tent in Jerusalem was the interim housing for the ark until the temple was built. (This did not occur until the time of Solomon.) Until then, Israel had two worship centers and two high priests: Zadok served in the tabernacle in Gibeon, and Abiathar served at the ark in Jerusalem.

WEEK 34 • SATURDAY   *1 Chronicles 17:1–27*

Why was David not allowed to build the temple?

David lived in a great palace, while the ark of the covenant sat under a tent. David told Nathan his plan concerning a temple (1 Chronicles 17:1–2). Nathan gave his approval. However, the Lord told Nathan that David would not build the temple, because David had "shed much blood on the earth" (1 Chronicles 22:8). The Lord Himself would build the temple using David's son Solomon to do so.

WEEK 35 • MONDAY   *1 Chronicles 18:1—20:8*

Why did kings go to war in the spring?

During the winter months, kings took advantage of undesirable weather conditions to plan their upcoming battles. Following the spring harvest when there was less agricultural activity, they went to war (1 Chronicles 20:1). Armies on the move could live off the land during times of battle. It was at this time that Joab led his forces out to defeat Rabbah, the capital of the Ammonites.

WEEK 35 • TUESDAY   *1 Chronicles 21:1–30*

Why was it sinful for David to count his fighting men?

After his many victories, David succumbed to Satan's temptation and took a census of Israel (1 Chronicles 21:1). Advised by Joab that his act was wrong in the eyes of the Lord, David persisted. Taking of the census was not wrong in itself. What made it wrong was David's motivation: he took great pride in the large number, thinking this was his accomplishment rather than a gift from God.

WEEK 35 • WEDNESDAY   *1 Chronicles 22:1–19*

Why did David stockpile all these materials when he couldn't build the temple?

David began to prepare for the building of the temple, even though God had chosen his son Solomon to carry out the task. Knowing that Solomon was young and inexperienced, David wanted to be sure that the temple was appropriate in size and splendor for reflecting God's glory (1 Chronicles 22:5). Thus David assumed much of the cost of the materials used in building the temple.

WEEK 35 • THURSDAY   *1 Chronicles 23:1—27:34*

Why did the temple need gatekeepers?

In order to help his son Solomon build the temple for the Lord, David gathered together many leaders and assigned them their responsibilities with respect to the temple, one of which was gatekeeping (1 Chronicles 23:4–5). Gatekeepers guarded the entrances to the temple and opened them for times of worship. They cleaned the temple, maintained the equipment used in the temple, and ordered and stored food supplies for the priests who served at the temple. Gatekeepers were men of high integrity, entrusted with the offerings and with the other gifts worshipers brought to the temple.

WEEK 35 • FRIDAY   *1 Chronicles 28:1–21*

Of all David's sons, why was Solomon chosen to be king?

In addressing the assembled officials of Israel, David explained that the honor of building the temple would not fall to him. Rather, God had chosen David's son Solomon to be the next king and to carry out the Lord's plan (1 Chronicles 28:5). Though God's will had overruled David's desire to build the temple, God's grace had given David more than his heart could have imagined. It was that same grace of God that chose Solomon to be the next king.

WEEK 35 • SATURDAY   *1 Chronicles 29:1–30*

Why was Solomon acknowledged king for a second time?

David celebrated with his entire assembly as he brought his gifts to the temple for building. The following day, after the people made their sacrifices to the Lord, they acknowledged Solomon as their king for a second time (1 Chronicles 29:22), anointing him before the Lord. Solomon's first appointment was carried out in a hurried fashion to take the steam out of Adonijah's coup (1 Kings 1). In the calmer days at the end of David's life, Solomon's ascent to the throne could be celebrated with proper solemnity.

WEEK 36 • MONDAY

2 Chronicles 1:1—2:18

Why did Solomon go to the high place at Gibeon to offer these sacrifices?

When Solomon became king, he called the leaders of Israel to join him at Gibeon (2 Chronicles 1:3), one of the hilltops northeast of Jerusalem. While mountaintops were usually off-limits to the Israelites because many were littered with pagan shrines, Gibeon was still the official location of the tabernacle. At Gibeon Solomon asked the Lord for the gift of wisdom (2 Chronicles 1:10).

WEEK 36 • TUESDAY

2 Chronicles 3:1—5:14

What is the significance of the cloud filling the temple?

When the temple was completed, Solomon placed in it the prescribed furnishings according to God's instructions. The priests and musicians were involved in the service as the ark of the covenant was brought into the temple. Then the temple was filled with a cloud (2 Chronicles 5:13–14). A cloud had signified God's presence since the time of Israel's wilderness wanderings (Exodus 14:19–20; 24:15–18; 33:20). The cloud, the sign of God's presence, hallowed the temple as God's dwelling place.

WEEK 36 • WEDNESDAY

2 Chronicles 6:1—7:22

Why did fire come down from heaven?

When Solomon finished his prayer of dedication, fire descended from heaven, consuming the offerings and sacrifices placed on the altar (2 Chronicles 7:1–2). As with the cloud (2 Chronicles 5:13–14), the fire signified that God had heard the prayers and had accepted the offerings. Because fire symbolized God's presence, the fire was kept burning on the altar from that time on. Fire had also descended from heaven at the dedication of the tabernacle (Leviticus 9:22–24).

WEEK 36 • THURSDAY
2 Chronicles 8:1—9:31

Where was Sheba?

Solomon's reputation as a wise ruler spread beyond the boundaries of Israel. The Queen of Sheba also heard of it and sought an audience with Solomon (2 Chronicles 9:1). Archaeological evidence suggests that Sheba was a mercantile kingdom in an area of modern-day Yemen. It profited from sea trade with India and Africa.

WEEK 36 • FRIDAY
2 Chronicles 10:1—11:23

Why did the Israelites send for Jeroboam?

When Solomon died, his son Rehoboam was crowned his successor. He was not, however, the only son eligible to take his father's place. Years before, the prophet Ahijah had predicted that Israel would be divided and that Jeroboam would rule the northern kingdom (1 Kings 11:26–40). Because Solomon found this announcement threatening, he tried to kill Jeroboam. Jeroboam fled to Egypt at that time but returned to Israel when he received word that Solomon was dead.

WEEK 36 • SATURDAY
2 Chronicles 12:1–16

Why did Rehoboam replace the gold shields with bronze ones?

When Shishak, king of Egypt, attacked Israel, he carried off the valuable treasures from the temple and the palace. In an attempt to replace these sacred articles, Rehoboam substituted the gold shields his father, Solomon, had commissioned with bronze ones (2 Chronicles 12:10), an inferior metal. (Rehoboam had no more gold to use.) In this way, Rehoboam used a pretense to maintain a semblance of the glory God had given his father.

WEEK 37 • MONDAY
2 Chronicles 13:1—14:15

Why did the cities have walls and gates?

When Asa became king of Judah, he tore down pagan shrines in the land. God blessed Asa's land and reign with peace. Peace usually brought prosperity and allowed the people to focus on building, instead of defending themselves. Asa took advantage of this time of peace by building walls and gates around major cities in the land (2 Chronicles 14:7). The walls, bars, and gates provided protection for the inhabitants of a city from any future, invading army.

WEEK 37 • TUESDAY
2 Chronicles 15:1—16:14

Why did King Asa depose his grandmother Maacah?

King Asa acted on the word of the Lord and "cleaned house" in Judah and Benjamin. Not only did he put to death those who opposed the Lord, he even deposed his grandmother—Maacah (2 Chronicles 15:16)! Even though Maacah was family, she had rejected the Lord by making an Asherah pole and encouraging pagan worship practices. Deposing her was a sign of God's work in Asa, leading the king to a commitment to serve only the Lord.

WEEK 37 • WEDNESDAY
2 Chronicles 17:1—18:34

How could God send a lying spirit to the prophets?

Ahab was already determined to go to war when he met with his in-house prophets. The prophets sensed his inclination and told him what he wanted to hear. Micaiah, a true prophet of the Lord, described the Lord as putting a lying spirit in the mouths of the false prophets (2 Chronicles 18:21). This was a way of saying that, while the Lord does not tempt people to do evil, He does sometimes use people's sins to advance His purposes.

WEEK 37 • THURSDAY
2 Chronicles 19:1—20:37

Why would King Jehoshaphat appoint judges?

Reprimanded by God for going abroad to join Ahab, Jehoshaphat restricted himself to activities he could initiate in Judah. Thus, in order to reform the country's judicial system, he appointed judges throughout Judah (2 Chronicles 19:5). These judges were to enforce the Law of the Lord without fear or favor, because in reality they were judging not "for man but for the LORD" (2 Chronicles 19:6).

WEEK 37 • FRIDAY
2 Chronicles 21:1—22:12

Why would Jehoram kill all his brothers?

Jehoram succeeded Jehoshaphat as king when he was 32 years old. His first order of business was to put his brothers to death (2 Chronicles 21:4). This bloody assassination of all potential rivals fit the patterns followed by the northern kings. Culturally acceptable in those times, this tragedy showing the wickedness of Jehoram was not sanctioned by the Lord or His Law.

WEEK 37 • SATURDAY
2 Chronicles 23:1—24:27

Why were the Levites slow to collect the money for temple repairs?

Joash had become king at the age of seven. When he was older, God led Joash to restore the Lord's temple. Joash sent the priests and Levites throughout Judah to collect a God-ordained temple tax to cover the cost of the repairs. While it is not entirely clear why the Levites delayed in their collection (2 Chronicles 24:5), Joash set up a collection box outside the temple gates. This removed the priests and Levites from the collection process and, presumably, speeded it along.

WEEK 38 • MONDAY
2 Chronicles 25:1—26:23

Why was it wrong for Uzziah to offer incense to God?

Uzziah grew more powerful as Judah's leader. Intoxicated by his own influence, power, and success, King Uzziah entered the temple to burn incense on the altar of incense in the Holy Place (2 Chronicles 26:16). Worship functions had been reserved by God for "the priests, the descendants of Aaron, who have been consecrated to burn incense" (2 Chronicles 26:18). This act of disobedience on Uzziah's part may have been a grab for priestly power. Or perhaps the king simply saw himself as above God's Law. In any case, the consequences were severe.

WEEK 38 • TUESDAY
2 Chronicles 27:1—28:27

Why would King Ahaz offer sacrifices to foreign gods?

In the midst of military conflict with surrounding nations, Ahaz approached Tiglath Pileser, king of Assyria, for help. Instead, the Assyrians attacked, causing even greater pressure on Ahaz. Rather than turning to the Lord, Ahaz became more faithless, sacrificing to the gods of Damascus, desecrating the Jerusalem temple, and shutting its doors (2 Chronicles 28:23). His divided spiritual loyalties angered the Lord and kept Ahaz away from his only source of true help—the Lord Himself!

WEEK 38 • WEDNESDAY
2 Chronicles 29:1–36

Why did the Levites carry everything that was unclean to the Kidron Valley?

The priests entered the temple and removed all the unclean items. The Levites then would carry this desecrated refuse to the Kidron Valley (2 Chronicles 29:16). The Kidron Valley, which separated the Eastern Gate of Jerusalem from the Mount of Olives, was the city dump, where pagan idols and relics were buried after being destroyed. King Asa had also burned pagan cult objects there (2 Chronicles 15:16).

WEEK 38 • THURSDAY — 2 *Chronicles 30:1—31:21*

Why did the Levites need genealogical records?

Hezekiah had rededicated the temple and was now restoring regular worship services, which had been suspended by his father. Thus, he established a system whereby the tithes and offerings could be inventoried in the temple storerooms, and he put priests and Levites on duty in and around the temple. Genealogical lists would assure that only true descendants of Aaron would serve as priests and only true descendants of Levi would minister in the ways the Lord's Law prescribed. Priests and Levites could not interchange their jobs.

WEEK 38 • FRIDAY — 2 *Chronicles 32:1–33*

How did blocking the springs help Jerusalem?

In the Old Testament era, cities were often built near natural water sources. Hezekiah blocked the springs outside the walls of Jerusalem in order to keep his enemy from using the water. This would also prevent the enemy from poisoning the water source, which the people of Judah would need when the war ended.

WEEK 38 • SATURDAY — 2 *Chronicles 33:1–25*

Was it right to worship the God of Israel at the high places?

During the first part of his reign, King Manasseh "led Judah and the people of Jerusalem astray, so that they did more evil than" the other nations (2 Chronicles 33:9). After Manasseh was defeated by the Assyrians and imprisoned, he repented and instituted many reforms aimed at restoring the true worship of God. The people, however, continued to sacrifice at the high places (2 Chronicles 33:17), though only to the Lord. These sacrifices encouraged mixed spiritual loyalties; the high places had been built by the Canaanites for pagan worship. By sacrificing at the high places, the people compromised their worship of the one, true God.

WEEK 39 • MONDAY
2 Chronicles 34:1—35:27

Why did Josiah kill priests?

Young King Josiah initiated a campaign to destroy the images and altars of pagan worship so entrenched in Judah at that time. According to 2 Kings 23:20, Josiah slaughtered priests who had been involved in sacrificing on the forbidden high places. He also burned the bones of deceased false prophets who had been involved in similar desecrations. By burning the bones of prophets, he cleansed the temple area of those who had dishonored the Lord. This was part of his purging the land before he went on to repair the house of the Lord.

WEEK 39 • TUESDAY
2 Chronicles 36:1–23

What was the "sabbath rest" for the land?

When Nebuchadnezzar conquered Jerusalem, he carried away exiles to Babylon. As a result, the land of Judah was left alone. Largely uninhabited, it lay fallow. The biblical writers referred to this inactivity as a sabbath rest (2 Chronicles 36:21). According to Leviticus 25:4, the people were to honor the Lord by leaving the ground inactive every seventh year. The Lord intended this as an extension of the weekly sabbath. Not only would that sabbath year replenish soil nutrients, it would also remind the people that their prosperity came not from their hard work or their skill as farmers, but from the Creator, their covenant Lord.

WEEK 39 • WEDNESDAY
Ezra 1:1—2:70

Why did Cyrus want to rebuild the temple?

In the first year of his reign, Cyrus, the king of Persia, issued an edict ordering that the temple in Jerusalem, razed by the Babylonians, be rebuilt (Ezra 1:2). Jeremiah and Isaiah had prophesied that this would happen. Cyrus was probably not a convert to Judaism, but he was very shrewd. By supporting the various religions of his people, Cyrus hoped to gain favor with the many nationalities in his empire. This is a good example of God using unexpected individuals to accomplish His purpose, even when the individuals themselves do not suspect the Lord's intentions.

WEEK 39 • THURSDAY

Ezra 3:1—4:24

Why were surrounding people opposed to rebuilding the temple?

The Samaritans mixed their worship of pagan gods with worship of the Lord. This mixed worship caused the exiles to reject the help of the Samaritans in rebuilding the temple. Thus the Samaritans began to oppose the temple—a hostility that lasted into New Testament times (John 4). They lobbied the Persian government for about 20 years to cut off funds for the rebuilding project. It worked. The rebuilding was stopped until the reign of Darius I.

WEEK 39 • FRIDAY

Ezra 5:1—6:22

Why did the people of Jerusalem send letters to Babylon?

Those who opposed the rebuilding of the temple did not give up when their ploys of criticism, intimidation, and intervention failed. Furious that the temple project was gaining momentum and nearing completion, the governor of Trans-Euphrates and his associates challenged the project by writing Darius, the king of Babylon, in an attempt to discredit the people to whom Cyrus had given permission to rebuild the temple. However, when Darius found the decree of Cyrus, he decreed that the work on the temple should continue.

WEEK 39 • SATURDAY

Ezra 7:1—8:36

Why did Ezra want Levites to accompany them on the trip?

To complete the rebuilding of the temple would require many men. Levites and temple workers were especially needed, because Ezra planned on reinstituting the temple worship services. Yet Ezra found few volunteers, perhaps because they did not relish leaving their homes and established lives in Babylon. So Ezra sent recruiters out to find Levites, who lived in great numbers at Casiphia. In all of this Ezra saw the gracious hand of the Lord, blessing His people and restoring them to the land He had promised Abraham (Ezra 8:18).

WEEK 40 • MONDAY
Ezra 9:1—10:44

What was the problem with intermarriage?

Since the days of Gideon, Samson, Deborah, and the other judges, the men of Israel had intermarried with pagan women of neighboring nations. As a result, they embraced not only their heathen wives, but also the pagan worship practices of those wives. From the beginning, God had prohibited intermarriage with pagans (see Exodus 34:11–16; Deuteronomy 7:1–4). Israel had been God's chosen people, the nation into which He would send the world's Savior. Compromise with paganism could potentially derail this plan. This fact made intermarriage with the heathen especially dangerous.

WEEK 40 • TUESDAY
Nehemiah 1:1–11

What was the cupbearer's position in a royal household?

Artaxerxes, the Persian king, had allowed the Jews to return to Jerusalem. Ezra had overseen the rebuilding of the temple, but the walls of the city remained as rubble. Nehemiah served as cupbearer to the king (Nehemiah 1:11). As such, he was responsible for tasting the wine and food before serving it to the king to make certain it wasn't poisoned. Thus, Artaxerxes trusted Nehemiah with his life; Nehemiah enjoyed the king's unreserved confidence. Not surprisingly, Nehemiah thus also served as an influential, though unofficial, advisor.

WEEK 40 • WEDNESDAY
Nehemiah 2:1—3:32

Why did Nehemiah inspect the walls of Jerusalem at night?

Nehemiah asked for, and received, Artaxerxes' permission to go to Jerusalem to rebuild the city walls. Three days after Nehemiah arrived in Jerusalem, he took a few men with him to inspect the city walls at night (Nehemiah 2:11–12). Many non-Jews lived in Jerusalem, and the city was a hotbed of political intrigue. Spies would willingly sell information to the enemies of the Jews. Apparently, Nehemiah wanted to avoid letting others know his plans in advance. That way, those who opposed him would have little opportunity to organize their opposition.

WEEK 40 • THURSDAY   *Nehemiah 4:1—6:19*

Why was usury a problem?

Nehemiah angrily confronted the Israelite nobles and officials who charged their fellow countrymen interest to borrow money (Nehemiah 5:6–7). The great task to which Nehemiah had called them, that of rebuilding the wall around Jerusalem, had taken entire families away from their regular work. To survive during this time of economic crisis, families who held no property had borrowed from the rich, putting up their own children as collateral. The people who complained to Nehemiah were justifiably panicked as their debts mounted. Nehemiah argued that they were all children of the same God, called to one great purpose—the rebuilding of their nation! The Gentiles were watching—and laughing—as the rich Jews got richer. After Nehemiah's public condemnation of their activities, the nobles and officers immediately relented and refunded the borrowers' interest payments.

WEEK 40 • FRIDAY   *Nehemiah 7:1—8:18*

What was the Feast of Booths?

The Feast of Booths, which the people now enthusiastically celebrated (Nehemiah 8:13–18), had its origins in ancient Israelite history. This feast was celebrated during autumn harvest after the crops from the orchards and vineyards had been harvested. The people constructed "booths," or temporary shelters, to commemorate the 40 years that their forefathers had spent wandering in the desert after their release from captivity in Egypt. The people's observance of this feast showed their desire to connect with their heritage and to see themselves as the Lord's holy, covenant people. Indeed there was reason for joy and celebration. The city walls were complete, and the Lord had led the people themselves back to His Word and worship.

WEEK 40 • SATURDAY
Nehemiah 9:1—10:39

Why did the people feel a need to make a binding agreement?

The commitment to a binding agreement (Nehemiah 9:38) came as a response to the teaching of Ezra and the reading of the Law. The writer of the book of Nehemiah also places this incident at the end of a long discourse on Israel's past disobedience and the acknowledgment that the current situation had come upon them as the direct result of their own sin and the sins of their ancestors. Here, the people testified that disobedience brought hardship but obedience to the Lord brought His blessing. The nation, led by the Holy Spirit, committed to change their ways and to learn the sad lessons of their people's history. They expressed this commitment in the form of a binding, written agreement, on which they affixed their seals.

NEHEMIAH • WEEK 41

WEEK 41 • MONDAY   *Nehemiah 11:1—13:31*

Why did the people exclude foreigners from the assembly of God?

The people's commitment to exclude non-Jewish people from participating in Israelite worship or living among the Israelite people (Nehemiah 13:3) was a radical move. It completed in practice what was symbolized in the construction of the wall—the Lord had called the Israelites to live as His children, His chosen people, the nation from whom the world's Savior would come. The Old Testament cites many instances where the Lord commanded His people to shun idols and other pagan practices. As the "cradle for the Christ," Israel was to live as God's holy nation. The people agreed to this separation, even to the point of dissolving their marriages with their foreign wives (Ezra 10:10–12). Praise God, He led them to this point of repentance and faith.

WEEK 41 • TUESDAY   *Esther 1:1—2:23*

How could a celebration last six months?

For six months, King Xerxes displayed his vast wealth for the benefit of his nobles and officials (Esther 1:4). The extended period over which this celebration occurred may seem strange, but Xerxes intended to pull together the leaders of the various parts of the Persian Empire and inspire their loyalty. In ancient times, wealth was seen as an indicator of military might. His empire was the largest (and wealthiest) the world had known up to that time. It's possible that Xerxes was gearing up for a major military campaign against Greece. His father, Darius, had failed in his attempt to conquer Greece, and Xerxes was determined to do what Darius had not. If that was the case, securing the loyalty of his civic and military leaders was essential.

WEEK 41 • WEDNESDAY
Esther 3:1—4:17

What is the significance of the king's signet ring?

When Xerxes gave Haman his signet ring (Esther 3:10), he handed over to him full authority to carry out his plan. The king's ring was used to seal official documents and decrees. These documents were either rolled or folded, and a small amount of hot wax sealed the two ends. The king pressed his ring into the wax as a sign that the document carried his full approval and endorsement. Haman had made his case that the Jews were a dangerous segment of the population. Having neither the time nor the energy to investigate this matter, Xerxes basically gave his loyal servant Haman a blank check—unlimited authority and resources—to do what he had proposed.

WEEK 41 • THURSDAY
Esther 5:1—7:10

Why did Esther plan two banquets for the king?

Esther planned not one but two banquets (Esther 5:7–8) for Xerxes and Haman as part of a careful plan to place the king in the right frame of mind. Esther's request to the king would dramatically change both his opinion of his right-hand man, Haman, and the history of the Jewish people. Such a request could not be rushed into or taken lightly. Esther had already explained to Mordecai the decorum and caution used in approaching the king (Esther 4:16). In going to the king uninvited Esther literally placed her life on the line. After receiving the king's initial favor, Esther strategically put Haman at ease and began to foster the good will of her husband. Esther's plan worked. When she finally brought Haman's murderous intentions to light, her request that the king save her and her people had its intended dramatic effect. The Lord used this Jewish queen to preserve His people—the nation from whom the King of kings would one day come to save all people.

WEEK 41 • FRIDAY
Esther 8:1—10:3

Why couldn't King Xerxes nullify his decree?

The laws made by the king of Persia could not be revoked (Esther 1:19). This point of law symbolized the king's absolute authority. Therefore, Esther asked for a new decree, one that would overrule Haman's original edict (Esther 8:5). Haman's decree had reached all the Persian provinces, and Xerxes could not afford to lose face throughout his vast kingdom. Knowing this, Esther presented an acceptable request, one that did not ask Xerxes to nullify his earlier decree. Xerxes had given Haman his signet ring as a symbol of his trust. Now Xerxes gave that ring to Mordecai, Haman's sworn enemy. Mordecai would use it to counter Haman's genocidal decree. With this ring Mordecai sealed a new decree, one which gave the Jews the right to defend themselves.

WEEK 41 • SATURDAY
Job 1:1–22

Who is Satan?

The Bible tells us that Satan (Job 1:6), a title that here means "accuser," is a real, living being. In other passages we discover that Satan was at one time an angel of God who rebelled against Him and was banished to the earth. He is therefore called the "prince of this world" and has power to move and act on earth. He is the enemy of the Lord and of all His people. Satan tempted Adam and Eve who succumbed to that temptation, plunging God's creation into sin and death. Satan roams the earth, looking for ways to destroy individuals and thwart God's activity. Peter warned us that Satan prowls around like a lion, seeking to devour us (1 Peter 5:8). Satan knows that he will be allowed to function only for a short while on the earth. His battle against God is really no contest. Christ has already defeated Satan and Satan's allies on the cross. In God's perfect timing, at the end of this age, Satan will be imprisoned forever in the lake of fire.

WEEK 42 • MONDAY

Job 2:1—3:26

Why did Job sit in ashes?

Job sat in ashes (Job 2:8) in a symbolic gesture of mourning. In ancient times, ashes symbolized a return to dust—a metaphor for death. We still use the image at the graveside: "Dust to dust, ashes to ashes." Other passages in the Bible describe people putting ashes on their head to symbolize grief and mourning. In his grief and pain Job removed himself from society and went to a place outside the city where rubbish was burned. He identified himself with the rubbish to bring a sharp poignancy to the depth of his despair.

WEEK 42 • TUESDAY

Job 4:1—5:27

Who are the holy ones?

In this phrase (Job 5:1), Eliphaz refers to the holy angels. Job needs a mediator, one who could state his case before God, one who could influence God's actions. In cruel words Eliphaz tells Job that no one will intercede on his behalf, that Job has brought his suffering upon himself by his own evil and foolish behavior. But Eliphaz was wrong. We have a "holy one," one who intercedes for us, one to whom we look for deliverance—the true Holy One, Jesus Christ. He willingly takes up our case before the Father. He has won our salvation in His death and resurrection. Even the demons recognized Him: "I know who You are—the Holy One of God!" (Mark 1:24).

WEEK 42 • WEDNESDAY

Job 6:1—7:21

What is a weaver's shuttle?

A weaver's shuttle (Job 7:6) was a pointed instrument used by one who wove fabric on a loom. The shuttle wove the horizontal threads through the vertical threads held by the loom. Expert weavers worked at an extremely rapid pace, which makes this an appropriate picture to indicate the brevity of life. Compared to eternity, our life here on earth is indeed very short. Job's suffering, both emotional and physical, is so intense that he wishes his life were over.

WEEK 42 • THURSDAY
Job 8:1—10:22

Who are the cohorts of Rahab?

Rahab here does not refer to the prostitute of Joshua 2. Rather, Rahab is the mythological sea monster who played an important role in the Babylonian creation myth (Job 9:13). In this myth, Rahab is defeated by another god, and her helpers (the cohorts) are captured. Job uses this myth to describe God's control of all of creation. Here Job paints a beautiful picture of God's greatness. The Lord even controls the powerful beings of ancient mythology.

WEEK 42 • FRIDAY
Job 11:1—12:25

Why was Job a laughingstock?

In the basic cause-and-effect world of the ancients, evil was punished and good was rewarded. Job had been highly respected, righteous, and blameless, but now his neighbor's made him the object of ridicule and contempt. Despite Job's emphatic personal defense, his friends and neighbors felt sure his troubles came because of some personal sin, known only to God. Now, in their minds, Job was receiving his just reward.

WEEK 42 • SATURDAY
Job 13:1—14:22

What is the significance of putting marks on the soles of feet?

Job's comments (Job 13:27) reflect the ancient practice of slaveowners who branded their slaves on the soles of their feet to identify them. It ties in with the image of shackles that Job also uses in this verse. Job was, in effect, saying that God had enslaved him by sending in these horrible circumstances. Job asks a haunting question: "Why do You . . . consider me Your enemy?" (Job 13:24).

WEEK 43 • MONDAY   *Job 15:1—17:16*

What is the significance of sackcloth?

Sackcloth was an extremely coarse and uncomfortable fabric, typically made of goat hair. People wore sackcloth during times of mourning or repentance. Together with ashes, sackcloth served as an outward sign of grief. Jacob wore sackcloth when he thought his beloved son, Joseph, had been killed by a ferocious animal (Genesis 37:34); the Ninevites wore sackcloth as a sign of repentance before the Lord for their wickedness (Jonah 3:6–8). In this passage, Job spoke of sewing sackcloth over his skin (Job 16:15) as a permanent sign to others of the depth of his grief and broken spirit.

WEEK 43 • TUESDAY   *Job 18:1—19:29*

What does Job mean when he speaks of his Redeemer?

Few passages in the Old Testament are more loved than these words of Job: "I know that my Redeemer lives" (Job 19:25). We sing it on Easter and at funerals as a bold and confident proclamation of our Christian faith. Here, Job's image of a "redeemer" reflects the practice of buying a person out of slavery. Job most certainly was referring to the Lord as the One who could, and eventually would, free him from his misery. Job's "friends" brought only accusation and more misery. But Job looks in hope to God and pleads for mercy. From a New Testament perspective, we see our Lord's ultimate deliverance from despair, sin, and death that Jesus worked for us on Calvary's cross. Since our Redeemer lives, we know that we, too, will live eternally by faith in Him.

WEEK 43 • WEDNESDAY   *Job 20:1—21:34*

What was meant by rivers flowing with honey and cream?

Zophar said the wicked would not enjoy "rivers flowing with honey and cream" (Job 20:17), a reference to what was commonly understood as prosperity or the good life. It presents an image of paradise, where the best things come to someone with virtually no effort on his or her part. We heard this poetic language and saw this pastoral image earlier, when Canaan was described as a land flowing with milk and honey (Exodus 3:8).

WEEK 43 • THURSDAY   *Job 22:1—24:25*

What are boundary stones?

Job asked why the godly have to wait in vain for the Lord, wondering when He will judge the wicked. Job lists several specific examples of wrongdoing, including the moving of boundary stones (Job 24:1–2). Boundary stones were heaps of rock or large boulders that marked the edges of one's territory (Deuteronomy 19:14; 27:17). A thief could easily move the stones, thus stealing his neighbor's possession. Land was an inheritance, a gift from God. To change boundaries offended God and wronged one's neighbor. People of faith, including Job, relied on God to set the lines. As the psalmist indicates with the words: "The boundary lines have fallen for me in pleasant places" (Psalm 16:6).

WEEK 43 • FRIDAY   *Job 25:1—28:28*

What was the gliding serpent?

The gliding serpent of Job 26:13 is Leviathan, a mythical creature of ancient Mid East folklore. Leviathan, along with the creature Rahab referred to earlier (Job 9:13; 26:14), represented the forces of evil, over which God had complete control (see also Isaiah 27:1). In Jesus, the Lord Himself has defeated evil and all its consequences. This victory shook the world. Some day, His suffering children will see the end of pain and death. For now we trust that He will preserve us in faith and save us from despair.

WEEK 43 • SATURDAY   *Job 29:1—31:40*

What did Job mean when he said, "I go about blackened"?

Job tells us that his condition was "not by the sun." Therefore, this must be a reference to the discoloration of his skin caused by the disease that wracked his body (Job 30:30). It could also refer to the scabs that covered him from head to toe. His physical appearance caused his associates and even family members to reject him in utter disgust.

WEEK 44 • MONDAY
Job 32:1—34:37

Why did Elihu wait to speak?

Elihu waited in deference to the older men with him (Job 32:4). With the respect that was expected in this culture, the younger Elihu stood by in silence and listened to the entire dialog between Job and his "comforters." Only after he was certain that the older men had nothing more to say did he presume to speak. As Elihu points out, "It is not only the old who are wise" (Job 32:9). Youthful and vigorous, Elihu has a great deal of wisdom to add to the discussion.

WEEK 44 • TUESDAY
Job 35:1—37:24

What were shrine prostitutes?

Prostitutes, both male and female, performed acts of ritual prostitution as part of the worship in pagan religions (Job 36:14). Sexual activity, both homosexual and heterosexual, was seen as symbolic of the forces that nature exerted on the earth; engaging in such activity was believed to encourage and direct those forces. The corrupt and immoral nature of cultic worship was well known by those who, like these men, believed in the living God. The Lord explicitly and on a number of occasions warned His people against these detestable practices (Deuteronomy 23:17–18; 1 Kings 15:12).

WEEK 44 • WEDNESDAY
Job 38:1—41:34

What is the behemoth?

Behemoth is a Hebrew word that means "beast par excellence." The behemoth in this passage refers to a large land animal, possibly an elephant or a hippopotamus (Job 40:15). The beast, made by God, has undeniable strength and power, and even the forces of nature cannot control it. Here again the Lord uses an animal image to highlight the differences between humans and Himself. Although a man wouldn't approach one of these great beasts, God, its Creator, has no hesitation to do with His creation what He wills.

WEEK 44 • THURSDAY

Job 42:1–17

What was significant about Job's daughters receiving an inheritance?

The last chapter of this book mentions Job's daughters specifically (Job 42:13–15). The beauty of a man's daughters, in this culture, was seen as a symbol of divine blessing on the father. In addition, only sons typically were named as inheritors, in this patriarchal culture. The fact that Job's daughters also received a portion of Job's vast wealth speaks to the peace and unity found in Job's family.

WEEK 44 • FRIDAY

Psalms 1:1—6:10

What is chaff?

The psalmist contrasts the life of the godly and that of the ungodly. The godly are like a tree that produces annual fruit (Psalm 1:3). But the ungodly are like chaff (Psalm 1:4). Chaff is the outer membrane that protects a kernel of grain from the elements as it reaches maturity. In harvesting the grain during Bible times, the chaff and the kernel were crushed and tossed into the air. Because the chaff was lighter, it blew away, while the valuable grain fell to the earth where it could be gathered.

WEEK 44 • SATURDAY

Psalms 7:1—11:7

What did the psalmist mean by curses?

One of the more common kinds of prayer in the psalms is that of complaint. Complaint psalms sometimes resulted from an attack by the ungodly on God's faithful people. Such an attack included curses, lies, and threats (Psalm 10:7). This kind of cursing was not using the Lord's name in vain. Rather, it called down the powers of a god to destroy someone. Many ancient Near Eastern people took these verbal assaults as seriously as we consider a legal contract.

WEEK 45 • MONDAY   *Psalms 12:1—17:15*

How was silver refined?

While silver was plentiful in the ancient world, it had only modest value until the accompanying alloys and impurities were removed. Using charcoal and primitive bellows, refiners would light a fire in a small clay furnace called a crucible. The silver would melt when the ore was heated over such a furnace. The impurities would float to the top where they could be poured off. Often the process had to be repeated several times in order to remove all the impurities. The words of humankind are so often flawed by lies, deceit, pride, and hate. In contrast, the Word of God is like pure refined silver (Psalm 12:6).

WEEK 45 • TUESDAY   *Psalms 18:1—22:31*

What are the cherubim?

After David was delivered from the hand of his enemies (especially from King Saul), he wrote a psalm of thanksgiving (Psalm 18). Using wonderful images, David praises the Lord's faithfulness and power in delivering His servant. At one point David describes the Lord mounting the cherubim and flying through the heavens (Psalm 18:10). The cherubim are an order of mighty angels. Usually the Bible pictures them as guardians. Cherubim guarded the tree of life in Eden (Genesis 3:24) and the Most Holy Place in the tabernacle (Exodus 26:31–33). Even the lid of the ark of the covenant bore the likeness of two golden cherubim as a reminder of these angels' protective presence.

WEEK 45 • WEDNESDAY   *Psalms 23:1—28:9*

What is a stronghold?

In Old Testament military imagery, a stronghold was a fortified defense to which anyone could run for protection from enemies. These strongholds were fortresses or walled cities, built on the top of a hill. For David, as he fled from King Saul, life was fragile with many reasons for fear. In the midst of this dark, uncertain world, David takes courage from knowing the Lord as his light, salvation, and stronghold (Psalm 27:1).

WEEK 45 • THURSDAY   *Psalms 29:1—34:22*

What is a lyre?

A member of the harp family, the lyre's strings were stretched over a wooden sounding board. Played by strumming or plunking the strings, the lyre is distinguished from the harp by its two vertical columns joined by a crossbar. Praise is always an appropriate response to God, who delights in caring for those called by His name. In Psalm 32, a new song to the Lord, David calls for singing and the music of a 10-stringed lyre (Psalm 33:2).

WEEK 45 • FRIDAY   *Psalms 35:1—41:13*

What is a buckler used for?

A buckler and a shield serve similar functions; both are used for defense. The Hebrew word, often translated "buckler," refers to a large shield designed to protect the whole body. The Hebrew writers and the English translators use the terms *shield* and *buckler* interchangeably. The psalmist was quick to call on the Lord when he was in trouble. He recognized his defenselessness and helplessness against his enemies, and so he asked the Lord to fight on his behalf by taking up the shield and buckler and coming to his defense (Psalm 35:2).

WEEK 45 • SATURDAY   *Psalms 42:1—47:9*

What are myrrh, aloes, and cassia?

In Psalm 45, a wedding song written for Israel's king—myrrh, aloes, and cassia perfume the royal robes (Psalm 45:8). The term myrrh probably refers to a fragrant gumlike substance exuded from the leaves of the cistus rose or from a balsam tree that grew in Arabia. It was used externally for perfume and was taken internally as a pain reliever. The Wise Men brought myrrh to Jesus (Matthew 2:11), and years later myrrh was applied to honor the infant Jesus' body after His death (John 19:39–40). Aloe is a spice that most likely came from aromatic wood (like sandalwood). It was used in Old Testament times for making storage chests and ornamental boxes. Cassia was a perfume made from the flowers of cinnamon trees.

WEEK 46 • MONDAY
Psalms 48:1—53:6

What is hyssop?

In confessing his sin, David asks God to cleanse him with hyssop (Psalm 51:7). Hyssop, a bush with fragrant leaves, grew in ancient Palestine. The priest used a hyssop branch to sprinkle the blood or water of Old Testament cleansing ceremonies on the worshiper (Numbers 19:18; Leviticus 14:6). Such a sprinkling pointed forward to Christ, the One who poured out His lifeblood for the forgiveness of the world's sin.

WEEK 46 • TUESDAY
Psalms 54:1—60:12

What does it mean to hide in the shadow of God's wings?

Psalm 57 is a prayer for deliverance from fierce enemies, written by David when he hid from Saul in a cave. In this prayer David longs to be hidden in the shadow of God's wings (Psalm 57:1). This is a metaphor or word picture that describes God's protective power. To shield her young from the intense heat of the sun or to protect them from prowling predators, a mother bird would shelter her offspring underneath her wings. This picture is used elsewhere in the Old Testament (e. g., Exodus 19:4; Psalm 17:8) and by Jesus in describing His care for sinners (Matthew 23:37).

WEEK 46 • WEDNESDAY
Psalms 61:1—66:20

Why is God compared to a rock?

While the exact background of Psalm 61 is uncertain, David probably wrote it at a time of exile while he hid from King Saul's murderous hatred. Yet, despite his troubles, David trusts God will deliver him as He so faithfully has done in the past. Renouncing trust in his own power, David confesses God as the rock who is higher than he is. The security David seeks is beyond his reach; only the Lord can bring David to the safe place he seeks (Psalm 61:2). This word picture conveys God's unfailing love as the believer's fortress, refuge, and place of safety and security.

WEEK 46 • THURSDAY   *Psalms 67:1—72:20*

What is the book of life?

Psalm 69 is the third most quoted psalm in the New Testament (right behind 22 and 110). Like Psalm 22, it paints a graphic, prophetic description of Christ's suffering. The psalmist in his immediate need asks for the execution of divine justice on godless persecutors in terms matched for vehemence only in Psalms 35, 109, and 137. As a zealous servant of the Lord, the psalmist calls out for God to save him and even asks God to blot out of the book of life those who are persecuting him (Psalm 69:28). The book of life, mentioned in both the Old (Daniel 12:1) and New (Philippians 4:3; Revelation 3:5; 21:27) Testaments, is the heavenly register of the elect, those who are saved by God's grace in Christ Jesus.

WEEK 46 • FRIDAY   *Psalms 73:1—77:20*

What does it mean to lift up one's horn?

Psalm 74 asks how long enemies will mock God and His believers. Psalm 75 answers that the enemy will continue in arrogance until God, who raised these enemies up as instruments of judgment against Israel, brings judgment on them in their turn. Trust in the promise that the Judge is at the door (James 5:9) is so firm that this psalm begins and ends in thanksgiving to God. These psalms use a common figure of speech: horns signify power and vigor. Attacking bulls and fighting mountain goats use their horns as powerful weapons. Thus, to lift up one's horn was a figure of speech for defiant opposition.

WEEK 46 • SATURDAY   *Psalms 78:1—82:8*

What happened at the waters of Meribah?

Psalm 81 begins with an invitation to worship the Lord because He delivered His people from slavery in Egypt (Psalm 81:1–7). In verses 8–10 the psalm gives God's warnings against idolatry. It concludes in grief over the fact that Israel chose curses instead of blessings and thus received God's judgment. In the Exodus the Lord rescued the Israelites from slavery in

Egypt. Israel crossed the Red Sea, and almost immediately began to complain about the lack of water. In the middle of the desert God commanded Moses to strike a rock with his staff. From that rock flowed water sufficient for the people's needs. Because the people had tested the Lord, Moses named the place Massah. And because the people had quarreled and murmured against God, Moses also called it Meribah.

WEEK 47 • MONDAY
Psalms 83:1—89:52

What was the significance of being the firstborn?

In Psalm 89:27, the Lord says, "I will also appoint [David] my firstborn." The firstborn of a king was usually heir to the throne. He enjoyed the highest privilege and position in the kingdom under the monarch himself. King David was not the firstborn of his father Jesse, nor of God. (David had seven older brothers; see 1 Samuel 16:10.) Thus, the "David" the psalm describes is the Christ, Jesus, God's only begotten Son. The psalmist declares his confidence in God's faithfulness to the covenant promises He made to David. After the terms of this covenant (Psalm 89:1–4), the psalmist goes on to praise the Lord's power, which upholds the covenant (Psalm 89:5–18). The Lord's faithfulness gives His people security. Next, the psalmist turns specifically to David and the terms of the Davidic covenant (Psalm 89:19–37). The psalm concludes with questions concerning the apparent lack of fulfillment of God's covenant with David and a prayer that the Lord remember and keep His covenant (Psalm 89:38–52). Throughout this psalm, the psalmist has 2 Samuel 7:4–17 in the back of his mind. In these verses the Lord had promised David an eternal dynasty. Given all the evidence of Israel's history, the psalmist's question remains, "How will this be? Has the Lord forgotten His promises to David?" But despite all evidence to the contrary, the Lord would be true to His Word of promise.

WEEK 47 • TUESDAY
Psalms 90:1—95:11

Why were the righteous compared to cedars and palm trees?

God's deliverance of His people from their enemies gave believers an occasion for praise. The unending theme for such praise is the Lord's steadfast love and faithfulness of which all His works are evidence. It may seem that the wicked flourish, but in reality they are only like the grass that is soon cut down or dries up (Psalm 37:2). The righteous—those made right by God through Christ Jesus—however, flourish "like a palm tree" (Psalm 92:12). A palm grows tall and straight, living a long time—a picture of the upright believer in the Lord. In this same verse, the righteous are also compared to the tall and sturdy cedars (some with a height of 120 feet and a circumference of 30 feet). Like such a tree, securely anchored, believers can stand firm against even the fiercest winds of temptation. We are rooted and grounded in Christ (Colossians 2:7).

WEEK 47 • WEDNESDAY   *Psalms 96:1—101:8*

What is meant by "the Lord's right hand and arm"?

The theme of Psalms 93–100 is, "The Lord reigns." Psalm 98 provides a variation on that theme—a new song, as it were. The new song proclaims God's marvelous deeds: the salvation He has worked by "His right hand and His holy arm" (Psalm 98:1). The right hand is a sign of honor, power, and strength, as is the arm to which it is attached. God, who is a spirit, describes Himself in terms of these human attributes so we can better understand Him. In Jesus Christ, who took on human flesh, hands, and arms, we have received marvelous things from God: forgiveness of sins and life eternal. With Mary we echo this psalm and proclaim that "the Mighty One has done great things for me" and "He has performed mighty deeds with His arm" (Luke 1:49, 51).

WEEK 47 • THURSDAY   *Psalms 102:1—106:48*

What is the leviathan?

Psalm 104 is a hymn to the Creator. It reflects Genesis 1, but also proclaims what God is still doing in His creation. Praise resounds not only from dry land or the high heavens, but also from the depths of the oceans. All living creatures—large and small—praise God (Psalm 104:25). The root word of leviathan suggests "one that gathers itself in folds." The word originally referred to a great sea monster, whale, or perhaps even a crocodile (Job 41). Despite the size and destructive power of the leviathans, they are but playful pets to our Creator-God.

WEEK 47 • FRIDAY   *Psalms 107:1—113:9*

What is a scepter?

David composed Psalm 110 for use at the coronation of his son Solomon. In it we read much that tells us of David's great future Son—Jesus Christ. This psalm has long been viewed as messianic, referring to the coming Messiah, Christ Jesus. This son of David would be king, sitting on David's throne, holding a scepter (a baton or a shepherd's staff used as an emblem of power and authority), and reigning over an eternal kingdom. While Solomon's reign foreshadowed some aspects of Christ's kingdom, this psalm finds its complete fulfillment in Jesus the Christ Himself, whom God seated at "His right hand in the heavenly realms" (Ephesians 1:20).

WEEK 47 • SATURDAY   *Psalms 114:1—118:29*

What is the cup of salvation?

A hymn of praise to the Lord for His deliverance from death, Psalm 116 overflows with ways in which praise expresses itself. While the wicked drink from God's cup of wrath (Psalm 11:6), the righteous—those who have been delivered by the grace of God—lift the cup of salvation (Psalm 116:13). A cup of salvation climaxed a thankoffering, celebrating and proclaiming deliverance by the Lord (Numbers 15:1–10). Such a cup also points to the cup of salvation Jesus would institute in the Lord's Supper. There we receive the Lord's body and blood with the bread and wine—all for the forgiveness of our sin. A true reason for thanksgiving indeed!

WEEK 48 • MONDAY   *Psalms 119:1–176*

What kind of lamp did the Israelites use?

Lamps common in this era were small, made from clay pottery, and had a reservoir for oil and a wick for the flame. Light from such lamps pointed down through the ages to Christ, the light of the world (John 8:12). Psalm 119 is a meditation on God's Word, written by an Israelite who passionately believed the Word of God was in truth the Word of life. In acknowledging his own errant ways, the psalmist knew firsthand both the pain and the fruit of God's corrective discipline. Even though he suffered much at the hands of those who had nothing but disdain for God's Word, the psalmist would cling to God's Word for dear life. That word was a lamp shining with light for the path through life (Psalm 119:105).

WEEK 48 • TUESDAY   *Psalms 120:1—125:5*

What are the songs of ascents?

The subtitles of Psalms 120—134 place them in a unique category, "songs of ascents." These hymns, written by the temple musicians, were intended to be sung as Hebrew pilgrims to the three high feasts commanded by God ascended the inclining slope to the city of Jerusalem, more than 3,000 feet above the Jordan Valley.

WEEK 48 • WEDNESDAY   *Psalms 126:1—134:3*

What does the psalmist mean when he speaks about a weaned child?

Psalm 131 is a confession of humble trust in the Lord. The psalmist does not attempt to strive to earn God's favor or to claim anything not given by God. Rather, the psalmist expresses the contentment of a weaned child— a child walking in trust beside his mother, no longer a baby howling for milk. In a similar way, children of the heavenly Father depend on His care and provision. The One who gave His only Son to give us eternal life and forgiveness will supply our earthly needs also.

WEEK 48 • THURSDAY   *Psalms 135:1—137:9*

What does the term Daughter of Babylon mean?

It pained the unknown poet of Psalm 137 to tears when he and his fellow exiles in Babylon were denied the privilege or worshiping in Jerusalem. What's more their captors ridiculed them for their inability to serve the Lord as His Law required. What a crime it would be for the poet and the other of God's people to forget Jerusalem, the place of true worship. The poet consigns those who try to frustrate God's kingdom to the Lord for His judgment and destruction. The term "Daughter of Babylon" is a personification of the enemy army of Babylon. The term also foreshadows those evil powers of the Antichrist described in Revelation 17–19.

WEEK 48 • FRIDAY   *Psalms 138:1—143:12*

How is prayer like incense?

Often prayed by the church in evening prayer, Psalm 141 is a prayer for deliverance from the wicked and their evil ways. While evildoers set traps and snares for innocent believers, their seeming success can tempt the faithful into similar evil deeds. The psalmist thus prays that the Lord will stand guard over the words of his lips, the thoughts of his heart, and the deeds of his hands. The Lord welcomes such a prayer, as the fragrance of incense that in the Old Testament sacrificial system covered the stench of burning blood and flesh (Psalm 141:2). As incense was placed on the fire, smoke would rise just as the prayers of the faithful rise to the heavenly Father.

WEEK 48 • SATURDAY   *Psalms 144:1—150:6*

What does it mean to exalt, extol, and praise God?

Exalt literally means to raise high, while *extol* means to praise highly. The psalmist(s) would raise high the mighty deeds of God by praising Him for those deeds. While a young child may have to be taught to say thank you for a gift, she does not have to be taught how to praise. The words just burst forth: "Look what Aunt Sally gave me!" Praise includes an element of thanksgiving, but because proclamation of God's saving work in Jesus Christ is the main thrust, praise also includes an aspect of witness to those around the proclaimer.

WEEK 49 • MONDAY
Proverbs 1:1—3:35

What is a proverb?

A proverb (Proverbs 1:1) is a concise, vivid statement or saying designed to teach wisdom. Underlying all of Scripture's proverbs is the premise of humankind's total dependence on God and responsibility to God. Every aspect and detail of life is under God's reign. Most proverbs consist of two lines, often following the characteristics of Hebrew poetry: "parallelisms" that include repetitions of a similar thought, two contrasting thoughts, or a second line that expands on the ideas of the first line.

WEEK 49 • TUESDAY
Proverbs 4:1–27

What is meant by straight paths?

Speaking through the writer of Proverbs (4:11), the Lord states that He guides us in the way of wisdom, leading us along a straight path. The straight path is the path of righteousness, the path of God, in contrast to the way the wicked (Proverbs 4:19), which is a way of sin and darkness. In the light of the New Testament we know that the straight path is Jesus Christ Himself, who is the way, the truth, and the life (John 14:6). He alone leads us in "paths of righteousness" (Psalm 23:3), all by His grace.

WEEK 49 • WEDNESDAY
Proverbs 5:1—6:35

What does it mean to strike a hand in a pledge?

Striking "hands in pledge for another" (Proverbs 6:1) is the equivalent of two people sealing an agreement with a handshake. All our material resources are gifts from God—gifts to be used wisely for the welfare of ourselves and those in need. This holds true when taking responsibility for someone else's debt, because abject poverty or slavery may result. Thus Solomon urges God's people to exercise caution in making commitments.

WEEK 49 • THURSDAY   *Proverbs 7:1–27*

What does "apple of your eye" mean?

The "apple of your eye" (Proverbs 7:2) is an expression that literally means "little man of his eye," a reference to the pupil of the eye. Since the pupil is the delicate part of the eye essential for sight, it must be protected. Just as the eyelid automatically flicks to protect the pupil of the eye, so the believer guards the teachings of our Lord and uses them to see all of life in the light of God's mercy and wisdom.

WEEK 49 • FRIDAY   *Proverbs 8:1–36*

What is the significance of the city gate?

In the ancient world, the city gates (Proverbs 8:3) were at the center of public life. Strategically placed and heavily fortified, the city gates provided the only entry points into ancient walled cities. Because most people passed through the city gates at least once a day, anyone who wanted to attract public attention—including merchants, teachers, the elders of the city, and those who came to plead for justice—gathered near the gates to be heard. In this passage, wisdom is personified as one who cries out at the city gate, pleading for an audience. Our Lord wants us to be "wise unto salvation" (2 Timothy 3:15), the salvation He has made available in Jesus. Those of us who know this wisdom, this salvation, proclaim it to the world!

WEEK 49 • SATURDAY   *Proverbs 9:1–18*

Why does wisdom build her house with seven pillars?

Wisdom is here personified as a woman preparing her house for guests (Proverbs 9). Her house has seven pillars, telling us that the house is quite large, able to host a large number of people feasting on the Word of God. Because seven is a biblical number signifying completeness, it indicates that all preparations have been made and that the house is ready for guests.

WEEK 50 • MONDAY
Proverbs 10:1—11:31

What/who are the righteous?

In contrasting the righteous (Proverbs 11:8) with the wicked, the question arises: What makes the righteous (godly) righteous? Because of sin no one is righteous before the holy God (Ecclesiastes 7:20). The only righteousness available to the sinner is that which comes from God Himself. There is only one who has the full righteousness of God: Jesus Christ. His death and resurrection have become our righteousness. Christ makes us righteous, just as He made Solomon and other Old Testament believers righteous. This righteousness—the right standing with God that belongs to us by His grace—leads us to act in right ways.

WEEK 50 • TUESDAY
Proverbs 12:1—13:25

Why were envoys and messengers so important?

Envoys and messengers (Proverbs 13:17) were the equivalent of today's (telephone, e-mail, and fax machine) for ancient rulers like Solomon. These couriers carried to the king the information he needed about the various parts of his kingdom. These same couriers carried decisions the king had made back to his subjects in far-off provinces. Thus messengers had to be reliable, accurate, and trustworthy.

WEEK 50 • WEDNESDAY
Proverbs 14:1—15:33

What is the fountain of life?

The Book of Proverbs (10:11; 13:14; 14:27; 16:22) makes frequent references to the fountain of life. In doing so, Solomon points to the natural springs and fountains of water sometimes found in the desert terrain of Palestine. Just as those springs supported and sustained life in the wilderness, so for the believer the Lord and His wisdom are the fountain of life. God not only creates physical life, He also gives us eternal life through the death and resurrection of His Son Jesus Christ.

WEEK 50 • THURSDAY *Proverbs 16:1—17:28*

Why would a high gate invite destruction?

Solomon uses a high gate as a metaphor for pride (Proverbs 17:19). It's akin to "keeping up with the Joneses." As soon as a homeowner built a gate in front of his house, his neighbor would put up a higher one. This picture illustrates a later proverb: "Pride goes before destruction" (16:18).

WEEK 50 • FRIDAY *Proverbs 18:1—19:29*

What was a citadel?

Cities at the time of Solomon not only were built on the highest point in a region, but they were also protected by walls, forts, and citadels. When an offense is given or when a dispute occurs, it tends to build an invisible wall between the people involved. Such walls can become very thick—as impenetrable as those of a citadel (Proverbs 18:19).

WEEK 50 • SATURDAY *Proverbs 20:1—21:31*

When was harvest time in Israel?

For Israel harvest was in the spring. Barley was harvested in April and May; wheat was harvested in late May. Even in our society with its broad business and industrial base, agriculture plays an important role. In Solomon's day agriculture was the primary business. Thus, when Solomon talked about the worthlessness of the lazy person, he was thinking in terms of planting and reaping, sowing, and harvest (Proverbs 20:4).

WEEK 51 • MONDAY
Proverbs 22:1—23:35

Why would a lion be in the street?

Solomon's father, David, had fought lions and bears that attacked his sheep. King Solomon, however, had little, if any, experience with wild beasts. When the wise teacher wrote of procrastinators seeing lions in the street (Proverbs 22:13), he referred to people who would use any excuse to cancel a commitment. Such behavior makes as much sense as worrying that one might step outside and find a lion at the door.

WEEK 51 • TUESDAY
Proverbs 24:1—25:28

What was the assembly at the gate?

The ancient walls of Near Eastern cities had gates, which consisted of a series of heavy wooden doors that opened in on each other. When shut, these doors provided a substantive reinforcement to deter would-be attackers. When the city was not under attack, the recessed wooden doors were open. At those times the gates became a town hall. Community leaders met at the city gate. Judges also held court there, when the wise of the city gathered, the fool had nothing to contribute to the discussion (Proverbs 24:7).

WEEK 51 • WEDNESDAY
Proverbs 26:1—27:27

Why did people take a garment for security?

In Proverbs 27:13, speculative business transactions are treated with subtle irony. The proverb seems to say that if anyone foolishly accepts responsibility for the debt of a stranger (whose reliability is unknown) or of a wayward woman (whose unreliability *is* known), he should be held accountable to the point of taking his garment. According to Deuteronomy 24:10–13, a person's garment could be taken as a security deposit. A co-signer of such a debt as these acts foolishly and will likely be left holding the responsibility for repaying the loan. Unless the creditor takes the co-signers coat in pledge, the creditor will likely never see his money again. See also Proverbs 20:16.

WEEK 51 • THURSDAY
Proverbs 28:1—29:27

What does it mean to fear God?

Fearing the Lord (Proverbs 28:14) means to solemnly revere the Lord for who He is and for what He has done, is doing, and will do for us. That reverence is best expressed by trusting the promises of the Lord. To fear Him is also to fear sin and its consequences. In Christ, our dread of sins' punishment evaporates. We know the joy and peace of eternal life. Perhaps surprisingly, this deepens our "fear" of the Lord in the sense that our reverence and adoration grow as does our desire to please the One who died and rose again for us.

WEEK 51 • FRIDAY
Proverbs 30:1—31:31

What are a distaff and spindle?

By concluding the Book of Proverbs with a tribute to a godly woman, the writer describes her as not only skilled in raising children and in business affairs but also in the art of weaving. Two common implements used in twisting wool fibers into thread (Proverbs 31:19) were the distaff, a stick-like rod that held the wool in place, and the spindle, a flywheel apparatus that allowed the wool to spin.

WEEK 51 • SATURDAY
Ecclesiastes 1:1—2:26

What does the phrase "under the sun" mean?

The idea that everything is meaningless forms a major theme of Ecclesiastes. The original idea behind the word "meaningless" is "breath." Just as a breath on a cold day is visible for but a moment, so also everything "under the sun" soon evaporates (Ecclesiastes 1:3). None of it has real value, substance, or permanence. The phrase "under the sun" includes not only this physical world and everything in it, but also every aspect of life. All of it has fallen under the curse of sin. Apart from the Lord, only despair would fill our days. But Christ died on the cross and rose to life again to forgive our sin and to give us new lives full of joy and meaning. Futility and despair do not have the last word in the lives of God's children.

WEEK 52 • MONDAY

Ecclesiastes 3:1—4:16

What is meant by the phrases *a time to hate* and *a time for war?*

Everything has its time, including hatred and war along with love and peace. The righteous—those made righteous by God in Christ—do hate the emptiness of this world. We also hate evil (Proverbs 8:13). Because our Lord has made us His new creations in Christ, we constantly war against "the powers of this dark world and against the spiritual forces of evil" (Ephesians 6:12). In times of both war and peace some Christians will be called to serve their country. Because of sin, hatred and war do also at times break out in our own personal lives. When this happens, the God of all peace confronts us with our sin and leads us to repentance and faith in Jesus' death and resurrection to remove our guilt.

WEEK 52 • TUESDAY

Ecclesiastes 5:1—6:12

What was the sacrifice of fools?

It is a sacrifice of fools (Ecclesiastes 5:1) to engage in outward rites of worship without the heart-filled intention of conforming one's life to the will of God (see Psalm 50:7–23; Amos 5:22–27). To the Hebrews, a fool was not someone lacking intelligence but rather a person lacking in morals and a right relationship with God. Better for the Christian to hear and take to heart the Word of God read and proclaimed as His people gather for public worship. As Jesus said, "Blessed . . . are those who hear the word of God and obey it" (Luke 11:28). In Him, we receive the power to do so.

WEEK 52 • WEDNESDAY

Ecclesiastes 7:1—8:17

How can someone be too righteous?

The righteous are those who have been made right by God. Thus, believers are often called "the righteous" (Romans 1:17). The phrase "Do not be overrighteous" (Ecclesiastes 7:16) does not refer to the righteousness that comes from God—we can never be too righteous in that respect. Rather, the point is this: don't be self-righteous, for it is impossible to become right with God by your own efforts. Don't put on a great show of piety to impress other people, either. They will see through your hypocrisy. What's the alternative? Let the Good News of Christ's righteousness settle down in your heart. Meditate on it. Praise them for it. Let it change you from the inside out. Let the Spirit use it to form in you the true Christlikeness no on will be able to reject or disregard.

WEEK 52 • THURSDAY   *Ecclesiastes 9:1—10:20*

What did it mean for someone to wear white clothes?

White clothes, a token of joy, were worn at festive times and celebration. While oil may have protected skin from the dryness of the hot climate, olive oil and white clothes were associated with joy and happiness. Thus, in a very real sense, believers can eat, drink, and be merry—enjoying the gifts of God. In the words of James (1:17), "Every good and perfect gift is from above, coming down from the Father of the heavenly lights." God intends that believers enjoy His good gifts and life itself as His good gift to us (Ecclesiastes 9:7).

WEEK 52 • FRIDAY   *Ecclesiastes 11:1—12:14*

What does it mean to cast bread on waters?

Wise living involves not only planning and counting the cost but also taking some risk. Thus comes the proverb "Cast your bread upon the waters" (Ecclesiastes 11:1), based on the example of a merchant engaged in trade and shipping on the seas. While a storm could sink his ships and fortune, this does not deter the wise merchant from investing in such risky ventures. Applied to wise living, God's people know that mercy and kindness are not bad investments. Rather, like ships sent out to sea, they return laden with rich dividends, though perhaps only after many days or years. Our relationship with Jesus makes it possible to take such risks. Knowing His infinite love, we can love others, even those who seem unlovable.

WEEK 52 • SATURDAY

Song of Songs 1:1—3:11

Why is this book called the Song of Songs?

Although some translations of the Bible call this book the Song of Solomon, the literal Hebrew is best rendered Song of Songs (Song of Songs 1:1). The title means the best of all songs. The song is an elaborate poem that depicts human love, often drawing from Solomon's experience. The song also points to the love between Christ and His people.

YEAR TWO

10-2-17

WEEK 53 • MONDAY
Song of Songs 4:1—6:13

What is the dance of Mahanaim?

Weddings in Solomon's day were festivals. The feasting and dancing lasted several days. Guests would watch the bride dance for her groom. In the dialog between the groom and the bride's friends, he refers to the dance of Mahanaim (Song of Songs 6:13). Two possible explanations come to mind. Judging from the words that follow in Song of Songs 7:1–9, the groom could be referring to a private dance in the bridal chamber. Alternatively, Mahanaim us a place about 15 miles east of the Jordan River. There Jacob encountered angels as he went to meet his estranged brother Esau (Genesis 32:2). The name Mahanaim means "two camps." Thus, the dance mentioned by Solomon may have been a folk dance involving two groups of people.

WEEK 53 • TUESDAY
Song of Songs 7:1—8:14

What are mandrakes?

Mandrakes are short-stemmed herbs that produce a fragrant purple flower. Among the ancients the mandrake was considered an aphrodisiac. The eating of this fragrant herb was thought to promote conception. Solomon's bride describes the mandrakes sending out their fragrance (Song of Songs 7:13). Mandrakes are also mentioned in Genesis 30:14–17.

WEEK 53 • WEDNESDAY
Isaiah 1:1—2:22

What were the sacred oaks?

Isaiah was a prophet who lived in Judah about 700 years before the birth of Christ. He preached repentance and salvation to the whole nation of Judah. By the Spirit of the Lord, Isaiah confronted the people about their evil ways, particularly their idolatry. He told them they would one day be ashamed because of the "sacred oaks" and disgraced because of the "gardens" they had chosen (Isaiah 1:29). These were both connected with Israel's idol worship. In the ancient Mideast, a garden shaded by oak trees was often used as a place for pagan sacrifice and the ritual prostitution of the Canaanite religion.

WEEK 53 • THURSDAY
Isaiah 3:1—4:6

Who was the Branch of the Lord?

Isaiah warned the people that God's judgment would come upon Jerusalem and Judah because of their disobedience. But Isaiah also offered hope. He foresaw the Branch of the Lord, who would "be the pride and glory of the survivors in Israel" (Isaiah 4:2). The Branch is a reference to the coming Messiah (Jeremiah 23:5). The term Branch is an appropriate name for the Messiah because He "sprouted" from a seemingly dead "stump"—that is, David's kingly line—and would bear fruit. The title "Branch" reminds us of Jesus' words that He is the Vine (John 15:5).

WEEK 53 • FRIDAY
Isaiah 5:1–30

Why did farmers build watchtowers?

Isaiah often used picturesque and figurative language to convey his message. In the "Song of the Vineyard," Isaiah sang of God's care for His vineyard—Israel. The vineyard was dug up and cleared of stones and planted with the best vines. He built a watchtower and a winepress in it (Isaiah 5:2). Vineyards were important and valuable in the land of Israel during both Old and New Testament times. A vineyard that was well taken care of could be quite profitable, especially for the wine produced from the grapes. Queen Jezebel had her neighbor, Naboth, killed for his vineyard (1 Kings 21). Because of the value of the vineyard, watchtowers were built in them. The watchtower was a stone structure from which to guard the vineyard against vandalism and theft.

WEEK 53 • SATURDAY
Isaiah 6:1–13

What is a seraph?

God commissioned Isaiah to be a prophet. This happened when Isaiah had a vision in which he saw God sitting on a throne and heard Him speaking. Above the throne were seraphs praising God (Isaiah 6:2). Isaiah 6 is the only reference in the Bible to seraphs. They were awe-inspiring and powerful angelic beings with six wings who were ardent in their zeal for the Lord. In this passage, they functioned as God's agents in commissioning Isaiah. Isaiah could understand them when they talked to him and when they praised God. Because they hovered around God's throne, they may have been heavenly attendants. Covering their faces indicated their humility before God. Covering their feet may have indicated service to God. Flying may be descriptive of their work of proclaiming God's holiness and glory.

WEEK 54 • MONDAY   *Isaiah 7:1—8:22*

What was the significance of the name Immanuel?

Isaiah prophesied to the people as he was directed by God. One of these prophecies told of a virgin who would give birth to a Son and call him Immanuel (Isaiah 7:14). The name Immanuel means "God with us." Immanuel as used in this passage has multiple meanings; it was meant to convince Ahaz that God could rescue him from his enemies, or it may be another name for Maher-Shalal-Hash-Baz (Isaiah 8:3). Immanuel also became a title for the Messiah and in that sense points to Jesus. Jesus was the final fulfillment of this prophecy, for He was "God with us" in the fullest sense.

WEEK 54 • TUESDAY   *Isaiah 9:1—10:34*

What did it mean for this child to have the government on His shoulders?

Isaiah prophesied of a future child that would be born. Unlike the previous prophecy in chapter 7, which had an immediate application as well as a later one, this prophecy was speaking specifically of the coming Messiah. This child would have the government upon His shoulders (Isaiah 9:6). This is a figurative phrase that refers to the kingly robe that would be worn by the Messiah. As King, the Messiah would rule over God's people and the world. In Isaiah's day, Judah's leaders were incompetent in governing the people, but the Messiah would govern properly. The Messiah's rule would bring wholeness and well-being to individuals and to society.

WEEK 54 • WEDNESDAY   *Isaiah 11:1—12:6*

What is the stump of Jesse?

Isaiah prophesied about the fate coming to Judah through the Assyrians, who would nearly destroy Judah, and the Babylonian exile that would bring the kingdom of Judah and David's dynasty to an end. But God's kingdom would rise by a shoot from the stump of Jesse; from his roots a Branch will bear fruit (Isaiah 11:1). The "stump of Jesse" is undoubtedly referring to God's promise to David, Jesse's son, that a descendant of his will rule over God's kingdom forever. When those descendants failed to meet the conditions of the promise, the tree was cut down to a stump. But from that stump a new shoot would grow—the Messiah. He would be greater than the original tree and bear much fruit.

WEEK 54 • THURSDAY   *Isaiah 13:1—20:6*

Did Isaiah really go around naked for three years?

Israel was considering an alliance with Egypt against the Assyrians. Isaiah graphically reminded Judah that they should not count on foreign alliances to protect them, for the Assyrians believed their advances could not be stopped. God told Isaiah to take off the sackcloth from his body and the sandals from his feet. Isaiah obeyed and went around stripped and barefoot (Isaiah 20:2). Isaiah probably was not completely nude, but he was undoubtedly shamed. *Stripped* means uncovered buttocks, which were a sign of humiliation. At the very least, Isaiah took off his sackcloth, the distinctive clothing of prophets. Isaiah was role-playing the part of captives, often stripped of their clothes and belongings as they were taken into exile. God was using Isaiah to demonstrate the humiliation that Egypt and Ethiopia would experience at the hands of Assyria, but the message was really for Judah.

WEEK 54 • FRIDAY   *Isaiah 21:1—23:18*

Why were graves cut out of the rock?

Isaiah, by God's direction, prophesied about the destruction of many of the surrounding nations by the mighty Assyrian army. Jerusalem would be destroyed as well. God also said that Shebna, a high court official, was not to make a grave out of the rock because he would die in a foreign country (Isaiah 22:16–18). Graves were cut out of rock to keep out wild animals and grave robbers. But there was also a sense of pride and permanence in carving a grave out of the rock, especially on the heights as Shebna was doing. One's place of burial was considered very important, and Shebna coveted a tomb worthy of a king. Perhaps he thought this would make his name live on in spite of the current conditions.

WEEK 54 • SATURDAY   *Isaiah 24:1—25:12*

What were the powers in the heavens above?

Isaiah had been warning about God's judgment upon specific cities, but now he broadened the word of doom to take in the whole world: destruction comes to all who sin. Isaiah 24:21 says that God will punish the powers in heaven and the kings on earth. This may refer to spiritual forces opposed to God—Satan and the fallen angels. Revelation 19:20 and 20:2 speaks of warfare among supernatural beings. The phrase might refer, however, to the stars. Just as many people of today believe in astronomy, many people in Isaiah's day believed that the stars had power over individuals and nations.

WEEK 55 • MONDAY   *Isaiah 26:1—27:13*

What does it mean that the Lord will thresh?

Isaiah prophesied that God would indeed punish Israel and they would be conquered. But the prophet also gave them the hope of deliverance. He said that God would thresh from the Euphrates River to Egypt, and gather up the Israelites one by one (Isaiah 27:12). In Isaiah's time, the farmers threshed the grain after it was cut. This was done by beating the grain stalks and then throwing it into the air. The worthless part (chaff) would blow away and the good grain would fall to the ground where it could be gathered. This is a promise of a coming event. Even though the Israelites would be scattered from Egypt to Babylon, God's people would again be gathered back to the Promised Land. Threshing was also often used as an image of punishment, so some suggest this contains the idea of judgment upon the nations that carried Israel away.

WEEK 55 • TUESDAY   *Isaiah 28:1—29:24*

What is the significance of the cornerstone?

Judah did not listen to God's words of upcoming disaster as Isaiah warned of disobeying the Lord and making a covenant with Egypt. God said that He would lay a precious cornerstone for a sure foundation (Isaiah 28:16). When anything is built, a firm base is needed. The Jerusalem leaders were trusting in other gods to save them from the Assyrians. But only the true God is the firm base for physical and spiritual salvation. The New Testament writers understood this cornerstone as being Christ—the only secure foundation on which anyone can build his or her life (1 Peter 2:6–7).

WEEK 55 • WEDNESDAY   *Isaiah 30:1—31:9*

What is Topheth?

God used Assyria to punish Israel, but after the punishment, it was time for Assyria to face the consequences of their own sin. Babylon would defeat Assyria and Assyria would be fit for nothing but Topheth (Isaiah

30:33). Topheth was a garbage dump outside Jerusalem, used to burn trash. During times when the Israelites were unfaithful to God, children were sacrificed to Molech, the god of the Ammonites, at that location. The Israelites generally regarded it as a place of shameful abominations.

WEEK 55 • THURSDAY   *Isaiah 32:1–20*

What does it mean to reign in righteousness?

Because the Lord would protect Jerusalem, He would also bring about a time when righteousness will abound. This would be a time of perfect government. A king would reign in righteousness, and rulers would rule with justice (Isaiah 32:1). The phrase "reign in righteousness" spoke of the Messiah. Judah longed for a strong king who would rule effectively. This would only happen when the Messiah reigned. Christ, unlike any other king, would reign in righteousness and wisdom. This righteousness would also be reflected in the people who serve Him. A perfect government could only be established under the Messiah.

WEEK 55 • FRIDAY   *Isaiah 33:1—35:10*

What is the sword of the Lord?

God declared His anger upon all nations that refused to honor Him and pronounced judgment upon them. The sword of the Lord was bathed in blood (Isaiah 34:6). This sword of the Lord represented God's judgment against enemy nations, even those living in luxury and ease. No one would be spared. It was bathed in blood because there would be many battles. Sometimes the Bible is also called the sword of the Lord because it pronounces judgment on unbelievers and tells of the punishment of eternal damnation that will befall people if they don't believe in the One He sent to earth—Jesus.

WEEK 55 • SATURDAY   *Isaiah 36:1—39:8*

Why would Hezekiah tear his clothes?

King Sennacherib of Assyria attacked all the fortified cities of Judah and captured them. Then he threatened King Hezekiah at Jerusalem and the Assyrian field commander told the people not to listen to Hezekiah. When King Hezekiah heard the report of this, he tore his clothes and put on sackcloth and went into the temple of the Lord (Isaiah 37:1). The custom of tearing one's clothes dates far back in the history of Israel. Garments represented personalities; to tear them indicated a grievous inner hurt. Hezekiah was disturbed because of the Assyrian threat and because the name of the Lord had been profaned by the Assyrians.

WEEK 56 • MONDAY
Isaiah 40:1—41:29

Why would a potter tread on clay?

Isaiah warned that Cyrus the Great, ruler of Persia, would come from the east and conquer Judah as he had defeated the Medes and the Lydians. Isaiah 41:25 describes Cyrus as treading on rulers as if they were mortar, as if he were a potter treading the clay. Potters would tread on clay to remove air bubbles. They would find clay in the ground, add water and some fine sand to get the right consistency, then remove the water. But it then had to be stomped to squash any air pockets that would weaken the final product. The Lord was using this familiar activity to illustrate how thoroughly Cyrus would crush all the nations that he conquered.

WEEK 56 • TUESDAY
Isaiah 42:1—43:28

What was the significance of the fat in animal sacrifices?

God told the people that they should not be afraid because He redeemed them and He was Israel's only Savior. God also reminded them of His care and mercy and lamented their unfaithfulness. God said that the Israelites did not make incense offerings or lavish on Him the fat of their sacrifices (Isaiah 43:24). The fat of the animal was considered the best part of the meat, and therefore it was offered to the Lord in the sacrifices. The Israelites had not only neglected to offer the fat of the animal in their sacrifices, they didn't sacrifice anything all. Instead, they ignored the entire sacrificial system.

WEEK 56 • WEDNESDAY
Isaiah 44:1—45:25

Why is Cyrus mentioned in this passage?

God, through Isaiah, reiterated that He alone is the true God and Israel's Redeemer. He reminded them that all idols are false gods and it is foolish to worship them or to think that the idols can do anything for them. In Isaiah 44:28, God spoke of Cyrus as His shepherd who would accomplish His purposes. Isaiah called Cyrus by name almost 150 years before he ruled! Later historians said that Cyrus read this prophecy and was so moved that he carried it out. One year after Cyrus conquered Babylon, he issued a decree that the Jews could return to Jerusalem and rebuild the temple. In doing this, Cyrus was serving God's purposes as if he were God's shepherd.

WEEK 56 • THURSDAY
Isaiah 46:1—47:15

Who are Bel and Nebo?

Isaiah continued to warn the Israelites against being drawn in by idolatry. This time he warned against the gods of Babylon. In Isaiah 46:1, Isaiah says that Bel bows down, Nebo stoops low. These idols are described as being borne by beasts of burden. Bel and Nebo were gods of Babylon. Bel (also called Marduk) was the chief deity of the Babylonians, known as the god of the sun. Nebo (also called Nabu) was Marduk's son; he was the god of the royal family and was honored in the name of Babylonian kings, such as Nebuchadnezzar. Nebo was the god of learning, writing, and astronomy. However, these "gods" needed men to carry them around and could not even save themselves from falling from a cart.

WEEK 56 • FRIDAY
Isaiah 48:1—49:26

What is the significance of engraving something on the palm of one's hands?

God reassured Israel that He would restore them at the time He decided to redeem His people. God said that they were not forsaken or forgotten, but were engraved on the palms of His hands (Isaiah 49:16). Tattooing was common in the ancient Mideast for religious and personal reasons. A person might tattoo the name of a loved one on their body. Likewise, the nation of Israel was inscribed or tattooed on God's palms. Therefore whenever God, figuratively speaking, lifted up His hands, He saw the nation's name, which reminded Him of His people. God used this symbol to express His constant concern for Jerusalem and Israel.

WEEK 56 • SATURDAY   *Isaiah 50:1—52:15*

What is the significance of draining the cup of wrath to its dregs?

Isaiah begged the Lord to act again as He did when He parted the Red Sea and the Israelites were saved from the Egyptians (Exodus 14:29). Then the prophet reprimanded the people for making God so angry. They drank the cup of His wrath and drained it to the dregs (Isaiah 51:17). Experiencing God's judgment was often compared to becoming drunk on strong wine. In their exile, the people of Jerusalem had experienced God's wrath fully—all the way to the bottom of the cup. Now God was going to do something—their calamity was coming to an end.

WEEK 57 • MONDAY
Isaiah 53:1–12

Why would the Servant be like a guilt offering?

Isaiah emphasized the purpose of God. Something great was happening, the prophet said. The Servant would make it happen, but it would ultimately happen because God willed it. The Lord would make the Servant's life a guilt offering (Isaiah 53:10). In the Israelite sacrificial system, a guilt offering was made for unintentional or unknown sins. The person brought an untainted ram to the priest for sacrifice, made restitution as necessary, and paid a fine. The Servant is Jesus whose death was the sacrifice that paid for our sins. Jesus had to die to satisfy the righteous demands of God.

WEEK 57 • TUESDAY
Isaiah 54:1—57:21

How would an everlasting covenant be different than previous covenants?

Through Old Testament history, God made many covenants with His people through Noah, Abraham, Moses, and David. Now God told the people that He would make an everlasting covenant with them, His faithful love promised to David (Isaiah 55:3). Some of the previous covenants were conditional and could be canceled if the people failed to live up to them. However, David had been promised an unending dynasty, one that would culminate in the Messiah. Jesus Christ came to earth to inaugurate that everlasting covenant with His own death. Christ's death and resurrection would free people once for all from the eternal consequences of sin. Those who believe in Christ can become God's people.

WEEK 57 • WEDNESDAY
Isaiah 58:1—59:21

What was true fasting?

God called for heralds to go about telling the nation of their rebellion and sins. Outwardly, the people seemed eager to want to know God and for God to be near them. God said that on the day of fasting, they did as they pleased and exploited all their workers (Isaiah 58:3). The people were going through the motions of religion without any inward reality of faith. God responded by pointing out that He was more interested in their obedience than in rituals. Their fasts did not alter their poor relationship with others. True fasting was a sign of humility and sincere repentance. It meant focusing their hearts on God and expressing their deep sorrow for their sins.

WEEK 57 • THURSDAY   *Isaiah 60:1—62:12*

What does it mean to raise a banner for the nations?

God promised a new name for Zion—one that fit the change in circumstances that would occur. A great and glorious coming of the Lord was foretold. A way would be prepared for the people. A highway would be built up, and the stones would be removed. A banner would be raised for the nations (Isaiah 62:10). To raise a banner was to announce something much like we would use posters or signboards today. A pole with a banner was often placed on a hill as a signal for gathering troops or for summoning the nations to bring Israel back home. The people were to prepare themselves for the coming of the Lord—all the nations were to be informed that He was coming to Jerusalem.

WEEK 57 • FRIDAY   *Isaiah 63:1—66:24*

What does "treading the winepress" mean?

A winepress was usually a shallow pit with a hole on the side leading out to a container. As individuals trampled on grapes in the press, the juice flowed through the hole into the container. The process left their feet and clothing stained by the red grape juice. In Isaiah 63:2 the prophet describes the Lord wearing clothing stained as the clothes of those who tramp in the winepress would be. But the stains are blood, not grape juice. The Lord has just returned from trampling and destroying the enemies of His people, specifically Edom.

WEEK 57 • SATURDAY

Jeremiah 1:1—2:37

What does the broken cistern in Jeremiah 2 mean?

Jeremiah 2:13 describes Israel as having forsaken God, the Spring of living water. Instead, the nation had dug for itself broken cisterns that could not hold water. A cistern was a pit hewn out of rock that collected rainwater. This water soon turned brackish, unlike spring water, which was always fresh. A broken cistern was practically useless; the collected water would quickly leak out. Jeremiah used this imagery to describe the foolishness of idolatry in Judah. He compared the nation's disobedience to someone who would abandon a spring of running water for broken cisterns that wouldn't even hold water. The flip side of this imagery of Law is the picture Christ painted of Himself in John 7:37–39. Here we see Jesus, the one who provides "living water" freely to His people.

WEEK 58 • MONDAY   *Jeremiah 3:1—4:31*

Why were trumpets sounded throughout the land?

Trumpets signaled the approach of enemy armies. They warned of impending doom. In Jeremiah 4:5, Jeremiah uses this fact to announce the judgment about to fall on Judah as the Lord unleashed Judah's enemies to the north. Destruction would come from Babylon when Nebuchadnezzar attacked. Even though some responded to Jeremiah's message of law in repentance and faith, most of Judah's citizens continued in sin and hard-heartedness. Thus Jeremiah's continuing message of doom.

WEEK 58 • TUESDAY   *Jeremiah 5:1—6:30*

Why did Jeremiah use the picture of someone "gleaning" from the "vines"?

When grape gatherers picked the grapes from the vine, they would miss some of the grapes. So, they would go back over the vines a second time to gather the leftovers. The vineyard owner wasn't satisfied until the vines were picked clean. Jeremiah used this picture to deliver a message of Law (Jeremiah 6:9). Like a landowner, Babylon wouldn't be satisfied until every person in Judah was plucked from the nation. Jeremiah's word came true: Babylon invaded Judah three different times and carried its people into exile.

WEEK 58 • WEDNESDAY   *Jeremiah 7:1—8:22*

Who is the Queen of Heaven?

In Jeremiah 7:18 the prophet refers to the Queen of Heaven. This was Ishtar, the Babylonian goddess of love, fertility, and war. Many ancient Mideastern cultures worshiped a similar goddesses, though the goddess was known by different names. Part of the worship ritual for Ishtar included cult prostitution. Through Jeremiah the Lord told the people of Judah how worthless their false religions were and how greatly they provoked Him to anger. Nonetheless, after the fall of Jerusalem, the refugees from Judah who fled to Egypt continued to worship her.

WEEK 58 • THURSDAY
Jeremiah 9:1—10:25

Who were the wailing women?

Saddened by the judgment that was to come upon Jerusalem, Jeremiah was nevertheless repulsed by the nation's sins. Through Jeremiah, the Lord called for "wailing women" (Jeremiah 9:17–18). These were professional mourners who were paid to grieve at funerals and other sorrowful occasions. Jeremiah called on them to lament the death of Jerusalem.

WEEK 58 • FRIDAY
Jeremiah 11:1—12:17

Why did Jeremiah want Judah to obey the terms of God's covenant?

The covenant that the Lord made with His people at Mt. Sinai could not have been more clear. Obedience would bring blessings and safety; disobedience would bring the curses about which Moses had warned. (See Deuteronomy 28.) Jeremiah loved his people and, like the Lord, he wanted them to be blessed. The Lord commissioned Jeremiah to remind the people of the covenant He had given them and to urge them to give up their disobedience (Jeremiah 11:3–4).

WEEK 58 • SATURDAY
Jeremiah 13:1—14:22

What is a linen belt?

The Lord often led His prophets to perform symbolic actions to teach important lessons. In one such dramatic demonstration the Lord told Jeremiah to buy a linen belt and put it around his waist. Linen symbolized holiness. The priest's garments were made from linen. Jeremiah wore this belt close to his skin. It symbolized holiness as a "kingdom of priests," and the formerly intimate relationship Judah had enjoyed with the Lord. The prophet was not to wash it (Jeremiah 13:1). In fact, after he had worn it for many days, he was to ruin it by burying it. (The trip to the Euphrates River was 500 miles one way!) The ruined condition of the belt showed how the people's disobedience, idolatry, and pride had ruined them, despite the covenant the Lord had made with them at Sinai.

WEEK 59 • MONDAY
Jeremiah 15:1—17:27

What is a winnowing fork, and how did people use it?

After farmers threshed the grain, they threw it into the air with a large, wooden winnowing fork. The wind blew away the chaff, while the grain, which was heavier, dropped to the ground. Judah's enemies would be the winnowing fork, throwing the unfaithful Jews as chaff (Jeremiah 15:7). This same figure of judgment is used in Isaiah 41:16 and in Luke 3:17, where John the Baptizer tells of the Messiah's activity.

WEEK 59 • TUESDAY
Jeremiah 18:1—19:15

What is the Potsherd Gate?

Each gate in the city walls of Jerusalem was named. The Potsherd Gate stood at the southeast corner of the main wall and was so called because it overlooked the main dump for broken pottery. This gate is also called the Dung Gate. Jeremiah used the imagery of potters and clay as he preached to the people of Jerusalem. The Lord told Jeremiah to buy a clay jar and to stand near the entrance of the Potsherd Gate to talk to the people (Jeremiah 19:2), using the jar as an object lesson.

WEEK 59 • WEDNESDAY
Jeremiah 20:1—22:30

Why does God swear by Himself?

Through Jeremiah, the Lord told the king of Judah and the other high officials that if they obeyed Him, the city of Jerusalem could be saved. But if they did not heed His commands, the Lord swore by Himself that the palace would become a ruin (Jeremiah 22:5). When humans swear, we do so by the name of a higher being. We take our oaths "before God." There is no greater name by which the Lord can take an oath. Because everything God says is absolutely true, He needs no oaths to back up His statements. Yet for greater emphasis and to underscore the seriousness of the message, the Lord used this expression. (See also Hebrews 6:13.)

WEEK 59 • THURSDAY   *Jeremiah 23:1–40*

What are false oracles and false prophets?

The word *oracle* means to lift, to carry, or to take. It can also refer to a load or burden that someone had to carry. God had laid on His true prophet the burden of His message of judgment on Judah's sin. And He warned the people against false prophets and their false oracles. These oracles and dreams did not come from God, and the prophet, priest, or anyone else who proclaimed them would be punished (Jeremiah 23:34). The false prophets claimed that God had given them new revelations in dreams, but their visions were only delusions. Their "new words" distorted the truth of God's Word. They led a willing people astray.

WEEK 59 • FRIDAY   *Jeremiah 24:1—25:38*

Who is Nebuchadnezzar?

Jeremiah had been prophesying to the people of Judah for 23 years, but they had not listened. They had not repented. Now the Lord's "servant"—Nebuchadnezzar—would completely destroy Jerusalem and take the people of Judah captive (Jeremiah 25:9). The word *servant* is used here in the sense of vassal or agent of judgment. Nebuchadnezzar, king of Babylon, did come just as Jeremiah had said. Nebuchadnezzar led the Babylonians and their allies in the conquest of Jerusalem. They completely destroyed the city. As God's servant, Nebuchadnezzar did God's bidding, executing the Lord's just judgment on Jerusalem.

WEEK 59 • SATURDAY   *Jeremiah 26:1—28:17*

To what does Shiloh refer?

God told Jeremiah to stand in the courtyard of the temple and speak to the people who came to worship. He was to tell them all of God's commands, omitting not a word. The Lord said if they did not listen and turn from their wickedness, He would make the temple like Shiloh (Jeremiah 26:6). Shiloh was the town in Ephraim where the ark of the covenant first rested in the Promised Land after the conquest of Canaan. Shiloh was the center of worship in the days of Eli, and the prophet Samuel received his call from God at Shiloh. Now, the destroyed and empty city was a vivid reminder that past glories did not shield the unrepentant people from the fury of God's judgment.

WEEK 60 • MONDAY   *Jeremiah 29:1–32*

Who were the exiles?

The Babylonians defeated the people of Judah and took them into an exile that would last 70 years. Then the Lord would bring them back. The Babylonian authorities let Jeremiah remain in Palestine, so he sent a letter from Jerusalem to the exiles in Babylon (Jeremiah 29:1–3). The letter includes a beautiful promise that the Lord gave to His people: He promised to listen to their prayer, to cause them to prosper, to bring them home. The lessons to be learned in exile were not easy ones, but the Lord's plans for the exiles were rooted in His love and mercy.

WEEK 60 • TUESDAY   *Jeremiah 30:1—32:44*

What is the new covenant?

Jeremiah told the people that after their time of exile was over, God would bring them back to Judah. God also promised to watch over them and bless them. The time was coming when the Lord would make a new covenant with Israel and Judah (Jeremiah 31:31). Unlike the old covenant at Sinai, written on stone tablets and conditioned on their strict obedience, the new covenant would be written by God Himself in His people's minds and on their hearts. As forgiveness in the old covenant was solemnized by the blood of sacrificial animals, the new covenant would be solemnized by the blood of Christ. More than that, the blood of Christ would remove the stain of sin and its guilt. The new supersedes the old and fulfills it in every way—Christ the sinless Lamb sacrificed once for all.

WEEK 60 • WEDNESDAY   *Jeremiah 33:1–26*

Why had Jeremiah been confined to the courtyard?

The Lord continued to give His message to the people of Judah through His prophet Jeremiah, even when Jeremiah was in trouble with the king of Judah. At one point in his ministry Jeremiah was confined to the courtyard of the guard in Jerusalem's royal palace (Jeremiah 33:1; see also 32:2). Jeremiah predicted Nebuchadnezzar's capture of both Jerusalem and the king of Judah. Such statements were considered treasonous by the king and his advisors. But God continued to speak through Jeremiah. No palace guard could stop the Lord or His Word.

WEEK 60 • THURSDAY   *Jeremiah 34:1—35:19*

Who were the Recabites?

Jehoiakim, king of Judah from 609 to 598 B.C., did not fear the Lord and had no desire to hear Jeremiah's prophecies. So God told Jeremiah to use the Recabite family as an example of following wise counsel (Jeremiah 35:3–16). The Recabites were an established, well-known clan family in Israel, descended from Jehonadab, son of Recab. Jehonadab had assisted Jehu in overthrowing wicked King Ahab (2 Kings 10:15–28) and thus in exterminating Baal worship from Israel. Jehonadab rejected a settled way of life, choosing instead the life of a nomad. This patriarch laid down some strict rules for his family. Ordinarily they traveled through the wilderness of the Negev but they were forced to move to Jerusalem when Nebuchadnezzar threatened Judah. The traditions and rules laid down by Jehonadab served as the glue that held them together more than 200 years after Jehonadab's death. By contrast, the Israelites had less respect for God's written Law than the Recabites had for the traditions and rules of their forefathers. The Recabites remained faithful to their ancestors, and the Lord wanted His people to consider and follow their example.

WEEK 60 • FRIDAY   *Jeremiah 36:1—37:21*

Why did the Babylonian army withdraw from Jerusalem?

Zedekiah was made king of Judah by Nebuchadnezzar, king of Babylon. Neither Zedekiah nor any of the people of the land paid any attention to the words of the Lord spoken by His prophet. When the Babylonians, who were besieging Jerusalem, withdrew from Jerusalem, Jeremiah told Zedekiah that they would return, attack the city, and burn it down (Jeremiah 37:5–8). The Babylonians had withdrawn because Pharaoh Hophra of Egypt stood at the southern border of Judah with his army at King Zedekiah's request. Zedekiah no doubt hoped that the Egyptians would force Babylon out of Judah. But the Egyptians were no help. As soon as the Babylonians marched against them, they retreated. This freed Nebuchadnezzar to turn his attention back to Jerusalem.

WEEK 60 • SATURDAY   *Jeremiah 38:1—40:16*

Why did the Babylonians set Jeremiah free?

As God had warned, the Babylonians under King Nebuchadnezzar completely destroyed the city of Jerusalem. They killed the nobles and blinded King Zedekiah. But Nebuchadnezzar ordered the imperial guard to free Jeremiah and look after him. They were to give the prophet whatever he wanted (Jeremiah 39:11–12). The Babylonians set Jeremiah free on King Nebuchadnezzar's direct order. Nebuchadnezzar had heard of Jeremiah—possibly through the letters the prophet had sent to Babylon or through the testimony of those who had defected to the Babylonians. Because Jeremiah had been imprisoned by his own people, the Babylonians assumed he was a traitor, on the side of Babylon. Once again, Nebuchadnezzar served as God's instrument. The Lord's promise to protect Jeremiah was fulfilled—through a heathen king!

WEEK 61 • MONDAY   *Jeremiah 41:1—43:13*

Why did the people want to go to Egypt?

Some of the poorest and least educated people of Judah were left behind by the Babylonians. Gedaliah was appointed governor over them, but Ishmael assassinated him in anger at not receiving the position himself. Johanan and his troops ran Ishmael off and recovered the survivors he had taken captive. This band of Jews decided to flee to Egypt (Jeremiah 41:17), where they thought they would be safe when word of the attempted coup reached the ears of Nebuchadnezzar. In this way the little band of Jews that hadn't gone into captivity defied the Lord's command to stay in the land, even though He had promised that they had nothing more to fear from Babylon. How ironic that God's stubborn people chose to return to Egypt, the land of slavery. There would be no safety there, and only a very few would survive Babylon's attack on Egypt.

WEEK 61 • TUESDAY   *Jeremiah 44:1—45:5*

Why did Jewish wives burn incense to other gods?

God was very angry with the Jews who wanted to flee to Egypt because He had forbidden them to do so. The people simply would not listen to or obey Jeremiah's warnings. They allowed their wives to burn incense to other gods (Jeremiah 44:15), and both men and women participated in the worship of idols. Apparently, the wives worshiped Ishtar (the "Queen of Heaven"), a Babylonian goddess of fertility. Women played a major role in her worship. In addition to burning incense, the women poured out drink offerings and made cakes in her image.

WEEK 61 • WEDNESDAY   *Jeremiah 46:1—49:39*

What was significant about the battle at Carchemish?

God is the Lord of all nations, and His prophet Jeremiah delivered a message against Egypt at the occasion of the battle of Carchemish (Jeremiah 46:2). Two major world powers, Babylon and Egypt, clashed in this battle. Babylon won. Egypt's defeat at Carchemish was one of the most decisive battles in the ancient world, ending Egypt's age-long claims and pretensions to power in Syro-Palestine. This was Nebuchadnezzar's first victory, establishing him in his new position as king of the Babylonian Empire.

WEEK 61 • THURSDAY   *Jeremiah 50:1—51:64*

Why would God punish the Babylonians?

Jeremiah's longest oracle against foreign nations concerns Babylon. Jeremiah said the Babylonians would be captured and defeated. The Lord would punish the king of Babylon and his land (Jeremiah 50:18). Actually, God vowed to punish the kings of both Babylon *and* Assyria for their destruction of His people. Though the Babylonians fulfilled God's purposes and acted as His instruments of judgment, they would suffer because they delighted in the downfall of God's chosen. They were proud and arrogant, taking credit for their victories. And so the Lord of all nations would cause this proud land of Babylon to fall, and her destruction would initiate the Jews' return to their own land. God was faithful to His promise to restore His people. As Bible history continued to unfold, the name *Babylon* would come to represent all enemies of Christ and His church (Revelation 14:8; 16:19; 17:5; 18:2, 10, 21).

WEEK 61 • FRIDAY   *Jeremiah 52:1–34*

Why was Jehoiachin honored after Zedekiah was disgraced?

Zedekiah was the last king of Judah. His brothers, Jehoahaz and Jehoiakim, and his nephew, Jehoiachin, ruled before him. When Jehoiachin was exiled to Babylon, Nebuchadnezzar made Zedekiah king. Zedekiah rebelled against Nebuchadnezzar, who captured him, killed his sons before his eyes, blinded him, took him to Babylon, and kept him in prison for the rest of his life. After 37 years in prison, Jehoiachin was freed (Jeremiah 52:31) by Nebuchadnezzar's son and successor, Evil-Merodach. He apparently saw no threat in the aging Jehoiachin, and, perhaps to celebrate his coronation, he set Jehoiachin free. Just as Jeremiah's prophecies of exile and destruction came true, so now his prophecies of blessing were beginning to be fulfilled. Jehoiachin's favored status was a sign of hope to the exiles that God's promised blessing and restoration would come.

WEEK 61 • SATURDAY
Lamentations 1:1–22

Why was Lamentations written?

Jeremiah, most likely the author of Lamentations, wrote this book in response to the fall of Jerusalem and the resulting exile of the people of Judah in 586 B.C. The book is organized in a series of five poetic laments, each expressing waves of grief and pain over what has happened. In the midst of suffering, Jeremiah calls the people to repent of their sinful rebellion and return to the Lord whose "compassions never fail" (Lamentations 3:22). Jeremiah continues to remind the people of the Lord's goodness, mercy, and faithfulness. In Him they will find hope and salvation (Lamentations 3:21, 26).

WEEK 62 • MONDAY
Lamentations 2:1—3:66

What did Jeremiah mean when he said the Lord was his portion?

Surveying the ashes of Jerusalem, it seemed to Jeremiah and God's people that they had lost everything. Their sinful faithlessness had earned God's judgment. No longer did they have land or possessions. Yet all was not lost—they still had the Lord! This situation placed all Judah in the position of the tribe of Levi, who according to the Law of Moses received no land or possessions but trusted the Lord to provide for them through His people's tithes (Numbers 18:20–23). Jeremiah knows confidently that the Lord will remain faithful to His promise and will provide for the needs of His people. Not land or possessions, but the Lord is their inheritance! He will take care of them.

WEEK 62 • TUESDAY
Lamentations 4:1—5:22

Why did the people think no one could conquer Jerusalem?

Because Jerusalem was built on a large hill surrounded by enormous walls, it had a strategic advantage. It also had its own internal water supply to rely on during long periods of siege. As a result, the people felt confident that no army could defeat them. But perhaps the greatest source of false security lay in the Lord's protection. Because He had protected Jerusalem against such mighty conquerors as Sennacherib, the people did not think the Lord would ever allow the destruction of His holy city, not under any circumstances. This false hope lulled them to sleep spiritually. They failed to take seriously Jeremiah's warning of God's judgment on their sin and what that would entail (Jeremiah 7:26).

WEEK 62 • WEDNESDAY
Ezekiel 1:1—2:9

Who was Ezekiel?

Ezekiel was born into Aaron's line in Judah and was therefore eligible to serve as a priest. In 597 B.C., however, Nebuchadnezzar deported King Jehoiachin and a number of Jewish people, including Ezekiel, to Babylon. In his 30th year, while Ezekiel was living along the Kebar River in

Babylon, God called him to become a prophet. Ezekiel was married and lived in his own house (Ezekiel 3:24; 24:15–18). His name means "God strengthens," and his mission included warning the Jews of the upcoming destruction of both Jerusalem and its temple due to the Lord's judgment on their sin. Ezekiel would also rally the exiles to a new spiritual understanding and heartfelt reliance on the Lord. Ezekiel affirms that even the Lord's judgments on His people reflect His grace, for His purposes involve a desire to renew and restore them spiritually.

WEEK 62 • THURSDAY   *Ezekiel 3:1—5:17*

Why did God call Ezekiel "son of man"?

After Ezekiel received God's call in a vision, the Lord asked him to listen to and prophesy what He told him. More than 90 times, the Lord addresses Ezekiel as "son of man," which can also be translated as "son of Adam." Perhaps He did this to remind Ezekiel of something important. Although the Lord had picked Ezekiel to proclaim His divine truth and was granting him special vision, He did not want Ezekiel to get an inflated opinion of his importance. Rather, He wanted Ezekiel to remember that he was still a son of man—a sinful human being. Without the Lord's Spirit, Ezekiel was incapable of being His messenger.

WEEK 62 • FRIDAY   *Ezekiel 6:1—7:27*

What is the significance of Ezekiel prophesying against the mountains?

After Ezekiel's vision of God's judgment on Jerusalem, the Lord told him to face Jerusalem and the mountains of Israel and prophesy against them (Ezekiel 6:1–2). The mountains and hills were high places where the Canaanite people had worshiped their false gods. When God's people first settled in Canaan, before the building of the temple, they were allowed to worship the Lord in these places. Eventually, they began to worship not only the Lord but also false pagan gods. By prophesying against these places, Ezekiel was letting the people know that because they had abandoned the Lord, He would abandon them, allowing their enemies to conquer or kill them. Since God's people did not respond to

His grace, He would show them through His judgment that their false gods were powerless; He alone is the true God.

WEEK 62 • SATURDAY   *Ezekiel 8:1—9:11*

What was the meaning of the detestable things in the temple?

The detestable things in the temple were part of a vision the Lord gave to Ezekiel. In the vision Ezekiel saw the people practicing various types of pagan worship within the temple itself, the place where the Lord dwelt with His people. The detestable things included a statue to Asherah, the Canaanite goddess of fertility, as well as crawling things and detestable animals, references to features of pagan worship in Egypt. While pagan worship was not actually occurring in the temple, God's people were worshiping pagan gods elsewhere. Ezekiel's vision pointed to the wicked ways of the people and how they had turned their backs on the Lord by welcoming false gods into their lives. Naturally, the Lord, who desired first place in their hearts, was angry at them for choosing to worship false idols, and He promised righteous punishment.

WEEK 63 • MONDAY
Ezekiel 10:1—11:25

What is the significance of God's glory departing from the temple?

Once again Ezekiel has a vision of what is to happen to God's people because of their idolatry. He sees the glory of the Lord, the visible sign of His loving presence, reluctantly leaving the temple. This happened because God's people had broken their covenant with Him and no longer loved Him above all else. Instead, they worshiped false gods. Since He was no longer first in their hearts and lives, the Lord was going to remove His presence from them, allowing a foreign nation to destroy the temple and Jerusalem and kill the people. While this judgment would be executed against those who had forsaken Him, the Lord does promise Ezekiel that He will not abandon His people completely. He will bring back some of those who are in exile with Ezekiel and give them a heart that is devoted to Him. They will be His people, and He will be their God (Ezekiel 11:17–21).

WEEK 63 • TUESDAY
Ezekiel 12:1—13:23

Why were the false prophets compared to jackals?

After God came to Ezekiel and told him he was living among a rebellious people, He commanded him to pack his belongings and go to another place. Ezekiel did as he was told. Then God came to Ezekiel and told him to prophesy among the prophets of Israel, who were like jackals among the ruins (Ezekiel 13:1–4). Jackals were related to the dog family and are found throughout the Near East. These animals traveled in packs and rummaged through debris, living off garbage and dead flesh. God compared the false prophets to these jackals to illustrate His contempt for them. They tolerated idolatry and sinful unbelief and proclaimed their own false message instead of speaking for the Lord.

WEEK 63 • WEDNESDAY
Ezekiel 14:1—15:8

Why are Noah, Daniel, and Job mentioned in Ezekiel 14:14?

Repeatedly, Ezekiel had warned God's people that Jerusalem would be destroyed because of the Lord's judgment on them for forsaking Him and worshiping other gods. Yet they continued to ignore what the Lord had to say. They felt safe, since they looked upon the righteous who lived in the city as a good luck charm. They reasoned that the Lord would not really destroy the city, for if He did, He would also have to punish those who were faithful to Him. The Lord, however, tells them that the destruction of Jerusalem is inevitable. Even if outstanding believers like Noah, Daniel, and Job lived there, they could save only themselves, not the city, nor those of His people who worshiped false gods.

WEEK 63 • THURSDAY   *Ezekiel 16:1—17:24*

Why does God compare Israel to a prostitute?

The Lord continues to express His righteous anger at the people whom He has chosen as His own. He compares Israel to an abandoned baby whom He rescued, cared for, and nurtured. Because of His love and blessings, she grew into a beautiful woman, whom He took as His bride. But she repaid His love by rejecting Him to chase after other gods. The Lord calls His people Israel a prostitute, because they have been unfaithful to Him in their worship of false gods.

WEEK 63 • FRIDAY   *Ezekiel 18:1—19:14*

What is the point of the proverb about eating sour grapes?

In response to Ezekiel's warning that the Lord would punish them for their sinfulness, God's people quoted the proverb about eating sour grapes. Rather than acknowledge their own sin, they accused the Lord of being unfair for punishing them for the sins of previous generations. In essence they were saying, "Our fathers sinned, but we have to suffer the consequences." This irresponsible attitude failed to recognize that the Lord looks at people on an individual basis and punishes sinners for their own sins. Through Ezekiel the Lord takes His people to task for saying this and tells them that His judgments are always fair. He is not to blame for their punishment, nor are their ancestors. Ezekiel also assures them that God takes no pleasure in punishing them and tells them to turn from their evil ways and receive the forgiveness He desires to give.

WEEK 63 • SATURDAY
Ezekiel 20:1—21:32

Why did the Israelites want to offer their sacrifices at high places and near leafy trees?

Ezekiel paints a vivid picture of how each generation of God's people continued to rebel against Him. The Lord had remained faithful to His covenant promise, delivering His people from Egypt and bringing them into the Promised Land. Yet, even there, His people became enamoured with the pagan fertility gods because they thought these gods could give them a good harvest. The people constructed a variety of images, stone altars, and Asherah poles in high places and near leafy trees and nominally dedicated them to the Lord. He was not pleased with this, however, because He saw the unfaithfulness deep in their idolatrous hearts. While the people wanted to be more like their pagan neighbors in their worship practices, the Lord called them to be set apart and to worship Him alone.

WEEK 64 • MONDAY
Ezekiel 22:1—23:49

What is the significance of cutting off someone's nose and ears?

Ezekiel continues to speak of the Lord's anger against His people by using the allegory of two adulterous sisters—Oholah, who represents Samaria, and Oholibah, who represents Jerusalem. In this allegory the Lord again compares the covenant relationship He has with His people as a marriage where His brides, Oholah and Oholibah, are faithless prostitutes. The Lord uses this analogy to show the people that what they are doing in their spiritual lives by forming alliances with other countries and worshiping their foreign gods is just as disgusting to Him as if they were involved in sexual prostitution. He also indicates that He will punish their idolatry and lack of faithfulness to Him. In the allegory (Ezekiel 23:25), the Lord directs His anger against the sisters by cutting off their noses and ears, apparently a common punishment used in the Middle East against those caught in adultery. He will also punish Judah and Jerusalem's spiritual prostitution. Just as a prostitute's beauty is lost when her nose and ears are cut off, so they will lose their beauty as His people when He allows foreign nations to overpower them.

WEEK 64 • TUESDAY
Ezekiel 24:1–27

Why wasn't Ezekiel allowed to mourn his wife's death?

In Bible times the customary way to mourn a loved one included weeping, tearing one's clothes, wearing sackcloth, going barefoot, and participating in a funeral feast. When the Lord told Ezekiel that his wife, "the delight of his eyes," was going to die, however, He told him not to observe these usual practices. Ezekiel obediently carried out the Lord's commands (Ezekiel 24:15–27). The Lord asked Ezekiel to do this as a sign to His people of how they would act when He took away the delight of their eyes, the temple. Instead of grieving in the usual way, the people would groan inside and waste away because they would realize their sinfulness had caused this great affliction. Then they would remember the Lord had predicted this event through Ezekiel's peculiar mourning ritual and would realize that the Lord was, indeed, the true God.

WEEK 64 • WEDNESDAY   *Ezekiel 25:1—27:36*

What did clapping hands and stamping feet mean?

The Ammonites were descendents of Lot who settled northeast of the Dead Sea (Genesis 19:36–38). They often joined forces with other nations against God's people. In their hatred toward God's people, they celebrated the destruction of the temple and clapped their hands in glee when the Babylonians took God's people into exile (Ezekiel 25:6). Because of this the Lord's anger burned against Ammon. Just as the Lord had punished Israel and Judah for their sins, so He promised to punish the Ammonites by allowing foreign nations to destroy them. When this came true, it would be a sign to them that He was Lord of all nations.

WEEK 64 • THURSDAY   *Ezekiel 28:1–26*

What is a guardian cherub?

The word *cherubim,* the plural form of *cherub,* refers to angelic beings whose assignment often included guardianship. For instance, God assigned cherubim to guard the tree of life in Eden (Genesis 3:24). Also, the golden cherubim on the ark of the covenant symbolically guarded the sacred objects inside. Ezekiel refers to Tyre as a guardian cherub (Ezekiel 28:14). Tyre, the capital of Phoenicia, was an important commercial center with two excellent harbors and a prominent fleet of trade ships. She enjoyed great wealth and beauty and was renown for her glassware and dyed materials. Because of her safe island location, Tyre was more than able to guard herself against any land attack. She was like "a guardian cherub." Even though Tyre seemed invincible, Ezekiel said the Lord would allow her destruction. Proud of her own success and elated over Jerusalem's fall, the greedy population of Tyre would face judgment and would have no defense.

WEEK 64 • FRIDAY
Ezekiel 29:1—32:32

What is significant about the cedars in Lebanon?

The mighty cedar trees in Lebanon, nourished by underground streams, were a valuable resource and symbols of majesty and strength. Because they provided the best building timber in the Middle East, Solomon used them in constructing the temple. In Ezekiel 31 the prophet warns Egypt of what will happen to her by first comparing her to Assyria and then comparing Assyria to a cedar in Lebanon. Like the stately and prized cedar, Assyria was once a great and powerful nation. Nevertheless, because of her pride, the Lord allowed Babylon to conquer Assyria, cutting her down as easily as a cedar is felled. In a similar way, the Lord would punish mighty Egypt for her pride.

WEEK 64 • SATURDAY
Ezekiel 33:1—34:31

What was a watchman supposed to do?

In an ancient walled city, the watchman held a trusted position of responsibility. In Bible times many people lived and worked outside the city. The watchman sat on the top of the city wall or in a high tower where he could scan the horizon for enemies. When danger threatened, the watchman would sound a warning trumpet. The people would then hurry inside the city walls, close the gates, and prepare for the approaching attack. If someone heard the watchman's warning, but paid no attention to it, he was responsible for what happened to him. If the watchman failed to give the necessary warning, however, he was held accountable for the lives of those who died. In much the same way, the Lord charged Ezekiel as watchman for the house of Israel. This was a position of trust, responsibility, and honor.

WEEK 65 • MONDAY
Ezekiel 35:1—36:38

How would God give the Israelites a new heart?

The Lord told Ezekiel that He would restore the land of Judah. Once again it would produce branches and fruit for His people. The Lord further promised to restore His people by spiritually cleansing them. He would give them a new heart (Ezekiel 36:26). He would change their sinful, unbelieving hearts of stone into hearts of flesh, softened by His love. He would breathe new life into them and make them open to His grace. Once again they would desire to live as His people according to His will and worship Him alone. By doing this the Lord would show not only the Jews but also the surrounding nations what kind of God He really is—a loving, providing God who keeps His covenant promises.

WEEK 65 • TUESDAY
Ezekiel 37:1—39:29

What did the dry bones represent?

The Lord granted Ezekiel the vision of the valley of the dry bones (Ezekiel 37:1–14) to confirm His promises to His people in exile and reassure them that He would restore them to their own land. In this vision Ezekiel is brought by the Spirit of the Lord to the middle of a valley full of dry bones. These bones represent God's people in captivity and their seemingly hopeless condition. Like unburied skeletons, they pined away, feeling as though they were dead. In the vision the Lord asks Ezekiel if the bones can live, and Ezekiel answers that only the Lord, who made the bones, knows, for only He can make them live. The Lord tells Ezekiel to say that He will make breath enter the brittle bones and they will come to life. And they do! So also the Lord would revive His people, Israel, and restore them to their land. This vision shows that Israel's restoration as a nation and renewed spiritual life as God's people depended on the Lord's power, not on their outward circumstances.

WEEK 65 • WEDNESDAY

Ezekiel 40:1—42:20

How did Ezekiel's vision of a new temple impact the exiles?

Fourteen years after the fall of Jerusalem and the destruction of the temple, Ezekiel saw a vision of the land of Israel. In his vision he saw buildings that looked like a city. A man who looked like bronze, possibly an angel, told Ezekiel to pay attention to what he showed him so Ezekiel could tell the exiles everything he saw (Ezekiel 40:4). Ezekiel went into lengthy detail to describe this new temple in words and pictures the people would understand. Through this vision, the Lord intended to give hope to His exiled people. Even though their nation and temple had been destroyed, He wanted them to know they were still His people. Ezekiel impressed upon them the great splendor the Lord had planned for them. His love and faithfulness in rescuing them from captivity pointed to an even greater deliverance He would bring about through the Savior, our Lord Jesus.

WEEK 65 • THURSDAY

Ezekiel 43:1–27

What is the significance of God's glory returning to the temple?

After Ezekiel had seen every detail of the new temple, he was brought to the east gate. There Ezekiel saw the glory of the Lord enter and fill the new temple (Ezekiel 43:4–5). Like the pillar of fire that guided Israel from Egypt to the Promised Land, the glory Ezekiel saw was a visible manifestation of the Lord's presence and power. Ezekiel had earlier described the devastation the Israelites felt when God's glory left the temple (Ezekiel 10:1–22). This dramatic reversal of that departure reminded Ezekiel that the Lord had not abandoned His people. He would one day reveal His glory to the world in the Person of His own Son, Jesus—the Messiah and Savior!

WEEK 65 • FRIDAY   *Ezekiel 44:1–31*

Why are the descendants of Zadok specifically mentioned here?

In Ezekiel's vision of the temple, the Lord gave him explicit directions concerning the regulations to be observed and the duties of the priests and Levites. The Lord said that the Levites who led Israel into sin by worshiping false idols were not allowed to serve in the temple in the same way as they had before. Only the descendants of Zadok were to minister before Him and offer sacrifices (Ezekiel 44:15). Zadok was appointed chief priest during Solomon's reign (and hence presided over the first temple). Zadok faithfully supported Solomon as king. His descendants also remained faithful to the Lord even when other priests led the people in false idol worship. The Lord wants those who serve Him to do so faithfully. He Himself makes it possible for us to do that (2 Thessalonians 2:13–17).

WEEK 65 • SATURDAY   *Ezekiel 45:1—46:24*

Why was the east gate to remain open on the day of the New Moon?

In Ezekiel's vision of the temple, the Lord gave him regulations about offerings and holy days. The east gate was the one through which the glory of the Lord had entered the temple, and so the east gate of the outer court was permanently closed out of reverence for the Lord. The east gate of the inner court was also closed on the six working days, but on the Sabbath day and the day of the New Moon it was opened (Ezekiel 46:1). The New Moon festival was both a religious and civil festival celebrated at the beginning of each month. It was a day of celebration, rest, increased offerings, and worship. By keeping the east gate of the inner court open on these days, the prince, who was the secular head of God's people, could observe the priest offering the sacrifices on the great altar in the inner court.

WEEK 66 • MONDAY

Ezekiel 47:1—48:35

What is the significance of the river flowing from the temple?

After Ezekiel had "toured" the temple in his vision, seen all of the temple, and heard the regulations concerning sacrifices and special days, his angelic guide brought him back to the door of the temple. There, Ezekiel saw a river of water flowing out from the south side of the temple. The river was so deep one could swim in it (Ezekiel 47:2, 5). This river is similar to the river of the water of life flowing from the throne of God in Revelation 22:1–2. The river mentioned in Ezekiel's vision symbolizes life from the Lord and the abundant blessings He provides. This vision was an encouragement to the exiles to remain hopeful. The Lord would see to their return home and once again His blessings would flow from among them to others.

WEEK 66 • TUESDAY

Daniel 1:1–21

Why did Daniel and his friends not want to eat the food provided by the king?

When Nebuchadnezzar returned to Babylon from the invasion of Judah, he brought with him the spoils of that victory—valuables from the temple and young men as captives—to signify Judah's submission to Babylon. These men were to be trained for government service and fed the finest food. The program was a rather elaborate and sophisticated brainwashing effort designed to produce a shift in loyalty from foreign governments to Babylon's rulers. But Daniel and his friends would not eat the royal food or wine; they asked for only vegetables and water (Daniel 1:8, 12). The royal food and drink offered did not conform to Mosaic law, which allowed only meat from "clean" animals properly prepared. Because Gentiles prepared the food for the captives, it was unclean. In addition, the food served at Nebuchadnezzar's table was first offered to the pagan idols, thus making all the food unclean for the Jews.

WEEK 66 • WEDNESDAY   *Daniel 2:1–49*

Where did the king's magicians, enchanters, sorcerers, and astrologers get their power?

Daniel 2 tells us that a recurring dream plagued King Nebuchadnezzar. Since dreams were considered messages from the gods, the king summoned the magicians, enchanters, sorcerers, and astrologers to interpret it (Daniel 2:1–2). Magicians were involved in occult practices, while enchanters claimed to soften the heart of the gods with song. Sorcerers cast spells, and astrologers supposedly received special knowledge through the stars. Ultimately, Satan was the source of all these "powers."

WEEK 66 • THURSDAY   *Daniel 3:1—4:37*

What was the purpose of the blazing furnace?

The Babylonians often worshiped before statues of their gods, and so Nebuchadnezzar hoped to use a statue of himself to unite the nation and to solidify his power. (Note too that, given the statue worshiping customs in Babylonian culture, Nebuchadnezzar made a not-so-subtle claim to *be* a god when he erected a statue of himself.) Nebuchadnezzar ordered that at the sound of music everyone was to fall to the ground and worship his image, overlaid with gold. Anyone refusing to bow disobeyed the king and showed disloyalty to Babylon and its gods. The penalty, typical in Babylon (Jeremiah 29:22), was death by fire in a blazing furnace (Daniel 3:6). Like a kiln for firing bricks, this furnace was used exclusively for executions.

WEEK 66 • FRIDAY   *Daniel 5:1–31*

Why did drinking from gold goblets prompt God's judgment?

The Persian army held Babylon under siege. Despite the serious threat, King Belshazzar gave a banquet for his nobles. Such feasts had religious overtones; they were sometimes given to appease the gods. Belshazzar ordered that the gold and silver goblets his father, Nebuchadnezzar, had taken from the temple in Jerusalem to be brought to the banquet hall so he and his nobles could drink wine from them (Daniel 5:2). Belshazzar desecrated these gold goblets, originally dedicated for worship in God's temple, by storing them in the temple of Bel. By giving these vessels to his gods, Belshazzar insulted the Lord. By doing this Belshazzar ridiculed the Lord who claimed to be the only true God but who apparently was helpless to protect His people from captivity and prevent His temple from being robbed and destroyed.

WEEK 66 • SATURDAY   *Daniel 6:1–28*

Why were lions kept in a den?

Despite temptations and a nearly 70-year exile from his own land, Daniel remained faithful to the one true God. By grace Daniel acted courageously when he knew praying to God would mean being thrown to the lions. King Darius gave the order, and Daniel—then probably almost 80-years old—was thrown into the lions' den (Daniel 6:16). Lions roamed the countryside and forests in Mesopotamia. Kings often hunted lions for sport. The Persians captured lions, keeping them in large parks or using them as a means of execution (Daniel 6:24).

WEEK 67 • MONDAY   *Daniel 7:1—8:27*

Who is the Ancient of Days?

In a nighttime vision, the Lord revealed a picture of judgment in which He has history's last word just as He had the first at creation. Daniel saw the Ancient of Days presiding over the proceedings in the heavenly courtroom (Daniel 7:9). The title, Ancient of Days, used only here in all of Scripture, belongs to God. It contrasts His steadfast, unchanging nature with the instability of all we know in creation and in human relationships. Long before the empires of the world appeared, the eternal, majestic God flung the stars into being. Daniel's description of the Ancient of Days resembles that penned by the apostle John in Revelation (1:14–15).

WEEK 67 • TUESDAY   *Daniel 9:1–27*

What is the abomination that causes desolation?

Daniel receives a vision from God that reveals redemption as an accomplished fact, a fact brought about by the Anointed One (Daniel 9:25), the Messiah. Gabriel comes to assure Daniel that God will shape the course of history to usher in and establish the eternal Kingdom of the Messiah. Before that kingdom comes, a destroyer would set up an "abomination" in the temple, perhaps an idol. This abomination would leave the temple desolate (Daniel 9:27). Some believed Antiochus IV Epiphanes fulfilled this prophecy when he butchered a pig in the temple and installed a pagan altar. The temple was desecrated again by Emperor Caligula, and yet again when the Romans finally destroyed Jerusalem. At that point, the temple became desolate. This pointed to the fact that the worship rituals God instituted at Sinai had found their perfect fulfillment in Christ. Now, those who worship the Father do so, not on a mountain in Samaria, not on the temple mount in Jerusalem, but as Jesus Himself said, "In spirit and in truth." (See John 4:21–24.)

WEEK 67 • WEDNESDAY   *Daniel 10:1—12:13*

Who is Michael?

The agents of Satan successfully threw many roadblocks in the way of the Israelite exiles who wanted to return to the land the Lord promised to Abraham and to his descendants. But the angels of God worked to counter that force. One angel who helped was Michael (Daniel 10:13). Daniel depicts him as one of the chief princes of the angelic realm, an archangel who protects the people of God.

WEEK 67 • THURSDAY   *Hosea 1:1—2:23*

Why would God tell Hosea to marry a prostitute?

Hosea prophesied during the tragic final days of the Northern Kingdom, during which six kings reigned within only 25 years. While Hosea proclaimed a message of judgment, he included and emphasized the Gospel as well. Like many prophets, Hosea enacted part of his message. God commanded Hosea to marry a prostitute (Hosea 1:2). The relationship between Hosea and Gomer, his unfaithful wife, depicted Israel's unfaithfulness to the Lord. Hosea himself represents the Lord, faithful in his love for his people. Unfaithful Gomer pictures the nation of Israel bowing before idols and figuratively prostituting herself with pagan gods. Gomer's unfaithfulness points us also to our spiritual unfaithfulness. We have no more rightful claim on God's love than Gomer had on Hosea's love. Yet the Lord does love us: "While we were still sinners, Christ died for us" (Romans 5:8). All who turn to Him in repentance and faith receive restoration and peace. What amazing grace!

WEEK 67 • FRIDAY   *Hosea 3:1—4:19*

Why did Hosea have to pay to get his wife back?

Before he married Gomer, God told Hosea that she would leave him for another man. When Gomer did leave, Hosea went after her and bought her back for 15 shekels of silver and about 10 bushels of barley (Hosea 3:2). Gomer had sold herself into slavery. Or maybe she had become the mistress of another man. Or perhaps she had even become a prostitute at a pagan temple. Hosea's redemption of Gomer and his taking her back as his wife pictured God's great love for Israel despite her gross unfaithfulness. It also pictured our Lord's deep love for all humanity, love He showed by sending His Son to live, die, and rise for us.

WEEK 67 • SATURDAY   *Hosea 5:1—6:11*

To what does the name Ephraim refer?

Throughout the Book of Hosea, the Lord cataloged Ephraim's unfaithfulness and warned of the judgment to come. The Lord knew all about Ephraim (another name for Israel, the Northern Kingdom) and about how its people had turned to other gods—to spiritual prostitution (Hosea 5:3). By promoting idol worship and all the related cultic practices, Israel's priests had turned their backs on their spiritual heritage. Because they served the Baals and because they only pretended to repent, the Lord withdrew Himself from them (Hosea 5:6). This should have turned Judah from idolatry, but it didn't. Blinded by sin, the people of the Southern Kingdom repeated the sins of Ephraim—the Northern Kingdom. Inevitably, they would reap the same crop—a harvest judgment.

WEEK 68 • MONDAY
Hosea 7:1—8:14

What is the calf-idol of Samaria?

With increasing clarity Hosea describes the punishment God will send down on Israel's idolatry and disobedience. While the Israelites claim that the Lord is still their God, they have broken their covenant with Him by rejecting what is good. Besides their unauthorized kings, Israel has bought deeply into idolatry, making silver and gold images of fertility deities. God ordered Israel to throw out its calf-idol in Samaria because His anger burned against them (Hosea 8:5). This calf-idol, worshiped at Bethel and Dan, was the image set up by Jeroboam to wean the people away from worship in Jerusalem. This golden calf is reminiscent of the one made by Aaron at Sinai. It also points to much in our own society that we have made into idols. Such sin needs God's forgiveness, which He gives freely because of His Son, Jesus Christ.

WEEK 68 • TUESDAY
Hosea 9:1—10:15

What is the bread of mourners?

Hosea warned Israel that their sacrifices would not please God because those sacrifices were "like the bread of mourners" (Hosea 9:4). Bread was made unclean by being in the same house with a dead body (Numbers 19:14–15). Thus, "bread of mourners" was unclean just as Israel would be—unclean because Israel would be taken captive to Assyria, unclean because Israel's sacrifices in Assyria would be mixed with the worship of idols.

WEEK 68 • WEDNESDAY
Hosea 11:1—12:14

What is the significance of God calling His son out of Egypt?

God proclaimed His love for Israel by reviewing His history with them. He had preserved Israel, His Old Testament child, from death in a famine by giving them refuge in Egypt at the time of Joseph, Jacob's son. God called the nation back to the Promised Land to carry out His plan of salvation (Hosea 11:1). The redeeming love of God, which called Israel out of Egypt and back into the Promised Land persisted through all Israel's disobedience, reached its full measure when God called His Son, Jesus, driven to Egypt by the enmity of King Herod, back to His people and land (Matthew 2:15). By His life and death, Christ fulfilled the promises God gave to Israel and in manifest mercy to the Gentiles (Romans 15:8–9).

WEEK 68 • THURSDAY   *Hosea 13:1–16*

What is the significance of being ransomed from the power of the grave?

The word of judgment for Israel is set aside for a moment in the Book of Hosea as the Lord describes His victory over humanity's great enemy, death. God will pay whatever price is necessary to ransom His people for Himself. Like the kinsman-redeemer (Ruth 3:12; 4:1–10) who buys back family property to keep it from passing into another's possession, so God pays the ransom price of His people with the life and death of His Son. Though Israel as a nation will die, God has His chosen remnant of believers in Israel. For them death in an Assyrian siege or exile in Mesopotamia will not mean the end of life with God because He will buy them for Himself from the power of death. Such promise and joy permeate Paul's quotation of this verse as he wrote his first letter to the Corinthians (15:55).

WEEK 68 • FRIDAY   *Hosea 14:1–9*

What is the fruit of our lips?

The only road to rebirth and new life leads through repentance (Hosea 13:13–14). The prophet pictures true repentance in the words he places on the lips of his judged and humbled people returning to the Lord their God. Unlike their prayer in Hosea 6:1–3, which did not acknowledge their sin and thus was unacceptable to God, this prayer confesses their idolatry and rebellious self-will. Renouncing dependence on any political or military power, this prayer expresses the people's will to live dependent on God's mercy alone. These words of repentance and thanksgiving are the "fruit of our lips" (Hosea 14:2)—a sacrifice of praise.

WEEK 68 • SATURDAY

Joel 1:1–20

Why were the Israelites afraid of locusts?

The coming "day of the Lord" is heralded by signs that bid God's people to be alert to it and to respond to it. One such sign is the plague of locusts. Through his warning, the prophet summons God's people to join in a lament, a cry to the Lord who is hastening toward the day of judgment and deliverance. To show the severe and complete destruction the locust plague would bring, Joel uses four different words for locusts. While these four words could be used for different kinds of locusts, they can also mean the four phases of the insect as it grows. A locust is an aggressive type of grasshopper whose plague can be as devastating as an invading army. Locust swarms, great in number, fly for miles devouring almost every piece of vegetation in their path. When locusts destroy one year's crop, they have in effect also destroyed the seed for the following year's crop. Following a locust plague, barns are empty and the people starve. Thus, there was good reason to fear the locusts.

WEEK 69 • MONDAY   *Joel 2:1–32*

What is "the day of the LORD"?

As Joel called the people of Judah to repentance, he called for them to fast and pray in the light of coming disaster. All the people were to tremble because "the day of the LORD is coming" (Joel 2:1) A common phrase in the Old Testament, "the day of the LORD" occurs five times in the book of Joel. It refers to the occasion—whether in the present, the near future, or the final period of history—when God actively intervenes to punish sin that has come to a climax. Though the punishment may come through an invasion, it could also come through a natural disaster such as an infestation of locusts (Joel 1–2). "The day of the LORD" is a day of wrath, on that day the Lord God will execute His judgment on the human race. When the phrase refers to a present event, it also serves to point to the day of the return of the Lord Jesus Christ at the end of the world. In another sense, Good Friday was "the day of the LORD." On that day God poured out His wrath on His Son in full, as Jesus absorbed the punishment we ourselves had deserved for our sin. Now, we need not fear Christ's return. Judgment Day will bring us into God's presence and into eternal joy.

WEEK 69 • TUESDAY   *Joel 3:1–21*

What does bloodguilt mean?

The Book of Joel describes God's judgment on the nations. The book ends with the blessings God has in store for His people. The Lord promises to pardon Israel's bloodguilt and to dwell in Zion (Joel 3:21). Bloodguilt results from bloodshed and can be traced back to Judah's wicked King Manasseh. He had "shed so much innocent blood that he filled Jerusalem from end to end" (2 Kings 21:16). Though God had at one time thrust Judah and Israel from His presence because of their wicked violence (2 Kings 24:20), now in Joel He promises pardon. This promise has its complete fulfillment in Christ's blood poured out on the cross; because of the cross the Lord forgives His people's wickedness and remembers their sin no more (Jeremiah 31:34).

WEEK 69 • WEDNESDAY   *Amos 1:1—2:16*

Why does Amos keep repeating the phrase "for three sins, even for four"?

After the Lord had called him, Amos put down his shepherd's staff and left Tekoa, his home in Judah, in order to do his work as a prophet in Israel, the Northern Kingdom. While Amos condemned the sins of Israel's enemies, he also rebuked Israel for their sins. In the first two chapters of Amos, the Lord repeats one phrase seven times: "for three sins of [a nation], even for four" (Amos 1:3; 2:6). The use of this phrase emphasizes not only the number of sins involved but especially the fourth one—the one named and detailed, the one that has brought God's patience to an end. Seven is the number often used in Scripture to indicate completion or fullness. The nations have sinned in every way and their guilt is completely worthy of judgment.

WEEK 69 • THURSDAY   *Amos 3:1–15*

Why does God call Israel "chosen"?

Because God had designated Israel as His chosen people, they felt that Amos had no right to threaten them with divine judgment. Israel had taken its chosenness, its election, for granted. The Lord reminds them, "You only have I chosen of all the families of the earth" (Amos 3:2). Nonetheless, this chosenness, in God's eyes, is not a magical protection from evil or a privilege. Rather election establishes a personal bond between the Lord and His people—a covenant. In love, the Lord chose Israel for His saving purpose. The world's Savior would be born from the descendants of Abraham, Isaac, and Jacob. Yet, Israel took their position and privilege for granted, even as they disobeyed and despised their Savior-God.

WEEK 69 • FRIDAY   *Amos 4:1—5:27*

Why are the women of Israel called cows of Bashan?

Despite Amos' warnings to affluent Israelites, they had not returned to the Lord in repentance and faith. Amos became more specific in Amos 4:1, calling the women "cows of Bashan" who oppressed the poor and needy. Strong bulls (Psalm 22:12) and fat cows were the pride of the land of Bashan, east of the Sea of Galilee. Amos uses this image to picture the women of Israel, concerned only with satisfying their own hunger and thirst at the expense of the poor. In the image we read an implied warning: just as fattened cattle are butchered, so Israel will meet destruction.

WEEK 69 • SATURDAY   *Amos 6:1–14*

Why would the people be afraid to mention the name of the Lord?

Amos pictures the severity of God's judgment by describing a city destroyed as God had threatened. So many are dead that, contrary to normal custom, the bodies are cremated. A kinsman arrives to perform the last rites. He finds only one person alive—and hiding in a corner. The destruction has so completely demoralized the survivor that he is afraid even to mention the name of the avenging Lord (Amos 6:10). By pronouncing God's name, he may give away his location and bring down on himself the same divine judgment that has emptied his family's house.

WEEK 70 • MONDAY
Amos 7:1–17

What does the plumb line represent?

In a vision Amos saw God standing by a wall that had been built true to plumb. God's hand holds a plumb line (Amos 7:7), a cord with a lead weight used by builders to construct straight walls. A plumb line could also test existing walls to see if they had settled and tilted. Those that had would be torn down. When the Lord dropped the plumb line of His Law to Israel, they didn't meet His standards and would need to be torn down before being rebuilt.

WEEK 70 • TUESDAY
Amos 8:1–14

Who is the Pride of Jacob?

God told Amos that the time had come for the people of Israel to be punished. The Israelites had let their pride interfere with true worship. The Lord God swore by the "Pride of Jacob" that He would never forget what they had done (Amos 8:7). Earlier in this book the Lord took an oath by Himself (Amos 6:8). Here God takes the same kind of oath, calling Himself the Pride of Jacob. Some believed God was swearing, not by His holy name, but by the land of Israel. Either way, God solemnly vows that He will never forget anything the Israelites had done—their sin, their disobedience, their idolatry.

WEEK 70 • WEDNESDAY
Amos 9:1–15

What did David's tent represent?

The Book of Amos closes on a note of hope. The Lord will restore David's fallen tent and repair its broken places, rebuilding it as it had once been (Amos 9:11). The original Hebrew word for tent meant "hut" or "rough booth" used for shelter. Such a shelter would recall David's humble beginnings and also point to the house (dynasty) of David and his kingdom of 12 tribes. David's dynasty, which had been like a protective canopy over all the people of Israel, had fallen. The Northern tribes had split from the Southern tribes. God's promise to restore David's fallen tent—a promise that had its roots in 2 Samuel 7:12–16—would find its complete fulfillment in Jesus Christ, the Son of David. The apostle James quotes this passage in Acts 15:16–18.

WEEK 70 • THURSDAY   *Obadiah 1–21*

What did Edom do to deserve an entire book written against them?

The Jews, descendants of Jacob through Judah, had a long-standing feud with the Edomites, descendants of Esau. While the brothers Jacob and Esau (sons of Isaac) eventually made peace with each other, a later generation of Edomites gloated when Babylon conquered Judah and led them off into captivity. The Edomites looted their defeated cousins, captured those who sought to escape, and turned them over to the enemy. For these reasons, Obadiah pronounced the Lord's judgment against Edom.

WEEK 70 • FRIDAY   *Jonah 1:1—2:10*

Why would throwing Jonah into the sea calm the storm?

By taking a ship to Tarshish, Jonah disobeyed God's command to preach repentance in Nineveh. When the storm threatened to sink the ship, Jonah knew that his attempt to escape the Lord had failed. Jonah confessed his sin to the sailors. Jonah knew he deserved death for his disobedience. Thus his request to be thrown into the sea was not a suicidal death wish nor fatalism. Rather, he placed himself, body and soul, into the Lord's hands.

WEEK 70 • SATURDAY   *Jonah 3:1—4:11*

Why did the Ninevites cover their animals with sackcloth?

The repentance of the Ninevites is one of the greatest miracles in all of Scripture. Renowned for their violence and wickedness, the people of Nineveh put on sackcloth, sat down in the dust, and called on God for mercy. Based on what Jonah had preached, they repented. The king issued a decree that sackcloth was to cover every living creature—humans and animals. This decree demonstrates recognition of how thoroughly sin had permeated the world of the Ninevites and how great was their need for forgiveness. In this account we see the Lord in grace granting both the gift of repentance and of faith.

WEEK 71 • MONDAY   *Micah 1:1—2:13*

Why would someone in mourning shave their head?

Shaving the head, tearing clothes, and putting on sackcloth all were signs of abject grief and mourning, especially in times of dire circumstances. Micah's words point to an inglorious end for the cities of Judah, one that would bring shame and disgrace on the chosen people of God. The prophet exhorts the people to shave their heads as "bald as a vulture" (Micah 1:16). This would be a sign of that mourning when Judah had lost "the children" of her delight, her people, "for they will go from you into exile."

WEEK 71 • TUESDAY   *Micah 3:1—4:13*

What does Micah mean by saying people would beat their swords into plowshares?

The beginning verses of Micah 4 are almost identical to the words of Isaiah 2:1–4. Both Micah and Isaiah use figurative language to describe what the Lord God will do in the days of the messianic age. Neither prophet describes a reshaping of the physical universe nor the formation of some political world empire. Rather, the "Jerusalem" God promises to create is constructed of "living stones" (1 Peter 2:5), "built on the foundation of the apostles and prophets, with Christ Jesus Himself as the chief cornerstone" (Ephesians 2:20). This new Jerusalem will embrace strangers and foreigners from all nations. Christ's coming will inaugurate peace through the preaching of the Gospel. As a sign of that peace, nations will no longer go to war but will "beat their swords into plowshares" (Micah 4:3), turning their energies from war to domestic pursuits.

WEEK 71 • WEDNESDAY   *Micah 5:1–15*

What was significant about Bethlehem?

Jacob's son Benjamin had been born in Bethlehem. Rachel, Jacob's wife and Benjamin's mother, was buried there. Ruth gleaned the fields of Boaz at Bethlehem. There too King David was born. And, as Micah points out, the Messiah would come from Bethlehem. This city was so small that it hadn't been named among the 100 cities belonging to the clans of Judah (Joshua 15). Yet Bethlehem was not too small for God's purposes, as Matthew points out in his Gospel (2:6). For the prophet Micah and the evangelist Matthew, little Bethlehem signifies that "God chose the weak things of the world to shame the strong. He chose the lowly things of the world … so that no one may boast before Him" (1 Corinthians 1:27–29).

WEEK 71 • THURSDAY   *Micah 6:1–16*

Why did Micah tell the people to plead to the mountains?

Through Micah the Lord presents before the mountains and hills His righteous case against His unfaithful people. The mountains and hills serve as judge and jury because they have witnessed God's goodness to Judah as well as Judah's unfaithfulness to the Lord. The Lord then challenges Judah to present its defense in this vast courtroom.

WEEK 71 • FRIDAY   *Micah 7:1–20*

What is the significance of gathering summer fruit and early figs?

Micah pictured his search for godly people in Judah like looking for summer fruit and early figs after the harvest had ended (Micah 7:1–2). None would be found. God's people were like a vineyard that no longer produced fruit (Isaiah 5:1–7). The Lord saw no fruits of repentance, only of evil and wrongdoing.

WEEK 71 • SATURDAY   *Nahum 1:1—3:19*

Why does God get angry at cities and nations?

Assyria, whose capital was Nineveh, conquered Judah, infected it with idolatry, and ruled over it in oppression and arrogance. Assyrian kings gloated over the gruesome punishment they inflicted on their conquered peoples. They conducted their wars with shocking ferocity. For such conduct they would have to answer to God. Because the Lord is slow to anger (Nahum 1:3), His judicial action is deliberate, not impulsive. All the same, Godís justice is sure (Nahum 1:3, 12–14).

WEEK 72 • MONDAY

Habakkuk 1:1—2:20

How could a prophet dare to complain to God?

Prophets often interpreted God's purposes in history. To Habakkuk history involved a series of agonizing questions to which he himself could not find answers. So with questions in hand Habakkuk turned to the Lord for understanding and interpretation of the history of Judah and its neighbors. People still ask these questions today: Why does evil seem to go unpunished? Why does God not answer prayer? (Habakkuk 1:1–4). In tense expectancy the prophet awaits an answer from the Lord, the only one capable of answering.

WEEK 72 • TUESDAY

Habakkuk 3:1–19

What do Teman and Mount Paran have to do with God's people?

The terms "Teman" and "Mount Paran" are poetic ways to express the history of the people of Israel with God Almighty (Habakkuk 3:3). Teman, meaning "southlands," is the northern district of Edom. Mount Paran is a mountain in Edom (Deuteronomy 33:2). In Habakkuk 3:3–5, the prophet describes a vision given by God. In the vision Habakkuk sees the Lord coming from Sinai as He did when He brought His people through the land of the Edomites into the Promised Land. Clothed in splendor and glory, the Lord brings with Him His terrifying power to destroy. Thus "Teman" and "Paran" mark the Lord's route as He advances from Sinai to Palestine.

WEEK 72 • WEDNESDAY

Zephaniah 1:1—2:15

What is so bad about stepping over a threshold?

When Zephaniah mentions those who avoid stepping on the threshold, he is referring to a superstition. Evil spirits supposedly exercised their influence on those entering a house, attacking them at the threshold. This superstition may date back to the time of 1 Samuel 5, when the Philistines placed the ark of the covenant next to the image of Dagon in order to demonstrate Dagon's superiority over the God of Israel. But the Lord reversed the symbolism by toppling the idol and braking it in pieces before the ark, time after time. From that day on none of the priests or worshipers of Dagon would step on the threshold (1 Samuel 5:5). Thus in Zephaniah 1:8–9, those who avoid stepping on the threshold are associated with idol worship.

WEEK 72 • THURSDAY   *Zephaniah 3:1–20*

Why did the people need to have their lips purified?

Matthew 12:34 declares that those who are evil cannot speak good—an apt description of the people of Judah, of its enemies, and of our world today. Through the prophet, God proclaims His judgment on sin and then brings comfort by describing the future of Jerusalem on the great "day of the LORD." On that day the speech of the nations will be made pure, and the Gentiles will break out in unanimous adoration of the Lord (Zephaniah 3:9). Just as the Lord purified Isaiah's lips (Isaiah 6:6–7), so also our lips as well as our lives are made pure by the blood of Jesus, which "purifies us from all sin" (1 John 1:7).

WEEK 72 • FRIDAY   *Haggai 1:1—2:23*

What did the Lord's signet ring represent?

A signet ring was a kind of seal that functioned as a signature (Esther 8:8) and was worn on one's finger (Esther 3:10). It could serve as a pledge or guarantee of full payment. A king's signet ring was a prized and jealously guarded possession. The king used the ring to impress his seal on documents to mark them as official business. God's name was stamped across the face of Zerubbabel. By this the Lord of hosts was putting His mark on history, marking it as His official business. Thus God would establish His kingdom in His way. His way was the One who is the way, the truth, and the life—Jesus, the Messiah.

WEEK 72 • SATURDAY   *Zechariah 1:1—2:12*

What is the significance of the different colored horses?

Born in exile, Zechariah was a prophet and a priest. As a young man he returned from Babylon to Jerusalem. In his first recorded vision Zechariah saw a man riding a red horse, and behind him were red, brown, and white horses (Zechariah 1:8). Despite many attempts to explain the colors, in the end, not much is really known about their meaning. Often the red horse is associated with war and the white horse with final victory. Revelation 6:1–8 describes a similar vision given by God to the apostle John.

WEEK 73 • MONDAY   *Zechariah 3:1–10*

What do the filthy clothes represent?

In Zechariah's vision, Joshua, the high priest, was dressed in filthy clothes
as he stood before the throne of judgment. The filthy garments of the
priest represent the sin and guilt of the priest and thus also the nation. The
Lord does not ignore the evil, but through the angel tells those present to
remove the high priest's dirty garments (Zechariah 3:3–4). The Lord
promises, "See, I have taken away your sin, and I will put rich garments
on you" (Zechariah 3:4). All of this points to Jesus Christ, our great High
Priest, "who has been tempted in every way, just as we are—yet was without sin" (Hebrews 4:15).

WEEK 73 • TUESDAY   *Zechariah 4:1–14*

What does the gold lampstand represent?

In his fifth vision from God, Zechariah saw "a solid gold lampstand with
a bowl at the top and seven lights on it, with seven channels to the lights"
(Zechariah 4:2). Similar to the lampstand in Israel's tabernacle and the 10
lampstands of Solomon's temple, Zechariah's lampstand was different in
that it was automatically filled with oil. The lampstand and the two olive
trees seem to indicate that under the watchful eye of the Lord, the divine-
ly instituted leaders of God's people will be the means by which God supplies His grace (oil) for life in the new Jerusalem and for worship in the
new temple.

WEEK 73 • WEDNESDAY   *Zechariah 5:1–11*

Why was the scroll flying?

In the sixth vision, Zechariah saw a scroll, 30 feet long and 15 feet wide
(Zechariah 5:1–2). The scroll, representing God's Law, was flying in the sky
and was spread out like a large sheet so it could be read on both sides. Like
a huge billboard, the scroll proclaimed God's judgment on all sin, particularly on the dishonesty of thieves and those who had sworn falsely.

WEEK 73 • THURSDAY   *Zechariah 6:1–15*

What was the significance of putting a crown on the head of the high priest?

God told Zechariah to take silver and gold to make a crown, and set it on the head of the high priest, Joshua (Zechariah 6:11). The Hebrew word for crown, not the same as the word used for the high priest's turban, refers to an ornate crown with many diadems. This prophecy finds its fulfillment in Jesus, the Messiah, who would serve as both King and High Priest to God's people. In the days of the kings and during the exile, Judah was ruled by two separate persons—the king, who ruled the political life, and the high priest, who ruled the religious life. Jesus holds both offices eternally.

WEEK 73 • FRIDAY   *Zechariah 7:1–14*

Why did the Israelites fast during certain months and hold festivals in others?

A delegation came to the priests and the prophets with the question: "Should we continue to mourn and fast in the fifth month as we have in the past?" Through Zechariah God answered by asking, in effect: "Your religion—is it for you or is it for God?" (Zechariah 7:5–6). The fast of the fifth month commemorated the destruction of Jerusalem and of the city and the temple by Nebuchadnezzar. The fast of the seventh month commemorated the murder of Gedaliah, the governor of Judah, during a time of civil strife after the fall of Jerusalem. Leviticus 23 describes the various festivals. The Lord's rhetorical question concerning Israel's fasting parallels the judgment Jesus passed on the fasting of the Pharisees (Matthew 6:16–18). In both cases, the fasting lacked sincerity and integrity; for fasting was supposed to express sorrow for sin and urgency in prayer, but it had become a piece of simple self-centered piety. Israel's self-centeredness had emptied their worship of any real meaning or value.

WEEK 73 • SATURDAY   *Zechariah 8:1–23*

What is the remnant of Israel?

God's promises, love, mercy, and grace may indeed seem too marvelous to the remnant of the people (Zechariah 8:6), but the Lord Himself declares that they are very real. The remnant included the small group of people who had returned to Palestine from Babylon. Though they desired to rebuild Jerusalem and the temple, life itself was a daily struggle for survival. This little group endured the added burden of hostile neighbors, and they often became discouraged. So the Lord continually reminds His people of His promises and love.

WEEK 74 • MONDAY   *Zechariah 9:1—10:12*

Why would a king ride a donkey instead of a horse?

God not only reigns over history but also reigns in history. The king whom God would send would be the opposite of "the pride of the Philistines" (Zechariah 9:6). God's king would be none other than the Word made flesh, Jesus Christ, who would approach His people in humility, riding a donkey (Zechariah 9:9). Contrasted with a stomping, snorting warhorse, the donkey was a lowly animal. David and his sons often rode donkeys, especially in times of peace. Zechariah's picture points to Christ's kingly entry into Jerusalem (Matthew 21:1–11). Christ's kingdom is not of this world. His only "weapon" is His Word, which offers peace to all. As the Servant King and Prince of Peace, Jesus is God's last word to the human race—that Word conquers the world and brings peace which the world cannot give.

WEEK 74 • TUESDAY   *Zechariah 11:1—12:14*

What is the significance of the two staffs named Favor and Union?

While the exact meaning of Zechariah 11 may be obscure, this much is clear: The people of God, His flock, are betrayed and exploited by outsiders and by their own leaders (their shepherds). These false shepherds must be destroyed if the flock is to survive. In their place, God sends the shepherd of His choice—a shepherd equipped with twin staffs, Favor (God's grace) and Union (unity). This shepherd tends the flock, judges the false shepherds, and yet is despised and rejected by the flock. As a result God's favor, His peace, is removed from the people. The unity between God and His people and the unity of the people with each other is broken and destroyed. True peace and unity would not be restored until *the* Good Shepherd, Jesus Christ, came. This Good Shepherd—rejected by His own—laid down His life for the sheep.

WEEK 74 • WEDNESDAY   *Zechariah 13:1–9*

Why would a prophet have wounds?

According to Zechariah 13:1 a fountain would open to cleanse the people from sin. As a result, idols will no longer have any significance, and false prophets will be wiped out. False prophets will find no support. No longer claiming the mantle of a prophet, the false prophets will think of themselves as farmers. They will claim that the telltale scars of self-inflicted wounds (similar to those of Baal's prophets in 1 Kings 18:28) came from carousing at a friend's house, rather than from the violent rituals performed at pagan altars—further proof of the deceit perpetrated by the prophets.

WEEK 74 • THURSDAY   *Zechariah 14:1–21*

What is the Feast of Tabernacles?

Since the Lord is king over all, He will be worshiped by all. The survivors of all the nations will join God's people to celebrate the Feast of Tabernacles (Zechariah 14:16). The Feast of Tabernacles (Leviticus 23:33–43), known also as the Feast of Ingathering, was a seven-day feast celebrated in our September or October. This Feast of Ingathering points forward to God's ingathering of all nations at the end of days. The feast itself echoed the Exodus, the first of God's acts of deliverance in Israel. It recalled the time when the Israelites dwelt in booths (tents, tabernacles) after the Lord brought them out of Egypt into the wilderness and from there into the Promised Land.

WEEK 74 • FRIDAY   *Malachi 1:1—2:17*

How could a loving God hate Esau?

Israel, God's chosen people, needed to be reminded of the Lord's elective love, especially now that they experienced the disillusionment of Persian domination. God's love initiated and sustained Israel's existence (Deuteronomy 7:7–8). The Lord continued to love His people despite their unfaithfulness (Hosea 11:1). Malachi illustrates God's love by contrasting the lot of the nation of Israel, descendant of Jacob, with the fate of the nation Edom, descendant of Esau. God's judgment lay heavy on Edom, that bitter and vindictive enemy of Israel. The Lord had removed His love from Edom—Esau "hated" (Malachi 1:3). So how could a loving God hate? From the enemies' point of view, only God's retribution and anger are in view. In the eyes of God's people, only God's love is in sight—His love that is the source of His protection. The idolaters of Edom had made themselves enemies of Israel and thus of the Lord (Numbers 20; Psalm 137:7). God hates evil and anything that stands in the way of His love. Through Jacob and his descendants, God's love was revealed more and more until it shone most brightly from the cross of His Son.

WEEK 74 • SATURDAY   *Malachi 3:1—4:6*

What is significance of God sending Elijah?

Malachi's concluding words first focus on God's Law. Then the prophet looks forward to the great "day of the LORD" (Malachi 4:5). In preparation for that day, Israel will receive warning from a prophetic voice, one who comes "in the spirit and power of Elijah" (Luke 1:17)—John the Baptizer. Like Elijah, John's message will work repentance in the hearts of people, restoring harmony between generations, and so making "ready a people prepared for the Lord" (Luke 1:17).

WEEK 75 • MONDAY   *Matthew 1:1—2:23*

Who were the Magi, and why did they want to see the King of the Jews?

Originally the name *Magi* referred to those from a Persian priestly caste, but by New Testament times it designated all magicians, astronomers, and astrologers from the east. These people had developed astrology into a sophisticated science, especially in Babylon. The Wise Men who came to see Jesus may have come from there. The Magi apparently knew something about the Old Testament prophecies concerning the coming Messiah, because when they observed the rising of a special star in the east, they connected it to "the King of the Jews." That motivated them to travel perhaps hundreds of miles to worship Him.

WEEK 75 • TUESDAY   *Matthew 3:1—4:25*

Why did John baptize people?

John the Baptizer prepared the way for the coming Savior. He announced the coming end of the age, which is both a great and dreadful event—dreadful for unrepentant sinners who will receive the Lord's judgment, but great for those who repent and receive His mercy. John called upon the people to confess their sins and be baptized (Matthew 3:1–6). Baptism, which means simply a "washing" in Greek, was a familiar ritual to the Jews. Many religious leaders in Judaism baptized Gentile converts into Judaism to signify the cleansing of their sins. John, however, called Jews—God's chosen people—to flee from the wrath to come by repenting of their sins and being baptized. This message caused quite a stir, reminding some of the pious, no doubt, of the prophecy found in Malachi 4:4–6.

WEEK 75 • WEDNESDAY   *Matthew 5:1—7:29*

Why are Jesus' teachings in Matthew 5 called the Beatitudes?

As crowds of people gathered to hear Jesus' Sermon on the Mount, Jesus took His disciples aside to explain what it means to be His followers. This series of teachings is often referred to as the Beatitudes (Matthew 5:1–12);

"beatitude" refers to "bliss" or "blessedness." The Beatitudes of Jesus are not a set of moral precepts for us to follow. That would be impossible for us sinners. Rather, the Beatitudes express the blessings Jesus' followers already enjoy because we are connected to Him.

WEEK 75 • THURSDAY   *Matthew 8:1—9:38*

Why didn't Jesus allow the man to bury his father?

While the man's request to go bury his father sounds reasonable, Jesus says no (Matthew 8:21–22). He knew the man's heart. Some think the man's father had not yet died. If so, then the man wanted to postpone support for Jesus. If his father had died, however, the disciple may have wanted to collect his inheritance. Whatever the reason, Jesus made it clear that His mission took precedence. He says (verse 22) that those who are (spiritually) dead can bury the (physically) dead. Following Him gives life. When we know and experience that life, then Jesus' life-giving mission becomes our highest priority.

WEEK 75 • FRIDAY   *Matthew 10:1—11:30*

What was the significance of shaking the dust off one's feet?

Jesus sent His disciples on an urgent mission to the people of Israel to extend to them the peace of God that comes only through faith in Him as the Messiah. If a town refused to welcome them as the Lord's representatives, the disciples were to shake the dust off their feet as they left these homes or towns (Matthew 10:14). Pharisees performed this symbolic act of rejection when they left an area that was ritually unclean. By telling the disciples to do this, Jesus indicates that those who refuse to believe in Him bear the responsibility for and the consequences of their unbelief. They face a more severe judgment than even Sodom and Gomorrah.

WEEK 75 • SATURDAY   *Matthew 12:1—13:58*

What was wrong with eating on the Sabbath?

As Jesus and His disciples moved through the grainfields on the Sabbath, they were hungry and so began to pick and eat some grain. The Pharisees saw this and charged them with disobedience to the law (Matthew 12:1–2). The Mosaic law prohibited harvesting—not picking and eating—on the Sabbath: "If you enter your neighbor's grainfield, you may pick kernels with your hands, but you must not put a sickle to his standing grain" (Deuteronomy 23:25). According to the ceremonial law as they had codified it, however, the Pharisees considered the disciples' action as reaping, one of the 39 kinds of work prohibited by custom on the Sabbath. Jesus did not dispute this with them. Instead, He pointed to His own lordship over the Sabbath as the One who instituted it.

WEEK 76 • MONDAY   *Matthew 14:1—15:39*

What was a tetrarch?

During the New Testament era a number of rulers had the name Herod, but not all of them had the same authority. Herod the Great, the ruler at the time of Jesus' birth, was appointed king of Judea by the Roman Senate in 40 B.C. After his death in 4 B.C., however, Herod's kingdom was divided among his three sons: Archelaus, Herod Antipas, and Herod Philip. These sons were tetrarchs, a Greek title given to minor rulers over a fourth part of a region controlled by a foreign nation. Herod Antipas ruled over the regions of Galilee and Perea for Rome. He was the ruler who arrested and imprisoned John the Baptizer prior to having him beheaded (Matthew 14:1–12). He was also the Herod to whom Pilate sent Jesus for a hearing after Jesus' arrest.

WEEK 76 • TUESDAY   *Matthew 16:1—17:27*

Why did the religious leaders want a sign from heaven?

Jesus had already done many miraculous signs—healing people of various diseases, feeding 5,000 people with a few loaves and fish, and turning water into wine. The Pharisees and Sadducees, however, were not satisfied with these miracles. They demanded instead a sign from heaven, something only God could give. In doing so they were really asking for proof that Jesus was indeed the Messiah as He claimed. Jesus reprimanded them, because He knew demonstrations of divine power do not bring people to faith. The Pharisees did not want a sign that would bring them to faith. Rather, they wanted a reason to continue in their unbelief. Jesus told them (Matthew 16:4) the only sign they would get was the sign of Jonah. Just as Jonah spent three days in the belly of the whale before he came "back" to the world of the living, so Jesus would die and rise from the tomb after three days.

WEEK 76 • WEDNESDAY   *Matthew 18:1—19:30*

How could people pay back their debts if they were in jail?

Jesus tells the parable of the master and his servant to help the disciples understand the unlimited nature of forgiveness. In the parable the master forgives his servant a huge debt, and so any limitation on the forgiveness the servant, in turn, shows to someone in his debt is unthinkable. Yet that is what happens. Because the servant fails to show mercy, the master revokes the forgiveness he extended and sends his servant to prison until his debt is paid (Matthew 18:21–35). In Bible times people who could not pay their debts went to jail. By this means creditors hoped to motivate a family to come up with the money, perhaps by selling the debtor's property. Sometimes family members were even sold as slaves to make payment. If all this failed, the debtor could be kept in jail for life!

WEEK 76 • THURSDAY   *Matthew 20:1—21:46*

Why did the people lay down cloaks and branches for the donkey to walk on?

Jesus rode into Jerusalem on a donkey as a great crowd spread their cloaks and branches on the road to pave His way (Matthew 21:8). Throwing flowers, leafy branches, cloaks, and other garments on the road to welcome the arrival of royalty and other important dignitaries was a common practice of the day. In this way, Jesus' entrance into Jerusalem reminded the people of Zechariah's prophecy about the coming Messiah (Zechariah 9:9–10). All Jerusalem was astir as the crowds shouted, "Hosanna to the Son of David." Many probably did not fully understand what these words of adoration truly meant or the nature of His kingship, yet their words communicated the truth: Jesus of Nazareth, the Son of David, is Savior of the world.

WEEK 76 • FRIDAY
Matthew 22:1—23:39

Who were the Sadducees?

The Sadducees were wealthy and influential Jewish religious leaders. While smaller in number than the Pharisees, they controlled the high priesthood and held a majority of seats in the Sanhedrin, the Jewish high council that decided civil and criminal cases not involving capital punishment. The Sadducees accepted only the five books of the Pentateuch (Genesis—Deuteronomy) as binding. They denied doctrines like the resurrection of the body, life after death, or angels. They frequently joined with the Pharisees in opposition to Jesus. When the Sadducees asked Jesus about what would happen in heaven to someone who had been married seven times on earth, they did not want an answer. Rather, they hoped to trap Him with a question He could not possibly answer (Matthew 22:23–24). Jesus responds that they err "because [they] do not know the Scriptures or the power of God" (verse 29). Then (verse 32) He quotes from Exodus 3:6, a book the Sadducees considered authoritative, to affirm the truth of life after physical death.

WEEK 76 • SATURDAY
Matthew 24:1—25:46

Why did the bridesmaids wait so long for the groom?

Jesus tells the parable of the 10 bridesmaids to illustrate the need to be ready when He comes again. In this parable, 10 bridesmaids wait for the groom to arrive. When He finally arrives, five of them are prepared, while the other five are not (Matthew 25:1–13). Just as we await the coming of Jesus, the bridesmaids in the parable awaited the coming of the groom so they could accompany him to the wedding banquet. Customarily, weddings took place after sunset. The ceremony began at the groom's house while the bride and bridesmaids awaited his arrival at her home, not knowing for sure when he would come. In this parable Jesus stressed the need for God's people to await His return faithfully. (The oil in the lamps represents faith.) No one knows when Jesus will come again. Only by remaining in Him, nourished by Word and Sacrament, will we be ready.

WEEK 77 • MONDAY   *Matthew 26:1—27:66*

What is the significance of Christ's Last Supper being instituted during the Passover meal?

In New Testament times all Israelite men were expected to go to Jerusalem during the week of Passover to celebrate Israel's deliverance from slavery. There the priests ritually slaughtered the Passover lamb in the temple as a sin atonement, and the people celebrated the Passover meal at the appointed time in homes within the city. Before Jesus died, He wanted to celebrate the Passover meal one last time with His disciples, and so they gathered in the Upper Room. The Passover meal included symbolic elements of roasted lamb, unleavened bread, bitter herbs, minor condiments, and four cups of wine. It was likely the third cup of wine that Jesus used to institute the Last Supper. In it, Jesus identifies Himself with the Passover lamb, for soon His own blood would stain the hill of Calvary so that our sins could be forgiven. Jesus fulfills the Passover, for the Old Testament sacrifices pointed to and found their completion in Him, the perfect and all-sufficient sacrifice for the sins of the world.

WEEK 77 • TUESDAY   *Matthew 28:1–20*

Why is it important to believe in the resurrection of Jesus?

Matthew and the other evangelists repeatedly witness to Jesus' bodily resurrection. They do this to underscore that our faith in Him as the Savior is not in vain. If Jesus had not risen from the dead, His death on the cross would have no power to atone for sin since anyone can claim to be the world's Savior and die. Jesus' resurrection from the dead proves He truly is the Savior of the world, for no mere man—only God—could do this. The resurrection also shows that Jesus' teaching is the truth; we can trust His Word (John 8:28). Jesus' resurrection proves that God the Father accepted Christ's sacrifice for the world's sin (Romans 4:25). Finally, Jesus' resurrection guarantees our own. Because He lives, we also will live eternally (John 11:25–26).

WEEK 77 • WEDNESDAY   *Mark 1:1—2:27*

What is the kingdom of God?

After Jesus was baptized by John, He began His ministry in Galilee, proclaiming the Good News—the Gospel of forgiveness through faith in Him. No earthly territory, the kingdom of God is our Lord's gracious rule in the hearts of His people. "Repent and believe the good news" describes the process by which God saves sinners. Both elements—repentance and faith—come to us as His gift. God's plan of salvation was at hand; the promised Savior had come into the world. By His life, death, and resurrection, Jesus would redeem us. His rule will continue throughout all eternity.

WEEK 77 • THURSDAY   *Mark 3:1—4:41*

Why did Jesus tell the evil spirits to be quiet?

A large crowd of people from Galilee and elsewhere followed Jesus, hearing Him teach and seeing Him heal those with diseases. The evil spirits who possessed some of the people recognized Christ for who He is—the Son of God (Mark 3:7–12). Yet Jesus rebuked the spirits to silence them, for He did not want defeated demons that were to confess Him. Rather, those who had been delivered by God were to proclaim His mighty deeds and confess Christ as Lord. If Christ would have accepted the testimony of these evil spirits, He would have played right into the hands of the Pharisees, who later accused Him of being "possessed by Beelzebub" (Mark 3:22).

WEEK 77 • FRIDAY   *Mark 5:1—6:56*

What does it mean to be possessed by a demon?

As Jesus traveled the region of the Gerasenes, a man possessed by a demon fell on his knees before Jesus (Mark 5:1–20). The demon's name was Legion, meaning that a multitude of demons were involved. When the demons recognized Jesus, they begged permission to enter a large herd of pigs. After Jesus granted permission, the newly possessed pigs rushed down a steep bank into the lake and drowned. Demon possession is not a mental aberration but a spiritual condition in which one is possessed by an evil mind and evil will that are not one's own. Jesus came to destroy the work of Satan (1 John 3:8). This incident illustrates that deliverance and looks forward to the full release from bondage to Satan that Jesus would win at Calvary.

WEEK 77 • SATURDAY   *Mark 7:1—8:38*

What is Corban?

In Mark 7:1–13, the Pharisees and teachers of the Law saw Jesus' disciples eating with unwashed hands. (Tradition required a ritual, ceremonial rinsing. This had nothing to do with hygiene, but symbolized cleansing from having touched anything profane.) When the Pharisees questioned Jesus about this, He answered by stating that they (the Pharisees) were hypocrites who honored God with their lips but whose hearts were far from Him. The Lord went on to cite one example of their hypocrisy— Corban. Matthew (15:5–6) translates this word as "devoted to God." A son may have had property to use for the support of his elderly parents. But that son could dedicate the property to God, thus making the property unavailable for secular use. The sacredness of that vow would withhold the support from the parents, even if the son did not actually give the property to God. This technicality nullified God's clear command to honor and love one's parents.

WEEK 78 • MONDAY
Mark 9:1–50

What is the significance of Elijah and Moses appearing with Jesus?

Peter, James, and John were with Christ on the mountain where He was transfigured before them (Mark 9:2–4). Moses represented the Old Testament Law (Torah), which included the Ten Commandments along with the entire good and gracious will of God. Elijah, the great prophet, had been taken to heaven without suffering death. Though Elijah taught rather then wrote, his presence with Moses confirms Jesus as the One who fulfilled the Law and the Prophets (Matthew 5:17). As much as this impressed the disciples, it pointed to an even greater glory—the glory of God's grace revealed at the cross, where Jesus gave up His life for the life of the world.

WEEK 78 • TUESDAY
Mark 10:1–52

What did James and John mean by asking to sit next to Jesus?

While on the way to Jerusalem, Jesus predicted His death for a third time. Then James and John made their request to sit next to Jesus in His glory (Mark 10:35–37). James and John expected a kingdom of royalty and kingship. They hoped to be among Jesus' highest officials. Jesus' response shows they had everything wrong. The way to the throne leads through service and suffering—His own suffering and death. Those who "reign" with Him do so by serving others in self-forgetful love. His is the way of the servant: the "Son of Man did not come to be served, but to serve, and to give His life . . . for many" (Mark 10:45). He gave up His life even for power-grabbers like James and John, you and me.

WEEK 78 • WEDNESDAY
Mark 11:1–33

Why would Jesus curse a tree?

The same day Jesus rode into Jerusalem, He and His disciples went to Bethany. The next morning they returned to Jerusalem. On the way back, Jesus, who was hungry, saw a fig tree and went over to pick some fruit for a snack (Mark 11:13). When He found nothing but leaves—empty promises, but no fulfillment—He cursed the fig tree. His words are harsh, pointing to Jesus' judgment on an empty piety that supported a costly temple and ritual but produces none of the fruit of repentance—mercy, service, and humility. This account sets up the cleansing of the temple which follows in verses 15–19. Jesus used the fig tree as an object lesson in verses 20–24. The religious leaders of Israel had hearts that had fallen from faith. In contrast to their hollow piety, Jesus holds up a faith that can move mountains because the power of God and His Word of promise supports it (Mark 11:22–25). The cursed, withered fig tree foreshadowed the judgment Israel would receive.

WEEK 78 • THURSDAY   *Mark 12:1—13:37*

How did people pay taxes in Jesus' day?

A delegation of Pharisees and supporters of Herod Antipas sought to trap Jesus in His words by asking Him about paying taxes. The tax they asked about was a poll tax paid annually by each male (Mark 12:14–15). From the earliest days, the Israelites had paid taxes to support the tabernacle. Later these taxes also supported the monarchy. When Rome occupied Israel, the Roman government demanded a tax also—one that funded the Roman government and its occupying forces in Palestine, but also funded the pagan worship of the Romans. The coin used to pay the tax was a Roman coin with the emperor's image on one side and this inscription on the other: "Tiberius Caesar Augustus, son of the divine Augustus." Thus, the Jews found the tax odious for several reasons: Their patriotism made supporting the Roman occupation distressing; their piety made supporting the Roman pagan rituals revolting; even touching the Roman coin with an image of an emperor who claimed to be a god turned the stomachs of any Jews who took Exodus 20:4 seriously.

The question Jesus' enemies asked was masterful in strategy. But as He pointed out, by using the Roman coin to pay their taxes, the Pharisees tacitly acknowledged Caesar's authority, thus answering their own question.

WEEK 78 • FRIDAY   *Mark 14:1–72*

What was the Sanhedrin?

After He was betrayed, Jesus was brought before Caiaphas (the high priest), who presided over the Sanhedrin, which sought a way to put Him to death (Mark 14:53–56). As the Jewish high court, the Sanhedrin consisted of 71 religious leaders—chief priests, elders, and teachers of the law. Its jurisdiction in civil cases was limited to Judea. It could order arrests but could not carry out capital punishment. Although the Sanhedrin was the legitimate ecclesiastical court of God's people, at the occasion of Jesus' trial, the court broke all of its own rules and made a mockery of justice. For instance, cases involving capital punishment had to have two trials separated by at least one day. Trials were to be held during daylight hours. Yet in their anger and haste to be rid of Jesus, the Sanhedrin played fast and loose with the laws of God and humans.

WEEK 78 • SATURDAY   *Mark 15:1–47*

Why was Jesus brought before Pilate?

The Sanhedrin found Jesus guilty of blasphemy, a crime punishable by death. In order to carry out its decision, the Sanhedrin turned Jesus over to Pilate for execution (Mark 15:1). Knowing that religious charges such as blasphemy would not hold up in Pilate's court, the Sanhedrin brought the political charge of treason against Jesus. Pilate's official residence was in Caesarea on the Mediterranean. But He took up residence in Jerusalem during Jewish holy days with the intent that his presence might prevent civil disorder. Pilate was the Roman governor of Judea from A.D. 26 to 36. Evidence of his tenure was unearthed in 1961 at Caesarea where a stone was found with Pilate's name inscribed on it.

WEEK 79 • MONDAY

Mark 16:1–20

Why were the women bringing spices to Jesus' grave?

After Jesus was crucified and laid in the tomb, Mary Magdalene, Mary the mother of James, and Salome brought spices to anoint Jesus' body (Mark 16:1) as a final act of honor and kindness to their Lord. Since embalming was not practiced by the Jews, spices were used for cosmetic purposes and to cover odors in the burial of the dead. Spices may have included aloe, balm, and cinnamon.

WEEK 79 • TUESDAY

Luke 1:1–80

What did it mean for a division of priests to be on duty at the temple?

During the time of King Herod, 24 divisions of priests served at the temple. Zechariah belonged to the priestly division of Abijah (Luke 1:5). Both Zechariah and his wife, Elizabeth, were descended from the line of Aaron. Each priestly division was to be on duty at the temple for one week twice a year. This duty included maintenance and care for the temple. One priestly task was to keep incense burning on the altar in front of the Most Holy Place, which required furnishing the altar with fresh incense in the morning prior to the sacrifice and again in the evening after the sacrifice. Assignments were chosen by lot, meaning God controlled who did what. While Zechariah was fulfilling this responsibility, the angel Gabriel gave him the amazing news that he and Elizabeth would have a son who would prepare the way for the Lord.

WEEK 79 • WEDNESDAY

Luke 2:1—3:38

Why did Joseph and Mary have to go to Bethlehem for the census?

The Roman emperor, Caesar Augustus, ordered a census to be taken during the time that Quirinius served as governor of Syria (Luke 2:1–2). Joseph came from the lineage of David and was required to travel to Bethlehem in Judea, the town of his ancestral origin. The government used information gathered by a census to draft men into the military and to aid in tax collections. Mary and Joseph traveled to Bethlehem from their hometown of Nazareth in Galilee—about 80 miles. The prophet Micah had foretold that the Messiah would be born in Bethlehem (Micah 5:2). As Ruler of all things, God uses both history and the human rulers who act in history to carry out His plans.

WEEK 79 • THURSDAY   *Luke 4:1—5:39*

How were synagogues different from the temple?

After Jesus' 40-day temptation by Satan in the desert, He returned to His hometown area of Galilee. During this time, Jesus taught in the synagogues (Luke 4:15–16), and news of Him spread widely. Synagogues arose during the time of exile when the Jews no longer had access to Jerusalem and the temple. Synagogues could be built in any area where a minimum of 10 Jewish families resided. The temple had been built solely for worship, whereas synagogues were used for a variety of purposes. In addition to being a place of worship, synagogues were used as a site for leaders to keep in touch with one another, a school for boys during the week, and a place for instruction in the Law. Synagogues had a special importance because of the scriptural scrolls kept there. On the Sabbath day detailed in Luke 4, Jesus read from one of those scrolls—the prophet Isaiah (Luke 4:18–19). Then He claimed to be the fulfillment of the prophecy.

WEEK 79 • FRIDAY   *Luke 6:1–49*

Why did Jesus choose only 12 apostles?

Before Jesus chose His 12 apostles, He went to a quiet place to pray (Luke 6:12–16). When morning came, He choose the inner circle of followers, those apostles who would be commissioned (sent out) to carry on Jesus' ministry after He returned to the Father. As there were 12 tribes of Israel, Jesus selected 12 men to be the leaders of the new Israel, His church. In teaching them, Jesus teaches us the same truths about Himself and His kingdom.

WEEK 79 • SATURDAY

Luke 7:1—8:56

What is a Roman centurion?

When Jesus entered Capernaum, a centurion who believed in Israel's God sent several Jewish elders to ask His help for his deathly ill servant (Luke 7:1–3). Centurions were Roman military officers in charge of a company of 100 soldiers. This particular centurion most likely served as an officer in Herod Antipas's forces. Yet the Jews respected him because he helped build their synagogue in Capernaum. The centurion displayed great respect for Jesus, sending the Jewish elders to plead his cause instead of coming himself, saying he was not worthy to approach Jesus (Luke 7:6–7). Jesus was amazed at the depth of this Gentile's faith.

WEEK 80 • MONDAY

Luke 9:1–62

What does it mean to take up one's cross?

After Jesus predicted His death and resurrection, He called on His disciples to deny themselves and take up their cross daily and follow Him (Luke 9:21–23). Jesus' words must have shocked them. The very word "cross" evoked thoughts of great physical pain, torture, and humiliation. The Romans used the threat of crucifixion to keep conquered peoples under control. The threat worked—there are few more ghastly ways to die. For the Twelve, as for us, following Jesus meant self-denial for His sake. More than coping with the common financial and health problems that plague daily life, "carrying the cross" involves a willingness to suffer for one's faith in the Messiah. Many of the Twelve indeed gave their earthly life for the sake of Christ and His kingdom.

WEEK 80 • TUESDAY

Luke 10:1–42

Who were the Samaritans?

Samaria was the province that lay between Galilee and Judea. Jesus told the parable of the Good Samaritan to illustrate what it means to love one's neighbor (Luke 10:25–37). In this parable, a Jewish man was stripped of his clothes, beaten, robbed, and left for dead. The only person who came to his aid was a Samaritan. While the Jews saw themselves as pure descendants of Abraham, they viewed the Samaritans with disdain as a mixed race, both physically and spiritually. Samaritans traced their ancestry back to the few poor Jews the Babylonians left in Canaan when they took the nation into exile. These Jews married the Gentiles Babylon imported into Canaan. Consequently, the Jews who returned from exile wanted nothing to do with the Samaritans and their religion—a mix of Judaism and pagan practices. Yet Jesus' parable made the Samaritan the example of true love for one's neighbor. God's love in Christ knows no limits, and our love for others is to reflect that.

WEEK 80 • WEDNESDAY
Luke 11:1—12:59

What was so bad about walking over unmarked graves?

Jesus accepted the Pharisees' invitation to eat with them. Yet the invitation was not entirely genuine. No doubt they hoped to catch Jesus in some error or another (Luke 11:37–54). Jesus rebuked the Pharisees for their hypocrisy, using six statements of woe. He compared the Pharisees to unmarked graves, which men walk over without even knowing it. Old Testament law proclaimed that people who came in contact with graves were ceremonially unclean for seven days (Numbers 19:16). Cleansing rituals took a lot of time and effort. Therefore, it was customary to whitewash tombs to make the graves easier to see and, thus, avoid. Jesus' point seems to be that the people who listened to the Pharisees were unknowingly made unclean through this contact. These spiritually "dead men" contaminated those with whom they came in contact.

WEEK 80 • THURSDAY
Luke 13:1–35

What is the significance of the kingdom of God being compared to a mustard seed?

The Jews had long expected God to intervene by sending the Messiah to free them from Roman rule. Although the Jews didn't know it, Jesus inaugurated the kingdom of God in coming to earth. Jesus compared God's kingdom to a mustard seed to illustrate that the kingdom would not come the way His people expected (Luke 13:18–19). The mustard seed was the smallest seed known at that time, but it grew into a tree that provided a sanctuary for birds to rest in its branches. The Israelites expected the Messiah's kingdom to come in conquering power. But the growth of God's kingdom would be gradual. From what seemed to be a small, unimpressive start, it would grow and spread to every nation, providing a place of rest for God's people.

WEEK 80 • FRIDAY

Luke 14:1–35

Who were the Pharisees?

A Pharisee invited Jesus into his home in order to trap Him in some theological error or to find a new reason to criticize Him (Luke 14:1–6). The Pharisees were a sect of Jewish lay leaders dedicated to preserving God's Law, both the commands written down and those handed down orally. They advocated strict adherence to the written Law as well as to tradition. Their roots were in the Hasidim, a group of godly scribes who continued preaching the Law just as their first leader, Ezra, did. In Jesus' day, these Jewish leaders were rarely challenged or questioned because they were regarded as the interpreters of the Law, the ones who best understood it. They gave the impression that if anyone could keep the Law perfectly, it was they. Jesus understood that the Pharisees were trying to earn righteousness through their good works. But their "righteousness" was a sham—they kept laws externally while breaking all of them inwardly. No one ever has or ever will attain righteousness in any other way than through Jesus Christ and His perfect work of redemption.

WEEK 80 • SATURDAY

Luke 15:1—16:31

Why was it offensive for the younger son to ask for his inheritance?

Jesus told the parable of the lost son to illustrate the depth of the heavenly Father's love for sinners who repent (Luke 15:11–32). The younger son went to his father and asked for his inheritance. As soon as possible, this disrespectful son left home and squandered his wealth. The son's request was offensive because the father was the head of the family. It was his place to decide when and if the inheritance would be divided among his children at an early date. An inheritance was usually transferred at death. There were times, however, when a father passed on his property to his sons before his death. When this happened, the father signed a deed as a gift during his life, which legally transferred the property to the son. The father then lived off the interest from the revenue. In this parable, the father went far beyond his obligations by transferring his younger son's inheritance to him upon his foolish request.

LUKE • WEEK 81

WEEK 81 • MONDAY   *Luke 17:1—18:43*

Why were tax collectors despised?

Jesus told the parable of the Pharisee and the tax collector to illustrate the danger of being self-righteous (Luke 18:9–14). As Jesus pointed out, the Pharisee prayed in front of others to show off his great piety. But his prayer was really no prayer at all—he simply gave all who listened a listing of his good works. The tax collector knew he was a sinner and so humbled himself before God. Jews despised tax collectors because they were considered traitors and thieves. They bought their position from Rome at exorbitant prices. In exchange, they received the right to collect taxes from the people. Anything they got, above the fee they had paid, was pure profit. This led, of course, to graft and corruption, which made most of the tax collectors wealthy. Besides their dishonest reputation, tax collectors worked for and with the hated Romans—Gentiles. The tax collector in Jesus' parable, however, repented of his sins and begged for God's mercy. His prayer was based on genuine change of heart and trust in God. In God's sight he, rather than the Pharisee, was justified, for he looked to God for righteousness and not to his own deeds.

WEEK 81 • TUESDAY   *Luke 19:1—20:47*

Why was Jesus so upset about people selling in the temple area?

After Jesus' triumphant entry into Jerusalem on the previous day, He entered the temple area. The activity going on there angered Him (Luke 19:45–46). Tradesman and moneychangers had created a flourishing business by displaying their wares in the limited space of the outer court of the Gentiles. In order to purchase animals to sacrifice at the temple, the religious leaders required people to use special temple coins. They considered Roman coins idolatrous because the coins had the image of Roman gods. The moneychangers used exchange rates designed to produce a tidy profit. Animals for sacrifice were also sold at exorbitant costs to out-of-towners who had come to worship and had no alternative means for acquiring the animals. Jesus expelled all those merchants for turning the temple, His Father's house, into a den of robbers.

WEEK 81 • WEDNESDAY

Luke 21:1—22:71

Why did Judas kiss Jesus?

Jesus knew the time of His death was drawing near. In deep anguish He prayed at the Mount of Olives. Although He asked His Father to take away the cup of suffering and wrath, He prayed that God's will, not His own, would be done. Judas approached Jesus in the Garden of Gethsemane (Luke 22:47). Previously, Judas had arranged with the authorities to betray Jesus. He would identify Jesus with a kiss, a common greeting also used to show honor and respect for one's teacher. Now the Teacher was betrayed by His own disciple, which surely was part of Jesus' anguish.

WEEK 81 • THURSDAY

Luke 23:1—24:53

What was the significance of the curtain in the temple tearing in two?

Jesus was nailed to a cross to die a horrible death between two criminals. At the sixth hour (noon), darkness covered the land until three o'clock. The curtain of the temple was torn in two, and Jesus called out to His Father before taking His last breath (Luke 23:44–46). The temple curtain was a large, heavy curtain that separated the Holy Place from the Most Holy Place. It kept people away from what was in God's throne room on earth—the ark of the covenant in the Most Holy Place. Only the high priest could enter the Most Holy Place, and then only once a year—on the Day of Atonement. He went in to sprinkle the blood of a bull on the mercy seat of the ark of the covenant. At Christ's death, God split the curtain that kept sinners from His holy presence, thus removing the barrier between Himself and all people. Christ, the perfect High Priest, gave Himself as the perfect sacrifice for sin and cleared the way for us to approach God directly. Now, believers have full access to the Father through His Son, Jesus Christ, who is both Victim and Priest. The wall of sin that separated us from our God is gone forever.

WEEK 81 • FRIDAY
John 1:1—2:25

Who or what is the Word?

John begins his Gospel by calling Christ the Word (John 1:1–5). The term *Word* (*Logos* in Greek) referred not only to the spoken word, but also to the governing principle of the universe. Today when so many talk of "mere rhetoric" or empty words, the term *Word* does not have the same power as it did in the Greek of John's day. In a strong sense God effects, or brings about, His gracious, saving will through the *Word*. In the beginning, God spoke the Word, and the Word created the universe. Yet the Word existed before creation: "The Word was with God, and the Word was God." This means that Jesus was both distinct from the Father, while also being true God and one with the Father. As true God, the Word surpasses all time and space. He has always existed: "He was with God in the beginning." The Word still active in creation, is the Word that recreates, that saves, as John's Gospel will describe.

WEEK 81 • SATURDAY
John 3:1–36

What does it mean to be born of water and the Spirit?

A Pharisee named Nicodemus came to Jesus secretly at night to seek some answers. When Jesus told him that no one could see the kingdom of God unless he was born again, Nicodemus asked how this could be. Jesus replied that it couldn't happen unless one was born of water and the Spirit (John 3:1–5). The water here refers to Christian Baptism; the Spirit refers to spiritual rebirth or regeneration by the Spirit. Water and Spirit together represent spiritual cleansing and regeneration, as indicated in Ezekiel 36:25–27. Jesus emphasized the need for spiritual rebirth, impressing on Nicodemus the importance of believing in God's Son rather than trying to earn entry into God's kingdom on one's own terms. Those who are reborn, born of water and Spirit, enter the kingdom and enjoy the citizenship God grants through Baptism.

WEEK 82 • MONDAY
John 4:1–54

What is the significance of the sixth hour?

As Jesus traveled from Judea to Galilee, He passed through Samaria and came to a town called Sychar. There, at the sixth hour, He met a Samaritan woman drawing water from Jacob's well (John 4:1–7). Women usually came to the well twice a day to get water. Because of the midday heat, they usually came in the early morning hours or during the cool evening. This woman, however, chose to come at the sixth hour, or 12 noon. This was almost certainly a strategic move on her part to avoid seeing others who despised her for her sinful life. But Jesus had come to talk to her about her past, her sins, and her need for the "living water" only He can give.

WEEK 82 • TUESDAY
John 5:1—6:71

Why would Jesus' testimony not be valid?

Jesus performed miracles and proclaimed His unique relationship with God by claiming to be God's Son. This provoked the Jewish leaders, who asked Jesus to answer their objections. As Jesus gave them explanations, He conceded that if His testimony about Himself was the only testimony, it would not be valid from their standpoint (John 5:31). Old Testament Law required at least two witnesses to establish something in a court of law. But many more "witnesses" had vouched for Him. At Jesus' Baptism in the Jordan River, John the Baptizer had verified Jesus' testimony by proclaiming Him the Son of God (John 1:32–34). Far more important is the testimony of God Himself, who spoke audibly from heaven that same day at the Jordan: "This is My Son" (Matthew 3:16–17). In addition, Jesus' words testify to His identity, as do the Scriptures and even Moses. But sadly, even after all this, His enemies still did not believe (John 5:38).

WEEK 82 • WEDNESDAY

John 7:1—8:59

Why did this woman deserve to be punished?

The Pharisees brought an adulterous woman before Jesus in order to test Him (John 8:1–6). They claimed that according to the Law of Moses, the adulteress should be stoned. But the Pharisees had already disregarded God's Law by arresting only the woman and not the man as well. The Law of Moses clearly called for both to be punished (Leviticus 20:10; Deuteronomy 22:22—though neither states that death should be by stoning). The Pharisees also claimed that the woman was caught in the act, but they produced no witnesses as required. So the Pharisees had twisted God's Law to fit their own purposes, setting the stage as a trap for Jesus. The woman certainly deserved punishment for her sin, but Jesus refused to fall into the trap laid by the hypocritical Pharisees. Instead, He forgave the woman and told her to leave her life of sin.

WEEK 82 • THURSDAY

John 9:1—10:42

What did Jesus mean when He said, "I am the gate for the sheep"?

Jesus had previously explained that He was the Good Shepherd. Just as a shepherd leads, protects, and guides his sheep, so Jesus shepherds those who put their trust in Him. He brought this truth into clearer focus when He also described Himself as the gate for the sheep (John 10:7). The shepherd enters the sheep pen by the gate; those who seek to enter any other way are thieves and robbers. Jesus, the Son, is also the gate to eternal life with God, the Father. He is, in effect, the one and only way of salvation because of His death and resurrection. Those who believe in Jesus hear the voice of the Good Shepherd who lovingly protects and saves. Through Him they enter the kingdom of heaven.

WEEK 82 • FRIDAY
John 11:1—12:50

Why was Lazarus wrapped in strips of linen?

Lazarus, the brother of Mary and Martha, became ill, so the sisters called for Jesus to help. When Jesus finally arrived, Lazarus was already dead and buried. Jesus came to the tomb and requested that the stone that had been rolled across the entrance be removed. Then He prayed to His Father and called for Lazarus to come out of his tomb. When Lazarus emerged, his hands and feet were wrapped with strips of linen and a cloth was over his face (John 11:43–45). These strips of linen were narrow dressings traditionally wrapped around the hands and feet and permeated with exotic perfumes. This was part of the burial ritual; there is no doubt that Lazarus had been dead and was now alive.

WEEK 82 • SATURDAY
John 13:1—14:31

Why did Jesus wash His disciples' feet?

As Jesus and His disciples celebrated the Passover meal, Jesus modeled an attitude of servanthood that showed His love for His disciples as well as giving them a lesson in humility and service. Jesus removed His outer garments, placed a towel around His waist, and washed His disciples' feet (John 13:1–5). Simon Peter was appalled by this gesture because it was a servant's responsibility to wash the feet of the master as well as the feet of guests. But Jesus insisted, and in this humble deed displayed His selfless love. The Suffering Servant was just hours away from the ultimate gift of selfless giving—His own life on Calvary's cross so that we could be cleansed by His blood.

WEEK 83 • MONDAY   *John 15:1—16:33*

Who is the prince of this world?

As Jesus talked with the 11 remaining disciples before His imminent arrest and crucifixion, He explained the Holy Spirit's upcoming ministry on earth. The Spirit would convict people of their guilt in regard to sin and righteousness and judgment. The prince of this world would already be condemned by Jesus' death on the cross (John 16:11). The title, "prince of this world," refers to Satan, who received it because of his desire to be equal with God (Isaiah 14:12–15). Due to his rebellion, God cast Satan and the angels who followed him out of heaven. The devil now roams the earth, leading sinners in their rebellion against God. But Satan did not triumph and still has only limited influence. Jesus Christ emerged from His tomb victorious over sin, death, and the devil. One day He will return in glory to judge "the living and the dead" and to cast Satan into the lake of fire. Satan is, indeed, powerful, but he will never amount to more than the "prince of this world." He has never and will never reign as King. Only Christ is Lord of all.

WEEK 83 • TUESDAY   *John 17:1–26*

How does the truth sanctify us?

As Jesus prayed for His disciples, He was well aware of Satan's power and cunning. He asked God to protect His followers from the evil one, that God would sanctify them in the truth (John 17:6–19). Christians are sanctified (made holy) by the Word of God, the means by which the Holy Spirit produces faith. In the case of adults, the Word that creates faith is the Word read and proclaimed to sinners. In the case of infants and young children that Word is the "visible Word," the water of Baptism connected to the Word by which God creates saving faith. In all cases, it is God's Word that rescues people from eternal death and gives eternal life. God's Word is truth and brings salvation. Indeed, *the* Word, Jesus, sanctifies Himself that His disciples, then and now, might also be sanctified.

WEEK 83 • WEDNESDAY   *John 18:1—19:42*

Why did the Jewish officials bring Jesus to Annas before bringing him to Caiaphas?

After Jesus was betrayed by Judas and arrested, He was immediately brought to Annas in the middle of the night (John 18:12–13). This was done because by the law, sentencing could not take place on the same day as the trial. However, the Jewish officials were anxious to condemn Jesus before any opposition could get organized. Annas was a former high priest who had been deposed in A.D. 15. He had been succeeded first by his son and then by his son-in-law Caiaphas and was still regarded as an elder religious statesman who retained significant authority. By taking Jesus to Annas, the Sanhedrin (the Jewish religious council) could claim to have had a preliminary hearing prior to Jesus' trial.

WEEK 83 • THURSDAY   *John 20:1—21:25*

Why did Mary speak in Aramaic?

As Mary stood outside the tomb crying, Jesus appeared to her. She did not recognize Him until He called her by name, at which time she responded by crying out in Aramaic, "Rabboni!" (John 20:15–16). The word *Rabboni* is a stronger version of the Hebrew word *Rabbi*, which means "my teacher." Most Jews of that day spoke Aramaic, and the apostle John, though writing in the Greek language, records Mary's words in her own language. For us who read it today, the scene is still very intimate. Through faith, all believers enjoy a close, personal relationship with the risen Savior.

WEEK 83 • FRIDAY   *Acts 1:1–26*

Why did the believers choose an apostle by casting lots?

The disciples asked the Lord to reveal His will concerning Judas's replacement as one of the Twelve. Two men had been nominated, and the disciples cast lots, a common practice in their day. Matthias was chosen. God's people frequently cast lots to determine His will, believing this practice allowed the Lord to make the decision instead of them—"The lot is cast into the lap, but its every decision is from the LORD" (Proverbs 16:33). Casting lots could be done in different ways, but most likely in Matthias's case, the names were written on pebbles, placed in a container, and shaken. Since Matthias's pebble fell out first, the disciples considered him to be the Lord's choice. This is the last time the New Testament refers to this practice. Post-Pentecost accounts emphasize the work of the Spirit in revealing the Lord's will.

WEEK 83 • SATURDAY   *Acts 2:1–47*

What is the day of Pentecost?

Pentecost, which means "fiftieth," is the Greek name for the Jewish Feast of Weeks, also called the Feast of Harvest and the day of firstfruits. Pentecost was one of the three major festivals of the Jewish year, a festival of thanksgiving for harvested crops. It took place 50 days after the Passover Sabbath. Pious Jews tried to celebrate this feast day in Jerusalem; those who could not, observed it in their local synagogues. Before Jesus ascended into heaven, He told His disciples to wait in Jerusalem for the coming of the Spirit. Jesus fulfilled His promise and sent the Holy Spirit on the day of Pentecost. Since then, the Christian church understands Pentecost as the day the Lord gifted His church with the Holy Spirit in order to equip believers to be His witnesses to the ends of the earth.

WEEK 84 • MONDAY   *Acts 3:1—4:37*

What were the temple courts?

The temple was the visible representation of the Lord's dwelling with His people, and so it was natural that Jesus' early followers would come to worship and pray there. Within the temple courts, Acts 3:1–2 tells us Peter and John encountered a man crippled from birth. The temple courts actually included four different courts—one for Gentiles, for women, for Israel (men), and for priests. Each court was more exclusive than the previous one because it was that much closer to the inner sanctuary and the Most Holy Place. A portico surrounded the outer court of the temple. On the east side this became a roofed porch, Solomon's Colonnade, a place where scribes debated and moneychangers set up shop. The temple gate called "Beautiful," one of several gates, was probably on this east side of the temple, leading from the Court of the Gentiles to the Court of Women. It was a high traffic area—a good place for begging. On this particular occasion Peter and John gave the man more than he had asked for. They told him about Jesus and then they healed him.

WEEK 84 • TUESDAY   *Acts 5:1–42*

Why did the religious leaders have Peter and the other apostles flogged?

The apostles healed many people and performed miracles and wonders as they witnessed to Jesus. The high priest and other council members became extremely jealous of the apostles' popularity with the people and also angry that they themselves were being blamed for Jesus' death. They had Peter and the apostles arrested, intending to put them to death. Gamaliel, however, persuaded the council to let the apostles go (Acts 5:35–39). Gamaliel's opinion held weight because he was a member of the Pharisees, the religious party with the most popular support among the people. The council also saw the wisdom in his advice, and they didn't want to risk a revolt. Still, they had Peter and the apostles flogged—whipped with 39 lashes—for not obeying the order to stop preaching about Jesus. They wanted to punish and disgrace the apostles publicly, as well as warn them not to disobey again.

WEEK 84 • WEDNESDAY

Acts 6:1—8:40

Why was there tension between Grecian Jews and Hebraic Jews?

Shortly after Pentecost two main groups of believers made up the church in Jerusalem. Both were Jews, but some were Grecian and some Hebraic. The Grecian Jews were born or had lived in various parts of the Roman Empire but had returned to Jerusalem. They spoke the Greek language and were influenced by the Greeks in their attitudes, dress, and outlook. The Hebraic Jews spoke Aramaic or Hebrew—the language of Palestine—and closely followed their Jewish customs and culture. The conflict arose between the two groups over the treatment of widows (Acts 6:1). While there was probably no malice intended, cultural differences as well as language barriers, led to a breakdown in communication and resulted in the Grecian widows being neglected in the distribution of food. The Roman government had no form of the social welfare programs we have come to expect today. When the issue of neglect came to the apostles' attention, they chose deacons to oversee this ministry.

WEEK 84 • THURSDAY

Acts 8:1—9:43

What is the significance of the baptism of the Ethiopian eunuch?

The Lord wanted to bring His saving message to the Gentiles as well as to the Jews. He directed Philip—one of the deacons appointed in Acts 6— through an angel to go "at noon" to a desert road south of Jerusalem. Because of the noonday heat and the road's desert location, one would not expect to find travelers on it, and yet, the Lord had already planned the encounter between Philip and the Ethiopian. The Ethiopian, a Gentile, was a treasurer in his queen's court, an official in a position to influence others. He was on his return home after a visit to Jerusalem. He apparently reverenced the God of Israel, but because he was a eunuch, he could not be come a full-fledged convert to Judaism. His conversion and Baptism by Philip, however, made him a full member of the body of Christ. His conversion fulfilled Isaiah 56:3–7, where the Lord specifically promises that eunuchs—along with everyone else who believes in the Messiah—will have a part in His kingdom.

WEEK 84 • FRIDAY

Acts 10:1—11:30

Why did Peter call these animals unclean?

Through a vision, the Lord told Cornelius, a centurion in the Roman army, to send for Peter. While Cornelius's servants were on their way, the Lord prepared Peter for their arrival by giving him a vision. In it, Peter saw a sheet come down from heaven filled with all kinds of animals. When the Lord told Peter to eat of them, Peter refused because the animals were "unclean" under the Mosaic code of the Old Testament (Acts 10:14). According to these dietary restrictions, certain animals, for instance, scaleless fish and swine, were designated as "unclean" (Leviticus 5:2) and therefore unfit to be eaten. In Peter's vision both clean and unclean animals appeared together. This mixing made all of them unclean. The Lord tells Peter, however, not to call unclean what He has cleansed. As Peter would soon see, the Lord's teaching about food also applied to people. Because the Lord had planned to include Gentiles in the community of faith, He showed Peter that though the Jews considered Gentiles unclean, the Lord Himself had declared them clean through Jesus' death and resurrection.

WEEK 84 • SATURDAY

Acts 12:1–25

Why did the Lord judge Herod so severely?

The ruler described in this passage was Herod Agrippa I, grandson of King Herod, who had ruled at the time of Jesus' birth. Herod Agrippa was popular with some of the Jewish people because he himself was considered partly Jewish. In order to earn the favor of those who did not recognize him as their legitimate king, Herod found it expedient to persecute and arrest "enemies" of the Jews—Christians. Herod had James executed and jailed Peter with the same intent, but an angel freed Peter. Acts describes how the Lord punished Herod for persecuting His church. In a hearing with the people of Tyre and Sidon, the people called Herod a god. When Herod didn't refuse their tribute and give honor to the Lord, an angel of the Lord struck him down. Herod was "eaten by worms" and died (Acts 12:23). Despite the early church's persecution and more important than Herod's being punished for his arrogance is Luke's assessment: "But the word of God continued to increase and spread" (Acts 12:24).

WEEK 85 • MONDAY   *Acts 13:1—14:28*

Why did Paul find so many Jewish synagogues in all those distant cities?

During the time of the Babylonian exile, when worship in the temple at Jerusalem was impossible, the synagogue arose as a local place for instruction in the Scriptures and for prayer. By New Testament times, Jewish people lived in many locations throughout the ancient world, and wherever a substantial number lived (10 or more families), they set up a synagogue. The temple in Jerusalem remained the only place where the priests offered sacrifices, but the synagogues became the central place for meeting, worshiping, and discovering the Lord's will through studying the Torah. It was natural for Paul and Barnabas to begin their missionary work by preaching in the synagogues (Acts 13:5, 15; 14:1). In so doing, they first brought the Lord's message of salvation to His chosen people, the Jews, but they were also making a point of contact with the God-fearing Gentiles who worshiped in the synagogues. Many of these Gentiles recognized in Jesus the fulfillment of the Old Testament prophecies concerning the Messiah and came to faith in Him.

WEEK 85 • TUESDAY   *Acts 15:1–35*

Why was circumcision such a problem in the early church?

Paul spent a great deal of time discussing circumcision with believers in the early church. Although many Jews accepted Jesus as the Messiah, they still found it difficult to give up what they had always believed regarding circumcision and the keeping of the Law. Some of these Jewish believers accepted that Gentiles as well as Jews could be saved, but they insisted that Gentiles still needed to be circumcised according to Mosaic law (Acts 15:1). In their view, circumcision remained an essential sign of the believer's relationship with the Lord. In contrast, Paul taught that Gentiles did not need to become Jewish first in order to be saved because all people, both Jew and Gentile, were saved through Christ alone.

WEEK 85 • WEDNESDAY   Acts 15:36—16:40

Why were the officers alarmed when they learned that Paul was a Roman citizen?

The Roman Empire recognized three classes of people: slaves, aliens, and citizens. Roman citizenship differed from what we expect citizenship to mean today. Still even Roman citizens had legal rights that exempted them from cruel or degrading forms of punishment. For instance, it was illegal for a government official to whip a Roman citizen, and every citizen had the right to a fair trial. For capital offenses, Roman citizens were beheaded rather than crucified. During the incident in Philippi the local magistrates had Paul and Silas illegally stripped, beaten, and put into prison without a trial (Acts 16:22–24). The next morning when the magistrates learned that the two were Roman citizens, they became alarmed (Acts 16:38). They knew that if a higher authority learned of what they had done, they would be in trouble. They personally came to the jail to appease Paul and Silas. They did, however, ask Paul and Silas to leave the city, perhaps fearing further civil unrest.

WEEK 85 • THURSDAY   Acts 17:1—18:22

What was the Areopagus?

Areopagus is Greek for "hill of Ares." Ares, the Greek god of war corresponded to the Roman god Mars, so the hill was also known as Mars' hill. Located northwest of the Acropolis in Athens, the hill overlooked the city marketplace and was the original place where the city council, the chief court in Athens, met to decide judicial matters. Because of the location where it met, the council itself also became known as the Areopagus. In New Testament times the council of Areopagus usually met in the marketplace. Made up of Stoic and Epicurean philosophers, the council did not enjoy the same legal authority it had in ancient Athens, but it still enjoyed considerable prestige and had special jurisdiction over matters of morals and religion. It was natural that Paul, who spoke of a foreign God, should be brought before this council for their opinion.

WEEK 85 • FRIDAY
Acts 18:23—21:16

Why didn't Agabus's prophecy stop Paul from going to Jerusalem?

While Paul was in Caesarea, a prophet named Agabus told Paul that if he went to Jerusalem, the Jews would capture him and hand him over to the Romans (Acts 21:10–15). Despite the protests of the believers in Caesarea, Paul was determined to go to Jerusalem because he wanted to take an offering from the Gentile believers to the Jewish believers there. Paul wanted to make this presentation to demonstrate that the Lord intends the salvation He provided in Jesus to bless both Jew and Gentile. His church is one. While Agabus's prophecy warned Paul of what was to come, it did not forbid him to go. In a way similar to Jesus submission in Gethsemane, Paul acknowledged the danger, yet was willing to face even death itself in obedience to the Lord's will.

WEEK 85 • SATURDAY
Acts 21:17—23:35

What is meant by "the Way"?

After his arrest in Jerusalem, Paul asked the Roman soldiers if he could address the crowd calling for his death. Amazingly, they agreed and Paul explained that before he had come to faith in Jesus, he had persecuted the followers of the Way, arresting men and women and throwing them in jail (Acts 22:4). The Way was the name the early Christian church used for itself. Christians may have started using this designation because of such passages as Isaiah 40:3, which talks about preparing the way for the Lord, and especially John 14:6, where Jesus refers to Himself as the only way to the Father. The term appears only in Acts.

WEEK 86 • MONDAY   *Acts 24:1—26:32*

What did it mean for Paul to appeal to Caesar?

When Paul appealed to Caesar, he was not trying to evade justice, but he wanted to remain within the jurisdiction of the Roman court, which was his right as a Roman citizen. He knew if he were sent back to be judged by the Jewish council, he would be found guilty, and that would hurt the cause of the Gospel. Appealing to Caesar did not mean that Caesar would hear the case, but it did mean that Paul would go to Rome to have his case tried before the highest court in the Roman Empire. This gave Paul the opportunity to bring the Gospel to Rome, something he had longed to do. Plus, if the Roman court ruled that his preaching was not illegal, Christianity would achieve the status of a legal religion. Paul was confident that no matter what happened in Rome, the Lord would work it for good both for Paul and the cause of the Gospel.

WEEK 86 • TUESDAY   *Acts 27:1—28:31*

Why wasn't Paul in prison?

By the time Paul arrived in Rome, he had become a trusted prisoner. The Roman officials knew Paul had committed no flagrant crime and was not a political threat. But they had to keep him under arrest until his trial. The officials kept Paul under house arrest, and he lived in quarters rented for that purpose. For two years at least one soldier guarded him at all times. Paul was not allowed to come and go as he wished, but he could receive visitors of his choosing. As soon as possible, Paul invited the local Jewish leaders to visit him in order to explain to them that Jesus was the promised Messiah. Being under house arrest instead of in prison gave Paul many opportunities to share the Gospel. Most likely he also wrote what are known as his Captivity Letters or Prison Epistles—Ephesians, Colossians, Philemon, and Philippians—while he was in Rome.

WEEK 86 • WEDNESDAY   *Romans 1:1—2:29*

How did Christianity spread to Rome before Paul got there?

Historical records indicate there was already a Jewish community in Rome as early as the second century B.C., but there is little evidence about the origin and early history of the Christian church there. Most likely, some Jews and converts to Judaism from Rome had been in Jerusalem on the day of Pentecost. Some of these had come to faith in the Lord during Peter's sermon that day. Upon returning to Rome, these believers would have shared the Gospel with others. Even if none of the Roman pilgrims came to faith that day, all roads in the empire eventually led to Rome. As believers moved out from Jerusalem into other areas, they would have arrived in Rome and established a church there. Despite physical distance and cultural differences, Paul felt a kinship with these believers.

WEEK 86 • THURSDAY   *Romans 3:1—4:25*

What did Paul mean by Christ being a sacrifice of atonement?

Old Testament believers recognized that sin caused a broken relationship between them and the Lord, a relationship they could not restore themselves. In His mercy, however, the Lord had made provision for cleansing them from sin through the sacrificial system. On the annual Day of Atonement the high priest entered the Most Holy Place to make atonement for the collective sins of the Israelite people throughout the year. The priest sprinkled the blood of the sacrificed lamb on the mercy seat, and the Lord forgave the sins of His people, making them "at one" with Him (Leviticus 16; 17:11). This sacrifice of atonement, repeated annually, pointed forward to the perfect sacrifice of Christ, the Lamb of God, whose shed blood once and for all time made atonement with the Lord for the sins of all people. No longer do God's people have to stand far off from the Lord as they did during the Old Testament sacrifices. In Christ, believers have direct access to God's throne of grace.

WEEK 86 • FRIDAY
Romans 5:1–21

What does it mean to be justified?

To justify is a legal term meaning "to acquit," "to declare righteous," "to be declared not guilty." When Paul talks about justification, he is referring to God's act of forgiving sinful people, those guilty of breaking His Law. God declares us righteous by His grace through faith in Jesus. God does this not because we deserve it, but because of His mercy in Jesus, who perfectly kept the Law for us and paid the penalty for all sin through His death and resurrection. Because we are declared righteous, we not only have pardon for sins but also peace from the Lord—access to Him and His blessings. As His justified people, we can be sure that nothing" will be able to separate us from the love of God that is in Christ Jesus our Lord" (Romans 8:39).

WEEK 86 • SATURDAY
Romans 6:1–23

What does it mean that our old self was crucified?

The old self is the "I" who doesn't know, love, and trust the Lord, the self who thinks, wills, and acts in opposition to Him. In Baptism, God unites us by faith to Christ and kills this sinful self so it can no longer dominate us. God gives us His Spirit, who supplies us with the will and power to know, love, and trust Him, breaking the control sin had over us.

WEEK 87 • MONDAY   Romans 7:1–25

What did it mean to be a slave in Paul's day?

In New Testament times people became slaves in a number of ways. Frequently, they were born into slavery or were made slaves by foreign powers or others who captured or kidnapped them and sold them into slavery. Sometimes people sold themselves or family members into slavery to get money to repay a debt. At other times prisoners became slaves to make restitution for their crimes. Slaves became their master's property and lost all legal rights. Their well-being depended entirely on their master's attitude toward them. According to the law of Moses, Israelites who placed themselves into indentured servitude had the option of buying their way out. If they never attained that goal, the Year of Jubilee (every 50th year) gave these slaves freedom. This law prevented the whole country from slipping into slavery. It also kept individuals, as we might imagine, from despair. The Roman system, however, did not have this provision. When Paul talks about being a slave to God's law, he means that his new nature, created by God's Spirit, desires to do the Lord's will. But he also recognizes that he has a sinful nature that still is in enslaved to sin and acts contrary to the Lord's will. The power of the sinful nature to force him into sin has been broken. Nonetheless, sin sometimes seduces even believers into attitudes and actions contrary to God's will.

WEEK 87 • TUESDAY   Romans 8:1–39

What is redemption?

Redemption means buying something or someone back. It involves more than simple deliverance; it is deliverance obtained at a price. For example, prisoners of war and slaves could go free if someone paid ransom money— the amount of money designated for their release. In Romans, Paul uses the picture of redemption to describe what the Lord does for sinners. He delivers us from sin and death by paying the redemption price—the blood of Christ. Believers, who have been bought at such a price, can now live in ways that show we belong to Him. In Romans 8:23, Paul talks about the redemption of our bodies. This refers to the day of resurrection, for on this day our physical bodies, also redeemed by Jesus' sacrificial death and resurrection, will be brought back from the grave. In Ephesians 4:30 Paul also refers to the day of resurrection as the day of our redemption.

WEEK 87 • WEDNESDAY   *Romans 9:1—11:36*

What was the stone people stumbled over?

In Isaiah 8:13–15, the prophet painted a word picture to show what was about to happen to God's people. Isaiah warned them that the Assyrian army would sweep over them like a great flood. But for those who trust in Him, the Lord will provide one place of refuge from the surging waters—a rock on which they can stand secure. Those who do not trust in Him will be swept away against this rock; to them that rock will be a stone that causes them to stumble, a rock that makes them fall. The New Testament writers use this same picture to describe Jesus. He is the Rock—the Messiah—provided by the Lord; those who trust in Him have salvation. In Romans 9:31–32, Paul says that those, like many in Israel, who trust instead in their own ability to keep the Law to save them will find Him to be a rock that makes them fall.

WEEK 87 • THURSDAY   *Romans 12:1–21*

What is the significance of the church being called "the body of Christ"?

In Romans 12, Paul compares the human body, with its multiplicity of parts each with its own function, to the church, with its many members from various backgrounds and with various gifts (Romans 12:4-5). The analogy underscores the essential unity we share as believers in Christ. Yet, it also helps us to appreciate the diversity and uniqueness of gifts that each member brings to the body of believers. Clearly, Paul did not think all believers should look and act alike. In fact, diversity, not uniformity, is the sign of the Creator's handiwork. While the Lord purposely equips each person with different gifts and abilities, believers are still connected to each other through Christ. They function together harmoniously as parts of the same body to accomplish the Lord's mission of spreading the Gospel throughout the world.

WEEK 87 • FRIDAY

Romans 13:1—14:23

Why did Paul call those who abstain from eating certain foods weak?

Paul knew and taught that Jesus set believers free from the burden of trying to keep the Law. The ceremonial and dietary laws belong to the old covenant. Christ fulfilled all of them in our place. Some of the Jewish Christians in Rome, however, were still immature and uninstructed in their new faith. They were unsure of how the Old Testament requirements of the Law, such as dietary restrictions and keeping the Sabbath and other special days, affected their new status in Christ. As a result some of them were unwilling to give these up. Paul calls these Christians "weak in faith" because they didn't yet fully understand the freedom Christ gives. Paul encourages those who are strong in faith—those who know that Christ has set them free from keeping the Jewish regulations—to bear with the failings of the weak and treat them in love, rather than judging or arguing with them.

WEEK 87 • SATURDAY

Romans 15:1—16:27

Who is the Root of Jesse?

The Scriptures use the term "Root of Jesse" to refer to both the faithful remnant of God's covenant people and to the Messiah who would come from this root. The Old Testament prophets often compared God's people Israel to a tree. When the nation became unfaithful to Him by worshiping other gods, He allowed foreign nations to "cut them down." Only a stump remained. The faithful remnant of believers, those from the house of Jesse, were the root of this stump. Because of the Lord's faithfulness to His covenant, He promised to keep this root alive and to cause a Branch or shoot to grow up from the stump of Jesse (Isaiah 11:1–9). This Branch is the Messiah, Jesus, who sprang from the lineage of Jesse's son—King David (Matthew 1:1–17; Luke 3:23–32). Later in Isaiah's prophecy, Jesus is also called the Root of Jesse. In Romans, Paul quotes Isaiah 11:10, pointing to Jesus as the Root of Jesse, the One in whom the Gentiles will hope. He is the Savior of all who trust in Him.

WEEK 88 • MONDAY   *1 Corinthians 1:1—2:16*

Why were there divisions in the church?

The divisions in the church at Corinth concerned the apostle Paul. They resulted from the sinfulness of human nature. Apparently, the believers there had a tendency to gravitate to one leader or another based on his personality or style of presentation. Some of the Corinthian believers then started to assert the authority of one leader over another. All this took the focus of the church off of Christ and His cross. It also gave some people an excuse to think of themselves as "better Christians" than other believers. In the strongest language, Paul condemned any factionalism in the church and asserted the believers' essential unity in Christ (1 Corinthians 1:10–17).

WEEK 88 • TUESDAY   *1 Corinthians 3:1—4:21*

What is the significance of being God's temple?

God gave very specific instructions for the building of the tabernacle (Exodus 25–31) and, later on, the temple. The overriding theme in Israel's place of worship was holiness. The Lord Himself had promised to dwell among His people on earth in the Most Holy Place! Paul picks up on this imagery when he reminds the Corinthians that together they are the "God's temple" (1 Corinthians 3:16). In the church, the Holy God dwells in grace among His people by His Spirit. Verse 17, then, gives a stern warning to anyone who would interfere with the building of the temple, especially to anyone who would tamper with its foundation—Jesus Christ alone!

WEEK 88 • WEDNESDAY   *1 Corinthians 5:1—6:20*

What did Paul mean when he said everything is permissible?

Here Paul possibly quotes a slogan or proverb popular in Corinth (1 Corinthians 6:12). Because we can never achieve righteousness by keeping the Law, believers no longer need to worry about observing every obscure detail. We have a new life in Christ, an eternal life. But Paul goes on to point out that not everything a Christian could choose to do would benefit the individual or the body of believers. While we live in freedom from the Law, we also live in the love of Christ. As He empowers us, we live unselfish, holy, Christlike lives. These lives bring us joy and peace, and they bless others around us, particularly other believers.

WEEK 88 • THURSDAY   *1 Corinthians 7:1–40*

What does it mean for this world in its present form to be passing away?

Ultimately, nothing in this world that might ensnare our affections will endure (1 Corinthians 7:29–31). God's good gifts—our possessions and relationships—can become idols. They can take our focus off Christ and His kingdom. By reminding the Corinthians that this world in its present form is passing away, Paul urged the Corinthians to pay attention to the things that really matter, the things that will continue into eternity.

WEEK 88 • FRIDAY   *1 Corinthians 8:1—9:27*

How did believers get food sacrificed to idols?

Animal sacrifice played a central role in the pagan temples of Corinth and other cities. At least some of the meat from those sacrifices ended up in butcher shops in the marketplace, where it was sold as food. Some new and weak Christians were hesitant to buy any meat from these sources for fear of somehow participating in or being tainted by pagan worship. Paul addresses this concern in 1 Corinthians 8. (See also Romans 14.)

WEEK 88 • SATURDAY   *1 Corinthians 10:1–33*

Why was idolatry a problem for New Testament Christians?

Idol worship flourished throughout the Roman Empire in Paul's time. Corinth housed several temples, and visiting worshipers brought welcome business to the merchants of the city. In addition, the pagan rituals often involved cultic prostitution. This feature appealed to the baser instincts of Corinth's citizens. Could Christians participate in this? Absolutely not, Paul said. Those who participated in the mystery of the Lord's Supper could not dabble with demons. Those who know the true God in His Son, Jesus

Christ, will flee in terror from the worship of false gods (1 Corinthians 10:20). Though the temptations to avoid offending the neighbors or one's customers were strong, love for Jesus was stronger still. His grace at work in the Corinthian believers would keep them from falling.

WEEK 89 • MONDAY   *1 Corinthians 11:1—12:31*

Why would women have to cover their heads?

Paul asked women to cover their heads in the public worship services in Corinth for two main reasons (1 Corinthians 11:2–16). The first involved a matter of Jewish culture and reverence—Jewish women had always covered their heads in worship, so if the new Gentile believers didn't do likewise, it would jeopardize the unity of the church. The second reason had to do with Gentile culture and custom. In the Corinth of Paul's day, only prostitutes appeared in public with an uncovered head or short hair. Thus, a Christian woman who worshiped in Corinth without a head covering would appear to have rejected God's command of sexual purity and marital fidelity. By continuing the practice of head covering, Christian women could avoid such scandal and outwardly signal their reverence for Christ and their love for one another in the church.

WEEK 89 • TUESDAY   *1 Corinthians 13:1—14:40*

Why were women admonished to remain silent in church?

That Paul is not commanding absolute, unqualified silence is evident from the fact that he permits praying and prophesying in 1 Corinthians 11. The silence mandated for women in 1 Corinthians 14 does not preclude their praying and prophesying. Accordingly, the apostle is not intimating that women may not participate in the public singing of the congregation or in the spoken prayers. Also, it must be underscored that Paul's prohibition that women remain silent and not speak applies specifically to the worship service of the congregation (1 Corinthians 14:26–33). Any other interpretation is artificial and improbable. Thus, Paul is not here demanding that women should be silent at all times or that they cannot express their sentiments and opinions at church assemblies. The command that women keep silent is a command that they not take charge of the public worship service, specifically the teaching-learning aspects of the service. Paul and the other apostles affirmed women and their service for the Lord's people.

Women held many positions of honor and responsibility in the early church, but God reserved leadership of the public worship service to men (Acts 2:17–18; 9:36–43; 18:24–28; and 21:8–9).

WEEK 89 • WEDNESDAY   *1 Corinthians 15:1–58*

What is the last trumpet?

At Jewish religious feasts and festivals, the priest would sound a long blast on a ram's horn to signal the beginning of the observance. As Paul writes about the last trumpet (1 Corinthians 15:52), he describes the beginning of the end, the time when the world as we know it will come to an end and God's throne will be established, fully and permanently, over His people. This trumpet heralds the Lord's return to judge the people of earth. The faithful will rejoice to hear that trumpet blast, but those who have remained outside God's grace will experience great fear and trembling.

WEEK 89 • THURSDAY   *1 Corinthians 16:1–24*

What was the collection for God's people?

Paul taught his Gentile converts that they owed a great debt to the Jews. After all, the world's Savior, Jesus, had been born into the Jewish family and the first Christians were Jewish. Paul also promoted the image of the church as the body of Christ, each part working together and tenderly caring for one another. So when Paul heard that the believers in Jerusalem were suffering poverty and famine, he called upon the Gentile churches to come to their aid. He encouraged the Corinthians to set aside money for this purpose until he could come in person to collect it and take it to Jerusalem (1 Corinthians 16:1–3).

WEEK 89 • FRIDAY   *2 Corinthians 1:1—2:17*

How is the Holy Spirit like a deposit?

In Baptism, our Lord has marked us as His own. His Spirit has taken up residence within us. He makes it possible for us to comprehend God's Word and to place our trust in God's only Son, our Savior. The Spirit is also our guarantee of heaven. Like the "earnest money" a home buyer gives the real estate agent, the Holy Spirit is a kind of "down payment," given us by God and assuring us that we will by grace one day receive the fullness of all God has promised us (2 Corinthians 1:22).

WEEK 89 • SATURDAY   *2 Corinthians 3:1—4:18*

What was the importance of teachers having letters of recommendation?

When Paul penned 1 and 2 Corinthians, the Good News of salvation was relatively new. Relatively few people could speak with authority about the Gospel of Jesus Christ and the truth God had revealed in Him. Paul warned his converts repeatedly about false teachers. In such an environment, it became important to authenticate genuine teachers, to give them some kind of official credentials. In fact, some false teachers went so far as to forge letters of recommendation supposedly signed by Paul. Concerned about false teachers, Paul also grew impatient over the Corinthians' doubts concerning his own ministry. How could the Corinthians ask Paul to prove himself? Their own faith provided ample evidence that he spoke the truth. The life of the Spirit in them and the witness of the Spirit to the truth were Paul's ultimate "letters of recommendation" (2 Corinthians 3:1–3)!

WEEK 90 • MONDAY   2 Corinthians 5:1–21

What does it mean to be Christ's ambassador?

An ambassador officially represents his own country in another country. In times of crisis, an ambassador may carry an important message from one head of state to another. In 2 Corinthians 5:20, Paul asserts that Christians are Christ's ambassadors. Citizens of heaven, we carry our Lord's message of reconciliation to the whole world. This is the message: God sent His Son to pay the penalty for our sin and to give us in exchange His own righteousness. What an honor! What a privilege!

WEEK 90 • TUESDAY   2 Corinthians 6:1—7:16

What does it mean to be unequally yoked with unbelievers?

Paul uses these words in 2 Corinthians 6:14 to warn against forming binding relationships in which we might find our loyalties divided. We cannot interpret Paul's words to mean that believers are to separate themselves entirely from the world, since in other contexts Paul cautions against isolationism (1 Corinthians 5:9–10) and against abandoning an unbelieving spouse (1 Corinthians 7:12–13). But Paul was aware that the deeper and more binding the relationship, the more important it is to agree on foundational beliefs and purposes. Paul urged Christians to seek out relationships with people who would encourage their faith in and obedience to Christ. Particularly our most intimate relationships need to involve spiritual unity and the harmony only our Lord can create.

WEEK 90 • WEDNESDAY   2 Corinthians 8:1—9:15

Why did Paul mention the generosity of the Macedonians?

To spur on the Corinthians to generous giving, Paul held up the example of the Macedonian churches—Philippi, Thessalonica, and Berea. These churches, in poverty and affliction, gave beyond their means (2 Corinthians 8:3), but not beyond the grace of God, which was the source of their giving. They join the poor widow in Mark 12:41–43 in exemplifying selfless generosity. Through their offerings the Macedonian Christians also expressed their fellowship, their unity in Christ, with the Jerusalem Christians.

WEEK 90 • THURSDAY   *2 Corinthians 10:1—11:33*

Who were the super-apostles?

Paul first used the term "super-apostles" in 2 Corinthians 11:5, but he does not state here or elsewhere in the letter who they were. The context shows that Paul used the term to refer to false teachers who proclaim in a polished, winsome way a different Jesus. Paul's concern was not so much their fine rhetoric or even the fact that these super-apostles charged a fee for their services. His concern was their dangerous message. Paul taught Christians to rely only on Jesus Christ, who lived, died, and rose for sinners. Paul wanted the Corinthians to rely completely on this Jesus and not be swayed by another gospel, a false gospel of human merit that would lead to eternal death.

WEEK 90 • FRIDAY   *2 Corinthians 12:1—13:14*

What is the third heaven?

In referring to the third heaven (2 Corinthians 12:2), Paul is probably borrowing terminology used by Jews of his day. In Judaic tradition, heaven was thought to have a number of levels, of which the third was the highest. Paul describes this place in terms of purest perfection and beauty. Rather than using the pronoun "I," Paul uses the third person—calling himself "a man in Christ." The nature and content of this vision and of this third heaven are unknown to us because Paul was not permitted to tell us.

WEEK 90 • SATURDAY   *Galatians 1:1—2:21*

What was the circumcision group?

The circumcision group (Galatians 2:12) consisted of Judaizers, Jewish Christians who insisted that Christians, like Jews, must be circumcised as a sign of belonging to God. At Antioch, Peter communed with uncircumcised believers, demonstrating the equality and freedom Gentile Christians enjoy in the Gospel. When the circumcision group arrived, Peter drew back and stopped eating with the Gentile believers. Paul confronted Peter for his inconsistent behavior and witness to the Gospel.

Peter knew full well that circumcision no longer indicated a person belonged to God. Rather, the Gospel proclaimed a God-given circumcision of the heart and justification by grace through faith in Christ.

WEEK 91 • MONDAY
Galatians 3:1–29

Why did Paul call the Galatians foolish?

Paul called the Galatians foolish not because they were mentally deficient but because they did not perceive that they were abandoning the very Gospel of Jesus, which had converted them. These Galatians accepted the Judaizer teaching that required observation of the Old Testament law in addition to faith in Jesus Christ (Galatians 3:1–3). Paul maintained that the Law did nothing but condemn all who broke even one iota of it (Galatians 3:10). He also taught that even those who, like he himself could boast of Jewish ancestry, were born Jews, were justified completely by faith (Galatians 2:15–16). Indeed, Abraham's own righteousness came to him by virtue of his faith in the coming Messiah and not because he kept the Law (Galatians 3:6–7). What was true of the Jews, then, was also true of the Gentiles—all are sinners and condemned; all are redeemed by God's grace in the death and resurrection of Christ.

WEEK 91 • TUESDAY
Galatians 4:1–31

What was wrong with observing special days, seasons, and years?

Paul points out in Galatians 4 that the Gentiles' way of life is marked by enslavement to pagan spiritual powers and philosophical ideas—idolatry. But those who insist on keeping the traditions of Judaism live for salvation marked by enslavement to rituals and the traditions of legalism—also idolatry. Both lead to bondage and death, not freedom or new life. Both are attempts by human beings to make themselves acceptable to God and worthy of salvation. The Judaizers, for example, observed dozens of special days, seasons, and years to earn God's favor (Galatians 4:10–11). The special "days" to which Paul refers include the Sabbath Day and the Day of Atonement. The "festivals of the new moon" were the monthly observances, while those that were seasonal included the Passover, Pentecost, and the Feast of Tabernacles. Festivals concerned with years were the Sabbath Year and the Year of Jubilee. Paul does not condemn the observance of any of these of themselves (In Romans 14:5 he consigns these to the discretion of individual believers exercising their Christian liberty). What Paul does attack, however, is the idea that these externals are necessary for salvation.

WEEK 91 • WEDNESDAY — *Galatians 5:1—6:18*

Why did Paul write in large letters?

In addition to Galatians 6:11, three other letters of Paul refer to his handwriting (1 Corinthians 16:21; Colossians 4:18; 2 Thessalonians 3:17). These references imply that Paul dictated these letters to a secretary. Thus, in order to help his readers distinguish his letters from forgeries that circulated among the early churches, Paul wrote a short section of each letter in his own handwriting, often in large letters, to draw attention to the letter's authenticity and to the importance of its content.

WEEK 91 • THURSDAY — *Ephesians 1:1–23*

What is the significance of Christ being at God's right hand?

In Paul's day and for centuries earlier, anyone seated at the right hand of a ruler shared that person's power and authority. It was a position of great honor and implied a relationship of trust. God's power, by which He raised Christ from the dead and seated Him at His right hand in the heavenly realms, is the same power at work in believers (Ephesians 1:19–21). Our Lord Jesus, who took on human flesh, reigns with God the Father and God the Holy Spirit, one God over all creation. We could not hope for better representation or identification than that we already enjoy with Christ, the Father's "right-hand Man."

WEEK 91 • FRIDAY — *Ephesians 2:1–22*

Who is the ruler of the kingdom of the air?

Paul refers to the ruler of the kingdom of the air, meaning Satan—the enemy of God and of all believers (Ephesians 2:2). Satan was thought to inhabit the region between earth and heaven, which is another way of saying that he is a spiritual force. But Christ, by His death and resurrection, triumphed over Satan, whose only kingdom consists of those who follow him. Even that will be taken from Satan when God brings all things into subjection under His Son, Jesus Christ (1 Corinthians 15:23–26). Before the Ephesians received the precious gift of the Gospel, they followed the ways of the world and of Satan, the great deceiver. But now they, who were dead in their sins, are alive with Christ, recreated in the image of Him who is Ruler over all.

WEEK 91 • SATURDAY   *Ephesians 3:1–21*

Why did Paul call himself a prisoner of Christ?

Paul was under house arrest in Rome. Calling himself a prisoner of Christ, Paul acknowledged that everything that happened to him was subject to the greater authority of God Himself (Ephesians 3:1). The religious leaders in Jerusalem had pressured the Romans to arrest Paul for causing rebellion among the Jews. Knowing that he could never get a fair trial in that city, Paul appealed to the emperor, which was his right as a Roman citizen. This transferred his trial to Rome. Paul saw all of this as part of God's plan for the sake of His church, and he firmly believed that God would use every circumstance of Paul's life for His own glory and the proclamation of the Gospel. Paul's claim to be a prisoner of Christ was reminiscent of Jesus' words before Pilate when He maintained that Pilate would have no power over Him unless God had granted it (John 19:11).

WEEK 92 • MONDAY

Ephesians 4:1–32

What is the significance of Christ leading captives in His train?

In ancient warfare, the conqueror exacted tribute from the cities conquered. This came in the form of spoils (any objects of value) and captives, who might become slaves of the conquering people. In His resurrection and ascension, Jesus is pictured as the victor over Satan, sin, and death. Those who once lived in the kingdom of darkness have been made believers, blessed captives of the victorious Christ and thus, now, children of light (Ephesians 4:8). This depiction of Christ as the conqueror reflects to the prophecy in Psalm 68:18, which Jesus fulfills in every way.

WEEK 92 • TUESDAY

Ephesians 5:1—6:24

Why did Paul tell slaves to obey their earthly masters?

There were several million slaves in the Roman Empire at the time Paul preached and taught. The Holy Spirit was bringing slaves and slaveholders alike to faith in Christ, and the new church had to confront the social dilemma in light of the Gospel. In his instructions, Paul neither condoned nor condemned the institution of slavery. Rather, he instructed both slaves and masters to have an attitude of mutual respect. Thus, he urged slaves to obey their masters and to serve wholeheartedly (Ephesians 6:5–8). He also urged masters to treat their believing slaves not as mere property but as brothers in Christ (Ephesians 6:9). In the long run, such an attitude would serve to undermine the institution of slavery from the inside by emphasizing humility and love of one's neighbor in contrast to hatred, greed, and exploitation.

WEEK 92 • WEDNESDAY

Philippians 1:1–30

What is the significance of the palace guard knowing about Christ?

God in His grace provided Paul unique opportunities to give witness to his faith even during imprisonment. One such opportunity involved the palace guard itself. Through Paul's words and character, the soldiers soon learned that Paul was no criminal. The members of the palace guard, or the Praetorian Guard, were elite imperial troops stationed in Rome. They heard about Christ through Paul and were impressed by his willingness to suffer imprisonment for the sake of the Gospel. No doubt the apostle's message touched many hearts, and more people came to faith. In this way Paul's chains advanced the Gospel—a dramatic irony made possible by the power of God's Word.

WEEK 92 • THURSDAY
Philippians 2:1–30

Why did Paul compare himself to a drink offering?

The Jews poured out a specified amount of wine along with their daily and monthly offerings to God (see Numbers 28). In a similar way, Paul saw himself as an offering poured out on behalf of his fellow believers. Paul knew that his suffering and even death for the sake of the Gospel would not be in vain. Led by the Holy Spirit, Paul would gladly sacrifice himself for the good of other believers and to advance the Gospel.

WEEK 92 • FRIDAY
Philippians 3:1–21

How did Paul's credentials strengthen his authority?

Prior to his conversion, Paul (then called Saul) belonged to the Pharisees, one of the most prestigious and powerful sects in Judaism. Highly educated in the Jewish religion, Paul was zealous for the letter of the Law; he calls himself "a Hebrew of Hebrews" (Philippians 3:5). The Pharisees adhered to a strict code of laws that went beyond that of Moses. The tribes of Benjamin and Judah were the most highly esteemed of the 12 tribes, in part because they were the ones to return to Canaan after the exile in Babylon (see Ezra 4). Jews of Paul's day would have found his credentials impressive (Philippians 3:5–6). Paul's pedigree was undeniable; when it came to Jewish heritage, his was second to none. Yet all these things meant nothing now that he had "gained" Christ. The majority of religious leaders had rejected Christ's claims, so Paul's firm convictions and willingness to give up his life were a remarkable and striking testimony to the change Christ had worked in him.

WEEK 92 • SATURDAY   *Philippians 4:1–23*

What did Paul mean by yokefellow?

In Philippians 4:3, Paul addressed one of his fellow believers as his loyal yokefellow. (This person may have had the proper name Syzygus, which means "yokefellow." If so, Paul was asking him to be true to his name.) Farmers in the ancient Mid East often yoked two oxen to pull a plow. Pulling together, the animals were reliable and powerful. Evidently, Paul saw this person as a partner or coworker with him in ministry. Together, they plowed the spiritual fields in order to bring forth God's harvest. Despite Paul's prominence, the Lord chose to use him in partnership with others, not in isolation. Trustworthy coworkers became even more important during Paul's imprisonments because they could deliver his messages and tend the flock of the Lamb.

WEEK 93 • MONDAY
Colossians 1:1–29

What is the mystery about which Paul writes?

The mystery Paul refers to in Colossians 1:26 is God's grand plan of salvation. It was not a secret to be revealed to a select few, like the mystery religions prevalent in Paul's day. Still, the fullness of God's plan had not been apparent until Jesus' life, death, and triumphant resurrection. God's Son came into the world, fulfilling all that the prophets had foretold about the coming Messiah. His sacrifice atoned for sin once for all. But in grace God extended the blessing of salvation and the gift of the Holy Spirit to the whole earth, Jews and Gentiles alike. Now the great mystery is made known, revealed by God so that all might believe. (See also Romans 11:25; 16:25–26; Ephesians 1:9; 3:2–6.) The Gospel is not a secret to be hidden but a divine revelation to be treasured and proclaimed to the ends of the earth.

WEEK 93 • TUESDAY
Colossians 2:1–23

About what deceptive philosophy did Paul warn the Colossians?

Paul warned the Colossians about a deceptive philosophy that threatened to divert them from the truth (Colossians 2:8). Any teaching that promises answers to life's ultimate questions outside of Christ is deceptive and dangerous. The heresy with which the Colossians struggled included a mixture of Jewish ideas and pagan philosophy. It taught strict adherence to specific rules about foods, festivals, and circumcision. It boasted of some "secret knowledge" (perhaps an early version of Gnosticism). But no human philosophy, no matter how elegant or sophisticated, can add anything to the sweet Gospel truth of God's grace and love for sinners made perfect in Christ. Human philosophy only adulterates the Gospel and robs it of its saving power.

WEEK 93 • WEDNESDAY
Colossians 3:1—4:18

Why did Paul mention the Greek and the Jew?

The church at Colosse had many tensions. Believers came from various ethnic groups and social classes. The Greeks were well educated and cultured, and they often looked down on those who did not share their worldview. Jewish believers embraced Jesus Christ as the Messiah of God's chosen people, the One proclaimed by their prophets through the centuries. At times they boasted, arrogant about their heritage as they looked down on members of other races. Some Jewish believers still clung to the notion that circumcision, the outward sign of God's covenant, was still necessary for salvation. Greek believers typically were not circumcised, nor did the apostles teach that they needed to be. In response to all the tension these conflicts provoked, Paul emphasized the oneness all believers share in Christ (Colossians 3:11). God's grace in Christ knows no barriers, geographic or ethnic. In fact, Christ bridges all the deep divisions that would separate people from each other as He draws people of every race and class to Himself.

WEEK 93 • THURSDAY   *1 Thessalonians 1:1–10*

What is the coming wrath?

The Bible teaches that Jesus will come again in final judgment. Jesus came to save sinners, and His blood cleanses all who put their trust in Him. But those who do not believe in Him will face God's judgment and ultimately, damnation. The church at Thessalonica was facing persecution. Therefore, God's Day of Judgment would bring rescue for the faithful but reckoning for their persecutors (1 Thessalonians 1:10). Still today believers wait in reverence and in hope for that coming day, because for them it holds no wrath, only the certainty of eternal life in heaven.

WEEK 93 • FRIDAY   *1 Thessalonians 2:1–20*

How could Satan stop Paul?

Paul had a deep longing and a personal desire to see the Thessalonian Christians again, to encourage and strengthen them in their faith. Evidently, he made repeated plans to journey there but was frustrated at every turn. According to 1 Thessalonians 2:18, Satan stopped him. Paul does not say that God had directed him to go to Thessalonica. Therefore, while Satan could derail the plans of Paul, he could not ultimately upset the plans of God. Paul was acutely aware of this reality, so in spite of his repeated frustration, he rejoiced in the faith of this young church and entrusted it to God's care.

WEEK 93 • SATURDAY   *1 Thessalonians 3:1–13*

Why did Paul send Timothy to Thessalonica?

Communication between the various cities in the Roman Empire was limited by the means of travel available. Word from faraway places was a rare luxury. If someone traveled on foot, on horseback, by ship, or some combination thereof, they might carry a personal message or letter to a friend in another city. Otherwise, relationships were limited by distance much more than in today's world. Under house arrest, Paul had even fewer communication options than most people. In order to send a trusted messenger, he deprived himself of his closest assistant for a time. Timothy had traveled with Paul, preaching and teaching the Gospel. He was young but had shown himself to be faithful and capable. He too had been in Thessalonica previously. So Timothy was the ideal person to go in Paul's place (1 Thessalonians 3:2). Timothy returned with the good news that the believers were standing firm in their faith.

WEEK 94 • MONDAY
1 Thessalonians 4:1–18

What is an archangel?

An archangel was an especially honored angel to whom the Lord assigned an important task. It is fitting that an archangel will announce Christ's triumphant arrival at His Second Coming (1 Thessalonians 4:16), though we don't yet know when that will be. The only archangel mentioned by name in the New Testament is Michael (see Jude 9).

WEEK 94 • TUESDAY
1 Thessalonians 5:1–28

Why was Paul concerned about people being idle?

Paul instructed the leaders of the Thessalonian church to warn those who were idle (1 Thessalonians 5:14). Specifically, he was concerned about a group of people who had convinced themselves that Jesus' return was imminent, causing them to stop all of the activities of daily life in order to wait for His Second Coming. These believers had shrugged off their responsibilities in the life of the community. In doing so, they ignored the clear teaching of Jesus and of Paul that warned believers not to try to guess the date of Christ's return (1 Thessalonians 5:2).

WEEK 94 • WEDNESDAY
2 Thessalonians 1:1–12

Why would Jesus return with blazing fire?

To encourage the Thessalonians in the midst of their suffering for Christ's sake, Paul stated Christ's promise that at His Second Coming they would find relief, while their persecutors would face judgment. Paul here paints a word picture in which Christ appears suddenly in blazing fire with His powerful angels (2 Thessalonians 1:7). The prophet Isaiah used the same imagery (Isaiah 66:15–16). This stands in stark contrast to our Lord's first coming, in poverty and weakness as the Babe of Bethlehem. The fire in Paul's picture symbolizes purity and judgment. Like a refiner of gold, the Lord in holiness burns away all that is tainted by evil, leaving only the precious metal behind (Malachi 3:2). The believers in Thessalonica, along with believers from every land and age, will be spared the fire of judgment because they have been rescued by this same Christ who will come again.

WEEK 94 • THURSDAY   2 Thessalonians 2:1—3:18

Why were people afraid of missing the "day of the LORD"?

Some false teachers, some even speaking in Paul's name, were actually going around telling the people that the day of Christ's return had already happened. Paul reminded them of his own teaching that certain significant events had to happen first. Clearly these had not yet occurred (2 Thessalonians 2:1–8). In every case of false teaching, Christians are to hold tightly to the Gospel as it has been revealed and taught.

WEEK 94 • FRIDAY   1 Timothy 1:1–20

What were the false doctrines being taught?

Paul instructed Timothy to stay in Ephesus long enough to silence those who were teaching false doctrine. These false teachers were specifically teaching that in order to be acceptable to God, one had to discover secret knowledge and engage in angel worship. Mythical stories were added to the Old Testament involving its history and genealogies (1 Timothy 1:3–4). Exclusivism and cliques abounded in the church. These false tenets were a part of early Gnosticism, a heresy that would gravely threaten the church a few years later. All of this ran contrary to the glorious Gospel, God's grace freely offered to sinners because of what Jesus Christ had done. Paul exhorts Timothy to "fight the good fight, holding on to faith" (1 Timothy 1:18–19).

WEEK 94 • SATURDAY   1 Timothy 2:1–15

What was wrong with wearing jewelry?

As Christians, women received unheard-of freedoms. They were allowed to study the Scriptures and were considered full members of the church. However, Paul wanted to be vigilant lest an abuse of these freedoms bring dishonor to Christ. Specifically, jewelry could be associated with the flaunting of wealth and pride in one's possessions. Furthermore, in the society of that day, certain kinds of jewelry were associated with loose sexual morals and even prostitution. Wearing such jewelry would ruin the testimony anyone seeking to bring honor to the name of Christ. In contrast to the outward emblems of beauty, Paul urged women to demonstrate true inward beauty through faith in Christ. The kind of gentle spirit given by the Holy Spirit would honor Christ and glorify God. (See also 1 Peter 3:3–5.)

WEEK 95 • MONDAY   *1 Timothy 3:1–16*

What did overseers and deacons do in the early church?

An overseer (the word *elder* is also used in Scripture; today we more often use the word *pastor*) led a local congregation. His duties included teaching, preaching, and shepherding. God set very high standards of conduct and character for this position. Paul indicated (1 Timothy 3:1) that to aspire to such a position was good. A deacon was, literally, "one who serves." Chosen for spiritual maturity and honesty, the deacon tended to practical tasks such as supplying the needs of the poor, the widows, and the ill within the congregation and collecting and dispersing the congregation's finances.

WEEK 95 • TUESDAY   *1 Timothy 4:1–16*

What is the significance of the elders laying their hands on Timothy?

The laying on of hands by a group of elders symbolized that the church as a body recognized God's call upon someone's life and affirmed God's gifting of that person for the work of His kingdom. It indicated to both the individual and the congregation the tremendous responsibility to which God through His church had called him. In his letter, Paul encouraged Timothy by reminding Timothy of the day the church publicly affirmed God's call and gifting in Timothy's life (1 Timothy 4:14).

WEEK 95 • WEDNESDAY   *1 Timothy 5:1–25*

What was the list of widows?

Already the psalmist David called God a "father to the fatherless, a defender of widows" (Psalm 68:5). The early church recognized that meeting the physical needs of its members was inextricably tied to Jesus' command to love one another. Widows were especially vulnerable, for there were few honorable ways for women to earn a living in Paul's day. Older widows who had no family to care for them sometimes vowed to serve the church in exchange for financial support. Paul wanted to make sure that these were mature, faithful women without prospects for remarrying. His concern was that they would build up the body of Christ rather than find temptation in idleness and false teaching and, thus, threaten the unity of the whole body of believers (1 Timothy 5:9–14). The church in Ephesus was to set certain qualifications of age (more than 60 years), need, and character before adding widows to its list. Paul charges family members to provide for widows who are not on the list.

WEEK 95 • THURSDAY   *1 Timothy 6:1–21*

How could godliness be a means to financial gain?

False teachers that plagued the early church displayed two chief charac-teristics. They stirred up strife among the believers, and they sought financial rewards for their role as teachers (1 Timothy 6:5). These false teachers demanded handsome remuneration, which seduced some peo-ple into thinking that they must be important and their teachings must be true. Paul set the opposite example and accepted no pay (see also 2 Corinthians 11:7). He didn't want anyone to question his motives, though he did accept support from some congregations (2 Corinthians 11:8–9; Philippians 4:14–16). Still today, a desire for wealth can scuttle a viable ministry.

WEEK 95 • FRIDAY   *2 Timothy 1:1–18*

What was the good deposit with which Timothy was entrusted?

The good deposit Paul mentions in 2 Timothy 1:14 is the Gospel message that is alive in Timothy's heart. The Holy Spirit had worked this faith in Timothy, and it had taken root, bearing fruit and building in this young disciple the mind of Christ. By the Spirit we are able to recall, understand, and practice Christ's teachings. Considering all the problems Timothy faced as he dealt with false teachers, Paul wanted to remind him to hold fast to the Gospel (2 Timothy 1:14). The same Spirit has deposited this same Gospel in our hearts also.

WEEK 95 • SATURDAY

2 Timothy 2:1–26

Who are the elect?

The elect are those whom the Lord has chosen from all eternity to be brought to faith in Christ. He will preserve them in the one true faith, and they will inherit eternal life. For their sake Paul will endure "everything" (2 Timothy 2:10). The doctrine of election presents questions beyond our ability to answer—why our Lord intends this doctrine to serve a different purpose. Rather than answering questions of curiosity, He intends to comfort those who believe. He wants us to rest secure in His love for us. He will not change His mind or His heart toward us. Confident in that love, we witness to people who need to hear the Word of God through which the Spirit works.

WEEK 96 • MONDAY
2 Timothy 3:1—4:22

In what sense is Scripture God-breathed?

God was actively involved in the writing and compiling of Scripture. The writers were inspired by the Spirit; Paul says Scripture is "God-breathed" (2 Timothy 3:16). While God retained and used each writer's own voice with his unique personal, historical, and cultural insights, He communicated precisely the things He wanted His people to know. This word-by-word involvement makes Scripture truly the Word of God, inerrant, infallible, and fully authoritative for the Christian's faith and life. Peter reaffirms this high view of Scripture, writing that "men spoke from God as they were carried along by the Holy Spirit" (2 Peter 1:21).

WEEK 96 • TUESDAY
Titus 1:1–16

Why did Paul quote a prophet from Crete?

Paul had left Titus on the island of Crete to organize the new church there. In his letter of instruction to Titus, Paul made the point that the congregation there had more than its share of unruly members, including false teachers who sought to profit from their own heretical versions of the Gospel. These false teachers advocated the need for circumcision, if a person wanted to be saved. In describing the problem and pointing toward a solution, Paul quoted Epimenides, a sixth-century B.C. Cretan poet (Titus 1:12), whom the Cretans highly esteemed. When Paul quoted this poet, he most likely thought this: Who could give a better commentary on the national character of a particular people than one of their own? The Cretans had earned a reputation as liars, brutes, and gluttons according to Epimenides. Paul reminded Titus that he must rebuke his flock where necessary; such rebuke was intended to lead to the believers' repentance and soundness of faith.

WEEK 96 • WEDNESDAY
Titus 2:1–15

Why would anyone despise Titus?

Titus faced a daunting task in Crete. The people there might well despise him (Titus 2:15). First of all, he was a Christian. The pagan religion of that area was totally contrary to everything the Gospel represented, and its inhabitants led an immoral life. Second, there were many Judaizers, or Christians of the circumcision party. These people advocated adherence to the rules and regulations of the old covenant, maintaining that no one could become a Christian without first becoming a Jew in every way. Also, Titus spoke words of harsh rebuke over their sin—not the way to win a popularity contest. Finally, Titus was a foreigner and was younger than some of the people he was sent to supervise. These factors might have made some people skeptical of him. It was important that Titus set a good example and show integrity and trustworthiness so that no one could find anything to criticize (Titus 2:7–8). This was no small task, but Paul encouraged Titus by reminding him that it was God's grace that taught him, the Cretans, and all believers to say no to ungodliness. He was there to preach and teach God's Word with authority given by God Himself.

WEEK 96 • THURSDAY
Titus 3:1–15

Why did Paul say genealogies are useless?

In a flurry of activity based on the premise that salvation came through the discovery of hidden knowledge and angel worship, some people in Crete and elsewhere in the first century invented mythical stories and speculative interpretations based on the genealogies of the Old Testament. The lists of ancestors were not in themselves useless, but they were being used to determine who was "in" and "out" of the kingdom. This nonsense damaged the church (Titus 3:9). Paul gave the same warning to the church in Ephesus (1 Timothy 1:3–4).

WEEK 96 • FRIDAY   *Philemon 1–25*

Why did Paul appeal to Philemon on behalf of Onesimus?

Onesimus was the runaway slave of Philemon, a rich man who was most likely a member of the Colossian church. According to Roman law, a runaway slave could be punished by death. Onesimus had taken refuge with Paul during his house arrest in Rome. He had become a believer and had proven very useful as a support to Paul during his imprisonment. Because the name Onesimus meant "useful," Paul used a play on the name to make the point that, as a rebellious slave, he had been little good to Philemon. Now Onesimus had been persuaded of his Christian duty to return to his master. For these reasons, Paul appealed to Philemon to set aside his legal rights, forgive Onesimus, and consider him a brother in Christ (Philemon 10–16). This little letter presents a beautiful illustration of Christian love. Paul's advocacy on behalf of Onesimus reflects Christ's advocacy on behalf of sinners. Christ, by His perfect life and sacrificial death, restored us runaways back to the Father.

WEEK 96 • SATURDAY   *Hebrews 1:1–14*

What are angels?

Angels, a word borrowed from the Greek language and meaning "messengers," are spiritual beings who do the work of God in heaven and on earth (Hebrews 1:5). Obeying God, angels carry His messages to His people (Judges 6:11–25; Luke 1:22–20, 26–38), bring help to those in need (1 Kings 19:5–7), and help execute God's judgment on the wicked (Matthew 16:27; Luke 12:8–9). Angels continuously glorify God the Father as they gather around His throne (Revelation 5:11). They are ministering spirits who still do God's work in the world today. The writer of Hebrews used the image of these powerful beings as a reference point in describing Jesus the Savior, who is far superior to the angels in power and position.

WEEK 97 • MONDAY   *Hebrews 2:1–18*

Why did Jesus have to be like us in order to make atonement for our sins?

The Book of Hebrews establishes the fact that Jesus was like us in every way (Hebrews 2:11–13), except that He was without sin, in order to save us from our sins. The three Old Testament passages that Hebrews quotes emphasize Jesus Christ's solidarity with humankind, for whom He performs His priestly service. The quotation from Psalm 22:22 pictures the righteous Sufferer calling humans His brothers. (This passage foretold both our Lord's incarnation and crucifixion.) The other two quotations in Hebrews 2:11–13 come from the prophet Isaiah and emphasize Jesus' humanity. From the earliest times sacrifices were performed to atone for sin. Yet these sacrifices could not in and of themselves remove it. Rather, the Old Testament sacrifices pointed ahead to the greatest sacrifice—the death of Jesus Christ on the cross. Jesus, the Lamb of God, suffered and died as the final, perfect sacrifice, satisfying God's demand for the just punishment of sin.

WEEK 97 • TUESDAY   *Hebrews 3:1–19*

Why did the author of Hebrews point out that Jesus is greater than Moses?

The original readers of this book were Jewish Christians who revered Moses (Hebrews 3:3), through whom God delivered the Israelites from Egypt and gave His Law. As great as Moses was as a deliverer and envoy of God, faithful in his service, greater still was the faithful service of Jesus. Moses served God's people as a servant in God's house; Jesus was faithful as a Son, Lord over God's house, because He is the builder of the house. Moses' service pointed to a greater future, while Jesus' work and Word ushered in the gift of eternal salvation for all in God's family (Hebrews 3:7, 13, 15). The house (household) over which Jesus reigns as Lord in the last days consists of those from all nations whose confidence and hope rest on Christ.

WEEK 97 • WEDNESDAY   *Hebrews 4:1–16*

What does Sabbath-rest mean?

The rest God created by His resting on the seventh day of creation endures (Hebrews 4:9). The promise of that rest was not exhausted when Joshua, Moses' successor, brought God's people into the Promised Land. Through David God continued the promise and opened up the prospect of a rest greater than Canaan could give. Jesus, greater than Moses and Joshua, gives that rest to those who believe in Him. That rest reflects the Sabbath, the seventh day of creation, a time when work ceases. Instead of trying to enter the Sabbath-rest by struggling futilely to do good works, the child of God enters by faith in Christ.

WEEK 97 • THURSDAY   *Hebrews 5:1–14*

What does it mean to be a priest in the order of Melchizedek?

The writer of Hebrews quotes Psalm 110 in reinforcing the fact of Christ's divine appointment to the priesthood. In particular the writer quotes Psalm 110:4 which pictures Melchizedek, a king who was also a priest (Genesis 14:18–20; Hebrews 5:6). In Genesis Melchizedek appears briefly as he meets and blesses Abraham returning from rescuing Lot. Moses, the author of Genesis, calls Melchizedek "king of Salem" and "priest of God Most High." The writer of Hebrews sees Melchizedek as a precursor to Jesus Christ, as one whose ministry foreshadowed that of Christ. Jesus did what Melchizedek could never do—as our Priest, Jesus sacrificed Himself on the cross for the forgiveness of sins and now reigns forever as King over His creation.

WEEK 97 • FRIDAY   *Hebrews 6:1–20*

What was the inner sanctuary?

The inner sanctuary refers to the Most Holy Place in the temple into which only the high priests entered, and then only on the Day of Atonement. It was a small room, separated from the outer chambers of the temple by a thick curtain. In this inner sanctuary, the Holy One sat "enthroned between the cherubim" (Psalm 80:1) of the ark of the covenant. Under the old covenant, the most Holy Place was considered God's "throne room" on earth. All of this pointed to Jesus Christ, our High Priest, who went through the curtain of the heavens to plead for us (Hebrews 6:19). He has gone before us and will one day bring us to Himself. Even now, we can approach our Holy God in confidence because by His death Jesus opened the way.

WEEK 97 • SATURDAY   *Hebrews 7:1–28*

What was the function and purpose of the Levitical priesthood?

The Levitical priesthood was established to make sinful humans acceptable to God (Hebrews 7:11), something this priesthood could not do. Though God gave the Mosaic law in support of the Levitical priesthood, laying down regulations about its operation, the fact remained that this priesthood was incomplete. It pointed ahead to the one great sacrifice by which sinners could be saved—the death of Jesus Christ, the eternal, perfect High Priest.

WEEK 98 • MONDAY   *Hebrews 8:1–13*

What does it mean that Jesus is the mediator of the new covenant?

The new covenant of which Jesus Christ is mediator is the covenant of grace. By His sacrificial death Christ did what the old covenant of the Law could not do—He stepped between sinless God and sinful humanity, serving as mediator of the new covenant. Christ's death covers our sins—past, present, and future. Now as heirs named in God's will, we receive the eternal inheritance made sure by Christ's complete sacrifice.

WEEK 98 • TUESDAY   *Hebrews 9:1–28*

What role did the tabernacle have in Old Testament worship?

The tabernacle, briefly described in Hebrews 9:1–5, served as the main location for the worship of the people of Israel during their wilderness wanderings. The tabernacle also served as the model for the temple Solomon later built in Jerusalem. The tabernacle, important in its day, was only "earthly," built by human beings according to God's instructions. By briefly mentioning the tabernacle, the author of Hebrews stresses not so much the earthly structures of the tabernacle, but rather the reality in heaven—the true altar which the earthly tabernacle could only symbolize. This earthly tabernacle and the animals sacrificed on it foreshadowed the sacrifice of Christ and the eternal, heavenly mercy seat on which Christ poured out His own blood in payment for our sins (Hebrews 9:11–15).

WEEK 98 • WEDNESDAY   *Hebrews 10:1–18*

What sacrifices were required by the law?

The sacrifices and offerings that were required by law (Hebrews 10:8) involved animals, grains, and wine. Moses detailed the various sacrifices the Lord required in Leviticus 1–7. Despite their use according to God's direction, animal sacrifices could only foreshadow the good things to come, the good things of salvation that Christ's sacrifice would bring. Animal sacrifices could not remove sin. They had to be repeated week by week, year by year. In contrast, the good things Christ's sacrifice has brought will last forever—forgiveness of sins, life, freedom, and hope.

WEEK 98 • THURSDAY   *Hebrews 10:19–39*

What does it mean to draw near to God?

Sin had separated human beings from God, keeping us from approaching Him in worship or prayer. The honor of drawing near to God (Hebrews 10:22) is the believer's blood-bought privilege—paid for by Christ's blood poured out on the cross. We now come to God in confidence because "our hearts [are] sprinkled to cleanse us from a guilty conscience" and "our bodies [are] washed with pure water" (Hebrews 10:22). This status stands in sharp contrast to the situation, even of believers, under the old covenant. Under that covenant, the high priest had to be ceremonially washed before he could enter the Most Holy Place and sprinkle blood on the ark of the covenant (Leviticus 16:4, 14). But Christ's death cleanses us from all sin, once for all. Christ's death removes the roadblocks of sin and guilt, giving us free access to our heavenly Father. We can pray and praise in confident joy.

WEEK 98 • FRIDAY   *Hebrews 11:1–40*

Why didn't these people of faith receive what they had been promised?

God commended the Old Testament saints showcased in Hebrews 11 for their faith. These people had received many promises from God and had seen many of those promises fulfilled. But Christ's coming to earth to die, His rising on the third day, and His coming again on the Last Day had not yet happened. They saw these promises from afar. Yet, these Old Testament heroes of faith are no second-class citizens of heaven, because Christ's cross and its redemption reaches back to them and forward to us and those yet to come. Though these people lived only in the foreshadow of Christ's coming, they lived by faith in God's faithful promises. By God's grace we too share that same faith.

WEEK 98 • SATURDAY   *Hebrews 12:1–29*

What is the cloud of witnesses?

The cloud of witnesses (Hebrews 12:1) includes those named earlier in the "hall of faith" (Hebrews 11), as well as all people of every time and place who have trusted Jesus Christ for salvation. Their lives, their words of confession and encouragement, their faith—all give us encouragement to persevere in the race of life. Yet they cannot strengthen us. The strength we need comes from Jesus. We fix our eyes on Him, the author and perfecter of our faith. Jesus Christ, the true God from all eternity became a true human being to live and die and rise for our salvation. Meditating on His deep love gives us courage and confidence as we run the race set before us.

WEEK 99 • MONDAY   *Hebrews 13:1–25*

What was the significance of going outside the camp?

In Old Testament times, individuals were banished to life outside the camp (Hebrews 13:13) because of ceremonial uncleanness. On the Day of Atonement, after animal blood had been sprinkled on the mercy seat, the bodies of the sacrificial animals were burned outside the camp, reminding Israel that its sin was removed. This too points to Christ, whose cross stood outside the city. Christ's blood, unlike that of the animal sacrifices, makes people holy, bringing them out of the darkness of sin into God's family of light. To go back to the old ways of life, to return to the regulations of Judaism, or to mix legalism with the new way of life that belongs to us in Christ is to leave the cross and lose its benefits.

WEEK 99 • TUESDAY   *James 1:1–27*

Who were the "twelve tribes" scattered among the nations?

By addressing the "twelve tribes scattered among the nations" (James 1:1), James speaks to the church, the new Israel, God's pilgrim people who have not reached their eternal home but live as scattered exiles in this world. The New Testament repeats this word picture several times (Galatians 6:16; 1 Peter 1:1, 17; 2:9–10). Such a reference does not necessarily mark James' first readers as Jewish. Still, many scholars believe the Letter of James was originally addressed to Jewish Christians, because of the references to the synagogue (James 2:2), to Old Testament examples, and to the sin of hypocrisy. While this sin plagued many Jewish believers, Gentile Christians found themselves more tempted by sins like sexual immorality and factionalism.

WEEK 99 • WEDNESDAY   *James 2:1–26*

What is dead faith?

In talking about dead faith (James 2:26), James combats not a doctrinal problem but a practical threat to faith. James' readers did not practice what they professed. (Compare Jesus' accusation in Matthew 23:3.) Out of love for his readers, James emphasizes that faith is union and communion with God. Such faith commits us wholly—in thought and action—to God. James will not let a brother destroy his faith and himself by making faith a mere intellectual acceptance of doctrines, empty of love and good works. Thus James speaks to Christian complacency, or what he calls dead faith.

WEEK 99 • THURSDAY   *James 3:1–18*

About what kind of teachers was James talking?

When James used the word *teachers* in James 3:1, he was referring to teachers in the house churches, those who taught and proclaimed the Gospel of Jesus Christ. Because the Gospel is the life-giving Word of God, those who teach it carry a special burden of responsibility to see to it that they don't dilute or pollute it with false teaching. This gives every Christian a reason to pray continually for those who preach and teach the Word.

WEEK 99 • FRIDAY   *James 4:1–17*

What does it mean to resist the devil?

Each Christian stands as God's outpost or beachhead in an alien and hostile world. Therefore, of necessity, we battle throughout life against Satan and his temptations. James warned that we should resist the devil (James 4:7), the author of all enmity against God. The best example (and commentary on) such resistance is the temptation of our Lord (Matthew 4:1–11). Jesus resisted the devil by using the Word of God—the same weapon we have available for our use against Satan. Although Christ's death and resurrection defanged Satan, our enemy still attempts to lure us into temptation and defeat us by our sin and guilt. Yet in Christ we enjoy ultimate victory over him.

WEEK 99 • SATURDAY   *James 5:1–20*

What were the autumn and spring rains?

James (5:7–8) encouraged his readers to consider the patience of the farmer who waits for the harvest. Farmers know why they must wait and for what they must wait—the fruit and grain that crowns a farmer's year with joy. In the dry and arid land of Palestine, farmers waited for the autumn (October, November) rains to come soon after they planted their seed. Then they waited patiently for the spring (March, April) rains to come just before harvest time to bring the crops to their full potential. Like the patient farmer, those among James' first readers who suffered oppression waited and endured their hardships. By God's grace, they trusted that Jesus would soon return to take them to Himself.

WEEK 100 • MONDAY
1 Peter 1:1–25

What is the significance of the lamb without blemish or defect?

The "lamb without blemish or defect" (1 Peter 1:19) suggests the Passover lamb (Exodus 12:5) by whose blood Israel was delivered from God's judgment when the firstborn of Egypt perished (Exodus 12:12–13). 1 Corinthians 5:7 points to Christ as our Passover Lamb—the Lamb without the blemish or defect of sin. Christ, the Lamb of God, takes away the sin of the world—including our own. As our Passover Lamb, He delivers us from sin, death, and Satan.

WEEK 100 • TUESDAY
1 Peter 2:1–25

What was the significance of Christ dying on a tree?

The Law of God demands perfection from every human being. Because of sin we are incapable of keeping that Law perfectly, and so we are condemned to death. In our place Christ Jesus became a curse (Galatians 3:13), taking our place under the curse of the Law—the curse of death (Deuteronomy 21:22–23). Hanging on "the tree," (another name for the cross), Jesus was crucified, taking away our sin, canceling our guilt, and defeating sin and Satan, hell and death. Bearing the sin of the whole world, Jesus bore the curse of God's judgment in order that we might live with God forever (1 Peter 2:24).

WEEK 100 • WEDNESDAY
1 Peter 3:1—4:19

Why was it important for believers to offer hospitality?

In the early church, generous hospitality was crucial to the functioning of the church and the spread of the Gospel. Early church leaders and teachers frequently traveled to other house churches to teach and encourage believers in their faith. These traveling teachers usually had little money and relied on the generosity of others to continue their work. Hospitality was one aspect of the life of love, a life lived to the glory of God through Jesus Christ.

WEEK 100 • THURSDAY
1 Peter 5:1–14

What does Babylon represent?

To his readers Peter brings greetings from her "who is in Babylon" (1 Peter 5:13), a reference to the church in Rome. Christianity borrowed this name for Rome from late Judaism. The Old Testament prophets had denounced Babylon as the ultimate world power at enmity with God and His people. In using the term, Peter reminded his readers that the hostile world they faced and which now had power to impose a fiery ordeal on scattered and homeless Christians, would someday meet the same fate as did Babylon of old—destruction under God's judgment.

WEEK 100 • FRIDAY
2 Peter 1:1—2:22

What was the sacred mountain?

Peter and the other disciples of our Lord were eyewitnesses to the great acts of God. This fact distinguished them and their teachings from the false teachers. On the "sacred mountain," the mountain of the transfiguration (2 Peter 1:18), Peter saw the majesty of the Lord Christ. On that mountain Peter, James, and John saw for themselves the power, honor, and glory that would be displayed in Christ at His Second Coming. These men had heard the voice of the Father proclaim: "This is My Son, whom I love; with Him I am well pleased" (2 Peter 1:17; Matthew 3:17). In Christ, the disciples saw God's Word accomplishing His purpose (Isaiah 55:11).

WEEK 100 • SATURDAY
2 Peter 3:1–18

How were Paul's writings being misused?

Peter states that some people misused the writings of Paul—writings they did not understand. (2 Peter 3:15–16). No one could deny Paul's letters as "weighty and forceful" (2 Corinthians 10:10), rich in thought and language concerning the free grace of God in Christ Jesus. At one point, Peter himself disagreed with Paul about what freedom in Christ meant for believers. In the end, though, their dispute was resolved on the side of the Gospel. Even so, some still saw freedom in Christ as a license to sin. They tried to reimpose the rules and rituals of Judaism on the new Christian church. To do so they had to twist Paul's letters and his intent. Peter warned his readers to be on guard so as not to be carried away by error.

WEEK 101 • MONDAY   *1 John 1:1–10*

Who is the Word of life?

God has spoken His ultimate Word, the Word of life (1 John 1:1), in the visible, historical person of His incarnate Son, Jesus Christ, the Word made flesh (John 1:1, 14). Because of the life and death of that Word—Jesus—God has admitted sinful human beings into fellowship with Himself and with one another.

WEEK 101 • TUESDAY   *1 John 2:1–29*

What is meant by the antichrist?

First John warns believers against false teachers who had arisen in the church. At the time of John's writing, these false teachers had either separated from the church or had been expelled, but they still constituted a threat. These teachers were not of Christ but were the very embodiment of the antichrist (1 John 2:18). First and foremost, they denied the deity of Christ (1 John 2:22; 4:3, 5; 5:5). John tells us that anyone who denies that Jesus is the Christ (1 John 2:22) and those who refuse to acknowledge Christ (1 John 4:3) as God coming in the flesh (2 John 7) is an antichrist. These "antichrists" follow the heresy of doctrine and life the final Antichrist at the end of the age will promote.

WEEK 101 • WEDNESDAY   *1 John 3:1–24*

What does "God's seed" mean?

To be born of God, to be God's seed (1 John 3:9), is the same as living or abiding in Him (1 John 3:6). Those born of God through the water and word of Baptism abhor sin because God's nature, His "seed," abides in them. This term ("seed") can also refer to God's Word and to His Spirit—both of which strengthen believers in our battle to resist sin.

WEEK 101 • THURSDAY
1 John 4:1–21

What does it mean to test the spirits?

"Don't believe everything you hear" is the advice John gave as he encouraged his readers to "test the spirits" (1 John 4:1). The problem of counterfeit teachers and false prophets—those who either distorted the pure Gospel or who preached the Word for their own personal gain—was rampant in the early church. The test of true belief is very clear: Does the teacher believe and confess that Jesus Christ is the Word of God made flesh (1 John 4:2)?

WEEK 101 • FRIDAY
1 John 5:1–21

What does it mean to come by water and blood?

The early Christians faced many heresies, especially one teaching that Jesus was a man among men, a superior man to be sure, but still merely a man. This heresy—an early version of what later became know as Gnosticism—claimed that at His Baptism, "the heavenly Christ" descended on Jesus, enabling Him to perform miracles. Just before His suffering and death "the heavenly Christ" left Jesus, and thus only the human Jesus died. John says (1 John 5:6) that Christ came by both water (Baptism) and blood (His death on the cross). These events marked the beginning and end of our Lord's earthly ministry. Both also point to the sacraments of the church—Baptism and the Lord's Supper. These sacraments, rooted in water and blood, bear witness to Jesus Christ as the Son of God and Savior.

WEEK 101 • SATURDAY
2 John 1–13

Who was the chosen lady?

Some think that John's reference to a "chosen lady" (2 John 1) refers to a specific, individual woman, a sister in the faith whom John "loved in the truth." The context of the letter also supports the possibility that John meant to refer to a congregation or group of congregations to which the letter is addressed. If that is the case, then the phrase "her children" refers to members of the church.

WEEK 102 • MONDAY   *3 John 1–14*

What is the Name?

God has always motivated His faithful Christians to be hospitable and to go out proclaiming the Name of Jesus. The Name of Jesus encompasses the entire Gospel, because Jesus means, "He will save His people from their sins" (Matthew 1:21). The freedom from sin we enjoy in Jesus' Name energizes hospitality, proclamation, and other good works of Christians (3 John 7—8).

WEEK 102 • TUESDAY   *Jude 1–25*

What was Balaam's error?

Balaam (Jude 11) was a prophet who, in Old Testament times, was hired by Balak to curse Israel for money. Even though God told him not to, Balaam went with Balak. Balaam was so stubborn that God stopped him by sending an angel and finally causing his donkey to rebuke him! Although Balaam wanted to curse the Israelites, God simply would not let him (Numbers 22—24). Thus Balaam exemplifies those who lead believers into idolatry and other great, shameful sins.

WEEK 102 • WEDNESDAY   *Revelation 1:1–20*

What is a revelation?

The word *revelation* means "the act of uncovering" or "unveiling" (Revelation 1:1). Jesus Christ Himself is the source of revelation given via an angel to John and ultimately to the church. This revelation is God's last word on the church, on history, on Jesus Christ, who triumphed over Satan and all the powers of darkness.

WEEK 102 • THURSDAY
Revelation 2:1–29

Who were the Nicolaitans?

The Nicolaitans were followers of Nicolas of Antioch (Revelation 2:6), a false teacher who taught that the believer's true nature was in the spirit and, therefore, it did not matter what he or she did in the body. This was an attempted justification of sexual immorality and other sinful practices that Jesus Himself specifically condemned in this passage. Nicolas and his followers advocated and defended a compromise with the paganism that surrounded the young church.

WEEK 102 • FRIDAY
Revelation 3:1–22

Why were these seven churches specifically named?

Through John's letter, Jesus the Victor addressed the seven specific churches, asking them to do the impossible in an intolerable situation—perversion of the Gospel from within and persecution from without. While each of the seven messages is different in content, they all have a common outline that serves a common purpose: to provide spiritual direction to a people called to live by faith in Christ and to be in the world but not *of* the world. Each letter begins with affirmation of what the church is doing right, followed by a correction and concluding with a promise. The seven churches were representative of the church as a whole.

WEEK 102 • SATURDAY
Revelation 4:1—5:14

What is the significance of the number seven?

These beginning chapters contain several references to the number seven: seven spirits (Revelation 4:5), seven seals (Revelation 5:1), seven churches (Revelation 2—3), and seven lampstands (Revelation 1:20). In God's economy, the number seven often represented perfection, completeness, and wholeness—concepts that are key in the Book of Revelation and in the rest of the Bible.

WEEK 103 • MONDAY
Revelation 6:1—8:5

What is the significance of the Lamb opening the seals?

The scroll of Revelation 5 contains the judgments of God. The Lamb—Jesus Christ—is the only One worthy to open the seals of the scroll (Revelation 6:1). Because of His death and resurrection, His defeat of death, sin, and Satan, Christ is worthy to open the seals. The opening of the seals reveals God's purposes and also their coming, their advent, their execution. The kingdom for which we wait in hope will come—soon. In God's time, we will witness the fulfillment of all His promises.

WEEK 103 • TUESDAY
Revelation 8:6—9:21

What is the significance of angels sounding trumpets?

The seven trumpets held by the seven angels (Revelation 8:2) were more than musical instruments. God's Old Testament people used rams' horns to signal temple worship, to direct warfare, and at the accession of kings. The sound of the trumpet was a call to attention that could not be ignored. The prophets wrote of the trumpet blast that would herald the coming of the day of the LORD (Joel 2:1; Zephaniah 1:16), while the New Testament speaks of Jesus' return, which will be accompanied by a mighty trumpet blast.

WEEK 103 • WEDNESDAY
Revelation 10:1–11

What was the significance of the scroll being both sweet and sour?

John ate the scroll and found it initially sweet but soon sour in his stomach (Revelation 10:10). This experience is common among all who incorporate God's Word in their speech. The servant of the Lord, meditating and savoring the Word of God, delights in what God has provided (see Psalm 34:8). God's Word is sweet to the taste, "sweeter than honey" (Psalm 19:10). Despite the sweetness of the Word, the Gospel of Jesus Christ, the Word is often rejected. The witness who proclaims the Word of God and sees the people reject of that Word experiences the bitterness of rejection in the pit of the stomach. Such also was the experience of

Jeremiah, Moses, Elijah, John the Baptizer, and our Lord Himself. Can we expect anything different?

WEEK 103 • THURSDAY   *Revelation 11:1–19*

What is the Abyss?

The word translated here as Abyss means "deep" or "a bottomless pit" (Revelation 11:7) like the chaos of deep waters. This place is unfathomable by air-breathing humans, and therefore frightening and mysterious. To the ancients, the Abyss represented everything that went against reason and order in creation. It came to represent a complete rebellion against God and His will. Therefore, the Abyss was seen as the home of demons, the source of everything evil.

WEEK 103 • FRIDAY   *Revelation 12:1–17*

What does the struggle between the woman and the dragon represent?

St. John retells the entire life of Jesus in a very few verses. This is not a quiet, gentle story, but one with cosmic significance. The lightning, thunder, and earthquake at the end of Revelation 11 focus our attention on the woman who appears in the sky that has become for John a theater screen. The woman (Israel, the Old Testament church) is pregnant. Her cries of pain during childbirth drown out the robust hymn sung by the 24 elders in the previous chapter. The seven-headed red dragon (Satan) is poised to devour the infant coming from the womb. The moment the child appears, the dragon lunges, but the child is rescued and lifted to the throne of God (the Ascension), while the mother (the New Testament church) escapes to a place of safety. The child is identified as one "who will rule all the nations with an iron scepter" (Psalm 2:9; Revelation 12:5)—the Messiah, Jesus Christ. The immediate consequence of Jesus' life, death, resurrection, and ascension is not a hymn of worship, but heavenly warfare in which the great dragon Satan is thrown out of heaven. As implied even in the Gospels of Matthew and Luke, Jesus' life excites more than wonder; it excites evil—first with Herod and later with Judas, Pilate, the crowds, and religious leaders. Finally, when Christ Himself ascends in glory, Satan attacks the believers left on earth. This chapter conveys the breath-taking scope of Christ's redemption and also the insane hatred Satan bears for the Lord and His people.

WEEK 103 • SATURDAY   *Revelation 13:1–18*

What does the number 666 mean?

The three sixes (666) of Revelation 13:18, sometimes known as "the mark of the beast," have been discussed more than other numbers in the Bible. The number 666 often is thought to give the name of the Antichrist and its followers. In both Hebrew and Greek, letters of the alphabet were used for numbers. By substituting the numerical value of each letter in a noun, a cryptogram of the noun could be made—one easily deciphered by those in the know. Most of that context is lost to us today. Nonetheless, the number 666 is symbolic as well as cryptic, for 666 is a triple failure to be a 777, the three-times perfect, whole, divine number. A sign of imperfection, 666 expresses intensified incompleteness, falling completely short of God and His glory.

WEEK 104 • MONDAY   *Revelation 14:1–20*

What is the significance of the 144,000?

In the vision of Revelation 14:1–5, the Lamb of God stands on Mount Zion, that is, heaven, with 144,000 of God's people. They are all the saints who have borne the names of the Lamb and the Father, which are stronger than the mark and number of the beast. The 144,000 is a symbolic number. We might think of it as 12 Old Testament tribes of Israel times 12 New Testament apostles times 1,000—the number of totality, all believers of all time and every place, safe in heaven with the Lamb. Compare the 144,000 believers "sealed" in Revelation 7:2–8. At that point, the believers lived on earth, subject to the rage of Satan and his human cohorts. Now John pictures a time when all have safely arrived in heaven. The Lord loses none who are His. As we consider the fury of our enemies, how good it is to know our Lord's care and power!

WEEK 104 • TUESDAY   *Revelation 15:1–8*

Why was the temple filled with smoke?

When God appeared to Moses on Mount Sinai, the mountain was covered with smoke (Exodus 19:18; 20:18). When Isaiah received his vision of heaven, "the temple was filled with smoke" (Isaiah 6:4). In John's vision, "the temple was filled with smoke" (Revelation 15:8). In describing this vision, John helps us understand the Old Testament passages, for he adds that the smoke was "from the glory of God and from His power." Thus the smoke was a sign of God's holy, omnipotent presence.

WEEK 104 • WEDNESDAY   *Revelation 16:1–21*

What is the significance of Armageddon?

Armageddon may be a transliteration of the Hebrew *Har Mageddon*, meaning "mountain of Megiddo." Or it may be a combination of *Harmah*, a place marked for destruction (Numbers 21:3; Judges 1:17), and *Megiddo*, a city some six miles from the southern end of Mount Carmel. Since it is not a specific geographical reference, we can think of Armageddon as a symbol of the final, complete, eternal defeat and destruction of all the forces and powers of evil.

WEEK 104 • THURSDAY   *Revelation 17:1—18:8*

Who or what is Babylon the Great?

The woman (*not* the same woman of Revelation 12) is identified as Babylon the Great, the "mother of prostitutes and of the abominations of the earth" (Revelation 17:5). In Old Testament times, the empire of Babylon had destroyed Jerusalem with its temple, along with Hebrew culture. Babylon thus earned a reputation as the great enemy of Israel. The new Israel, the church, saw Rome as its Babylon, the source of persecution and evil. "Babylon" in Revelation symbolizes the entire, ungodly world system of values and philosophy that opposes the Lord's truth and hates His people.

WEEK 104 • FRIDAY   *Revelation 18:9–24*

What is a millstone?

A millstone was a large flat stone that was used to crush grain (Revelation 18:21). It sat on top of a flat slab of stone onto which grain was poured. Household millstones were small and worked by hand. Larger millstones rotated on pivots and were turned by animals or prisoners. The angel of the Lord takes up the sign of judgment—the millstone—and hurls it into the sea, thus portraying the total destruction of Babylon.

WEEK 104 • SATURDAY   *Revelation 19:1–21*

What is the fiery lake of burning sulfur?

The fiery lake of burning sulfur is John's image of the place of final torment for the beast and the false prophet (Revelation 19:20). This place is the "eternal fire prepared for the devil and his angels" (Matthew 25:41).

WEEK 105 • MONDAY   *Revelation 20:1–15*

What do Gog and Magog represent?

The names Gog and Magog appear in the prophecy of Ezekiel (38—39) and represent the nations Satan beckons from all parts of the earth to wage war against the Lord (Revelation 20:8). Gog and Magog symbolize all enemies of the new Israel, the children of God by faith in Christ Jesus. Though Gog and Magog are great in number, the Lord defeats them.

WEEK 105 • TUESDAY   *Revelation 21:1–27*

Why is the new Jerusalem described as a cube?

One of the striking features of heaven is its symmetry. This feature symbolizes holiness. John's description of heaven, the new Jerusalem, resembles the cubic Most Holy Place in Solomon's temple (1 Kings 6:20). But in Revelation it has grown extravagantly. While the immense size may stagger us, the point of the picture is to give us a sense of enormous wholeness, holiness. This reduces all desecration and blasphemy to puniness. Just as God dwelt in the Most Holy Place of the temple, so God dwells now in this holy place that is heaven (Hebrews 9:24). The great walls of the city are inclusive, completely enclosing the final and eternal union and communion of God with all who are His own.

WEEK 105 • WEDNESDAY   *Revelation 22:1–21*

What is the significance of the tree of life?

The tree of life has a twin in the tree in the Garden of Eden (compare Revelation 22:2 with Genesis 2:9). In Eden, all humanity fell into sin when Adam and Eve ate from the tree of knowledge of good and evil, disobeying God's clear instructions. The Lord evicted Adam and Eve from Eden so they would not eat from the tree of life and live forever in sin, sickness, pain, and frustration. In Revelation, the tree of life reappears. It bears fruit every month, and its leaves are used for healing of all the nations. In heaven, God's people will be able to enjoy the fruit of this tree forever. All this because of an earlier tree—the cross—on which the Lamb was slain to redeem His people.

READING PLAN FOR THE TODAY'S LIGHT BIBLE

This daily reading plan will guide you through the Bible in two years. You can use *Frequently Asked Questions* as a reference tool, as you read through God's Word.

☐ Week 1
☐ Monday — Genesis 1:1–2:25
☐ Tuesday — Genesis 3:1–24
☐ Wednesday — Genesis 4:1–6:8
☐ Thursday — Genesis 6:9–8:22
☐ Friday — Genesis 9:1–10:32
☐ Saturday — Genesis 11:1–12:9

☐ Week 2
☐ Monday — Genesis 12:10–13:18
☐ Tuesday — Genesis 14:1–15:21
☐ Wednesday — Genesis 16:1–17:27
☐ Thursday — Genesis 18:1–19:38
☐ Friday — Genesis 20:1–21:34
☐ Saturday — Genesis 22:1–24

☐ Week 3
☐ Monday — Genesis 23:1–24:67
☐ Tuesday — Genesis 25:1–26:35
☐ Wednesday — Genesis 27:1–28:22
☐ Thursday — Genesis 29:1–30:43
☐ Friday — Genesis 31:1–33:20
☐ Saturday — Genesis 34:1–35:29

☐ Week 4
☐ Monday — Genesis 36:1–37:36
☐ Tuesday — Genesis 38:1–39:23
☐ Wednesday — Genesis 40:1–23
☐ Thursday — Genesis 41:1–40
☐ Friday — Genesis 41:41–57
☐ Saturday — Genesis 42:1–44:34

☐ Week 5
☐ Monday — Genesis 45:1–46:34
☐ Tuesday — Genesis 47:1–48:22
☐ Wednesday — Genesis 49:1–50:26
☐ Thursday — Exodus 1:1–22
☐ Friday — Exodus 2:1–25
☐ Saturday — Exodus 3:1–4:31

☐ Week 6
☐ Monday — Exodus 5:1–6:30
☐ Tuesday — Exodus 7:1–24
☐ Wednesday — Exodus 8:1–9:35
☐ Thursday — Exodus 10:1–29
☐ Friday — Exodus 11:1–12:51
☐ Saturday — Exodus 13:1–22

☐ Week 7
☐ Monday — Exodus 14:1–31
☐ Tuesday — Exodus 15:1–27
☐ Wednesday — Exodus 16:1–17:16
☐ Thursday — Exodus 18:1–27
☐ Friday — Exodus 19:1–20:26
☐ Saturday — Exodus 21:1–22:31

❏ Week 8
❏ Monday   Exodus 23:1–24:18
❏ Tuesday   Exodus 25:1–27:21
❏ Wednesday   Exodus 28:1–29:46
❏ Thursday   Exodus 30:1–31:18
❏ Friday   Exodus 32:1–35
❏ Saturday   Exodus 33:1–23

❏ Week 9
❏ Monday   Exodus 34:1–35
❏ Tuesday   Exodus 35:1–36:38
❏ Wednesday   Exodus 37:1–38:31
❏ Thursday   Exodus 39:1–40:38
❏ Friday   Leviticus 1:1–17
❏ Saturday   Leviticus 2:1–3:17

❏ Week 10
❏ Monday   Leviticus 4:1–6:30
❏ Tuesday   Leviticus 7:1–9:24
❏ Wednesday   Leviticus 10:1–11:47
❏ Thursday   Leviticus 12:1–15:33
❏ Friday   Leviticus 16:1–17:16
❏ Saturday   Leviticus 18:1–19:37

❏ Week 11
❏ Monday   Leviticus 20:1–22:33
❏ Tuesday   Leviticus 23:1–25:55
❏ Wednesday   Leviticus 26:1–27:34
❏ Thursday   Numbers 1:1–3:51
❏ Friday   Numbers 4:1–6:27
❏ Saturday   Numbers 7:1–8:26

❏ Week 12
❏ Monday   Numbers 9:1–10:36

❏ Tuesday   Numbers 11:1–12:16
❏ Wednesday   Numbers 13:1–15:41
❏ Thursday   Numbers 16:1–18:32
❏ Friday   Numbers 19:1–20:29
❏ Saturday   Numbers 21:1–35

❏ Week 13
❏ Monday   Numbers 22:1–25:18
❏ Tuesday   Numbers 26:1–27:23
❏ Wednesday   Numbers 28:1–30:16
❏ Thursday   Numbers 31:1–54
❏ Friday   Numbers 32:1–34:29
❏ Saturday   Numbers 35:1–36:13

❏ Week 14
❏ Monday   Deuteronomy 1:1–46
❏ Tuesday   Deuteronomy 2:1–37
❏ Wednesday   Deuteronomy 3:1–29
❏ Thursday   Deuteronomy 4:1–49
❏ Friday   Deuteronomy 5:1–33
❏ Saturday   Deuteronomy 6:1–25

❏ Week 15
❏ Monday   Deuteronomy 7:1–26
❏ Tuesday   Deuteronomy 8:1–20
❏ Wednesday   Deuteronomy 9:1–10:22
❏ Thursday   Deuteronomy 11:1–12:32
❏ Friday   Deuteronomy 13:1–18
❏ Saturday   Deuteronomy 14:1–15:23

❏ Week 16
❏ Monday   Deuteronomy 16:1–17:20
❏ Tuesday   Deuteronomy 18:1–19:21
❏ Wednesday   Deuteronomy 20:1–21:23

❏ Thursday   Deuteronomy 22:1–23:25
❏ Friday   Deuteronomy 24:1–22
❏ Saturday   Deuteronomy 25:1–26:19

❏ Week 17

❏ Monday   Deuteronomy 27:1–26
❏ Tuesday   Deuteronomy 28:1–68
❏ Wednesday   Deuteronomy 29:1–29
❏ Thursday   Deuteronomy 30:1–20
❏ Friday   Deuteronomy 31:1–30
❏ Saturday   Deuteronomy 32:1–52

❏ Week 18

❏ Monday   Deuteronomy 33:1–29
❏ Tuesday   Deuteronomy 34:1–12
❏ Wednesday   Joshua 1:1–18
❏ Thursday   Joshua 2:1–3:17
❏ Friday   Joshua 4:1–5:12
❏ Saturday   Joshua 5:13–7:26

❏ Week 19

❏ Monday   Joshua 8:1–9:27
❏ Tuesday   Joshua 10:1–43
❏ Wednesday   Joshua 11:1–12:24
❏ Thursday   Joshua 13:1–15:63
❏ Friday   Joshua 16:1–17:18
❏ Saturday   Joshua 18:1–19:51

❏ Week 20

❏ Monday   Joshua 20:1–21:45
❏ Tuesday   Joshua 22:1–34
❏ Wednesday   Joshua 23:1–16
❏ Thursday   Joshua 24:1–33
❏ Friday   Judges 1:1–36

❏ Saturday   Judges 2:1–23

❏ Week 21

❏ Monday   Judges 3:1–30
❏ Tuesday   Judges 3:31–5:31
❏ Wednesday   Judges 6:1–8:35
❏ Thursday   Judges 9:1–10:18
❏ Friday   Judges 11:1–12:15
❏ Saturday   Judges 13:1–16:31

❏ Week 22

❏ Monday   Judges 17:1–18:31
❏ Tuesday   Judges 19:1–20:48
❏ Wednesday   Judges 21:1–25
❏ Thursday   Ruth 1:1–2:23
❏ Friday   Ruth 3:1–4:22
❏ Saturday   1 Samuel 1:1–28

❏ Week 23

❏ Monday   1 Samuel 2:1–36
❏ Tuesday   1 Samuel 3:1–21
❏ Wednesday   1 Samuel 4:1–22
❏ Thursday   1 Samuel 5:1–6:21
❏ Friday   1 Samuel 7:1–17
❏ Saturday   1 Samuel 8:1–22

❏ Week 24

❏ Monday   1 Samuel 9:1–10:27
❏ Tuesday   1 Samuel 11:1–15
❏ Wednesday   1 Samuel 12:1–25
❏ Thursday   1 Samuel 13:1–22
❏ Friday   1 Samuel 14:1–52
❏ Saturday   1 Samuel 15:1–35

❏ Week 25
❏ Monday — 1 Samuel 16:1–23
❏ Tuesday — 1 Samuel 17:1–58
❏ Wednesday — 1 Samuel 18:1–19:24
❏ Thursday — 1 Samuel 20:1–21:15
❏ Friday — 1 Samuel 22:1–23
❏ Saturday — 1 Samuel 23:1–29

❏ Week 26
❏ Monday — 1 Samuel 24:1–22
❏ Tuesday — 1 Samuel 25:1–44
❏ Wednesday — 1 Samuel 26:1–25
❏ Thursday — 1 Samuel 27:1–29:11
❏ Friday — 1 Samuel 30:1–31
❏ Saturday — 1 Samuel 31:1–13

❏ Week 27
❏ Monday — 2 Samuel 1:1–2:32
❏ Tuesday — 2 Samuel 3:1–4:12
❏ Wednesday — 2 Samuel 5:1–25
❏ Thursday — 2 Samuel 6:1–23
❏ Friday — 2 Samuel 7:1–29
❏ Saturday — 2 Samuel 8:1–10:19

❏ Week 28
❏ Monday — 2 Samuel 11:1–12:31
❏ Tuesday — 2 Samuel 13:1–14:24
❏ Wednesday — 2 Samuel 14:25–16:23
❏ Thursday — 2 Samuel 17:1–18:33
❏ Friday — 2 Samuel 19:1–20:26
❏ Saturday — 2 Samuel 21:1–22:51

❏ Week 29
❏ Monday — 2 Samuel 23:1–39

❏ Tuesday — 2 Samuel 24:1–25
❏ Wednesday — 1 Kings 1:1–2:46
❏ Thursday — 1 Kings 3:1–4:34
❏ Friday — 1 Kings 5:1–7:51
❏ Saturday — 1 Kings 8:1–66

❏ Week 30
❏ Monday — 1 Kings 9:1–10:29
❏ Tuesday — 1 Kings 11:1–43
❏ Wednesday — 1 Kings 12:1–33
❏ Thursday — 1 Kings 13:1–14:31
❏ Friday — 1 Kings 15:1–16:34
❏ Saturday — 1 Kings 17:1–18:46

❏ Week 31
❏ Monday — 1 Kings 19:1–21
❏ Tuesday — 1 Kings 20:1–43
❏ Wednesday — 1 Kings 21:1–22:53
❏ Thursday — 2 Kings 1:1–2:25
❏ Friday — 2 Kings 3:1–4:44
❏ Saturday — 2 Kings 5:1–27

❏ Week 32
❏ Monday — 2 Kings 6:1–7:20
❏ Tuesday — 2 Kings 8:1–29
❏ Wednesday — 2 Kings 9:1–10:36
❏ Thursday — 2 Kings 11:1–12:21
❏ Friday — 2 Kings 13:1–14:29
❏ Saturday — 2 Kings 15:1–16:20

❏ Week 33
❏ Monday — 2 Kings 17:1–41
❏ Tuesday — 2 Kings 18:1–19:37
❏ Wednesday — 2 Kings 20:1–21

❏ Thursday	2 Kings 21:1–26
❏ Friday	2 Kings 22:1–23:37
❏ Saturday	2 Kings 24:1–25:30

❏ Week 34

❏ Monday	1 Chronicles 1:1–4:43
❏ Tuesday	1 Chronicles 5:1–8:40
❏ Wednesday	1 Chronicles 9:1–12:40
❏ Thursday	1 Chronicles 13:1–14:17
❏ Friday	1 Chronicles 15:1–16:43
❏ Saturday	1 Chronicles 17:1–27

❏ Week 35

❏ Monday	1 Chronicles 18:1–20:8
❏ Tuesday	1 Chronicles 21:1–30
❏ Wednesday	1 Chronicles 22:1–19
❏ Thursday	1 Chronicles 23:1–27:34
❏ Friday	1 Chronicles 28:1–21
❏ Saturday	1 Chronicles 29:1–30

❏ Week 36

❏ Monday	2 Chronicles 1:1–2:18
❏ Tuesday	2 Chronicles 3:1–5:14
❏ Wednesday	2 Chronicles 6:1–7:22
❏ Thursday	2 Chronicles 8:1–9:31
❏ Friday	2 Chronicles 10:1–11:23
❏ Saturday	2 Chronicles 12:1–16

❏ Week 37

❏ Monday	2 Chronicles 13:1–14:15
❏ Tuesday	2 Chronicles 15:1–16:14
❏ Wednesday	2 Chronicles 17:1–18:34
❏ Thursday	2 Chronicles 19:1–20:37
❏ Friday	2 Chronicles 21:1–22:12

❏ Saturday	2 Chronicles 23:1–24:27

❏ Week 38

❏ Monday	2 Chronicles 25:1–26:23
❏ Tuesday	2 Chronicles 27:1–28:27
❏ Wednesday	2 Chronicles 29:1–36
❏ Thursday	2 Chronicles 30:1–31:21
❏ Friday	2 Chronicles 32:1–33
❏ Saturday	2 Chronicles 33:1–25

❏ Week 39

❏ Monday	2 Chronicles 34:1–35:27
❏ Tuesday	2 Chronicles 36:1–23
❏ Wednesday	Ezra 1:1–2:70
❏ Thursday	Ezra 3:1–4:24
❏ Friday	Ezra 5:1–6:22
❏ Saturday	Ezra 7:1–8:36

❏ Week 40

❏ Monday	Ezra 9:1–10:44
❏ Tuesday	Nehemiah 1:1–11
❏ Wednesday	Nehemiah 2:1–3:32
❏ Thursday	Nehemiah 4:1–6:19
❏ Friday	Nehemiah 7:1–8:18
❏ Saturday	Nehemiah 9:1–10:39

❏ Week 41

❏ Monday	Nehemiah 11:1–13:31
❏ Tuesday	Esther 1:1–2:23
❏ Wednesday	Esther 3:1–4:17
❏ Thursday	Esther 5:1–7:10
❏ Friday	Esther 8:1–10:3
❏ Saturday	Job 1:1–22

❏ Week 42

❏ Monday   Job 2:1–3:26
❏ Tuesday   Job 4:1–5:27
❏ Wednesday   Job 6:1–7:21
❏ Thursday   Job 8:1–10:22
❏ Friday   Job 11:1–12:25
❏ Saturday   Job 13:1–14:22

❏ Week 43

❏ Monday   Job 15:1–17:16
❏ Tuesday   Job 18:1–19:29
❏ Wednesday   Job 20:1–21:34
❏ Thursday   Job 22:1–24:25
❏ Friday   Job 25:1–28:28
❏ Saturday   Job 29:1–31:40

❏ Week 44

❏ Monday   Job 32:1–34:37
❏ Tuesday   Job 35:1–37:24
❏ Wednesday   Job 38:1–41:34
❏ Thursday   Job 42:1–17
❏ Friday   Psalms 1:1–6:10
❏ Saturday   Psalms 7:1–11:7

❏ Week 45

❏ Monday   Psalms 12:1–17:15
❏ Tuesday   Psalms 18:1–22:31
❏ Wednesday   Psalms 23:1–28:9
❏ Thursday   Psalms 29:1–34:22
❏ Friday   Psalms 35:1–41:13
❏ Saturday   Psalms 42:1–47:9

❏ Week 46

❏ Monday   Psalms 48:1–53:6

❏ Tuesday   Psalms 54:1–60:12
❏ Wednesday   Psalms 61:1–66:20
❏ Thursday   Psalms 67:1–72:20
❏ Friday   Psalms 73:1–77:20
❏ Saturday   Psalms 78:1–82:8

❏ Week 47

❏ Monday   Psalms 83:1–89:52
❏ Tuesday   Psalms 90:1–95:11
❏ Wednesday   Psalms 96:1–101:8
❏ Thursday   Psalms 102:1–106:48
❏ Friday   Psalms 107:1–113:9
❏ Saturday   Psalms 114:1–118:29

❏ Week 48

❏ Monday   Psalm 119:1–176
❏ Tuesday   Psalms 120:1–125:5
❏ Wednesday   Psalms 126:1–134:3
❏ Thursday   Psalms 135:1–137:9
❏ Friday   Psalms 138:1–143:12
❏ Saturday   Psalm 144:1–150:6

❏ Week 49

❏ Monday   Proverbs 1:1–3:35
❏ Tuesday   Proverbs 4:1–27
❏ Wednesday   Proverbs 5:1–6:35
❏ Thursday   Proverbs 7:1–27
❏ Friday   Proverbs 8:1–36
❏ Saturday   Proverbs 9:1–18

❏ Week 50

❏ Monday   Proverbs 10:1–11:31
❏ Tuesday   Proverbs 12:1–13:25
❏ Wednesday   Proverbs 14:1–15:33

❏ Thursday   Proverbs 16:1–17:28
❏ Friday   Proverbs 18:1–19:29
❏ Saturday   Proverbs 20:1–21:31

❏ Week 51

❏ Monday   Proverbs 22:1–23:35
❏ Tuesday   Proverbs 24:1–25:28
❏ Wednesday   Proverbs 26:1–27:27
❏ Thursday   Proverbs 28:1–29:27
❏ Friday   Proverbs 30:1–31:31
❏ Saturday   Ecclesiastes 1:1–2:26

❏ Week 52

❏ Monday   Ecclesiastes 3:1–4:16
❏ Tuesday   Ecclesiastes 5:1–6:12
❏ Wednesday   Ecclesiastes 7:1–8:17
❏ Thursday   Ecclesiastes 9:1–10:20
❏ Friday   Ecclesiastes 11:1–12:14
❏ Saturday   Song of Songs 1:1–3:11

❏ Week 53

❏ Monday   Song of Songs 4:1–6:13
❏ Tuesday   Song of Songs 7:1–8:14
❏ Wednesday   Isaiah 1:1–2:22
❏ Thursday   Isaiah 3:1–4:6
❏ Friday   Isaiah 5:1–30
❏ Saturday   Isaiah 6:1–13

❏ Week 54

❏ Monday   Isaiah 7:1–8:22
❏ Tuesday   Isaiah 9:1–10:34
❏ Wednesday   Isaiah 11:1–12:6
❏ Thursday   Isaiah 13:1–20:6
❏ Friday   Isaiah 21:1–23:18

❏ Saturday   Isaiah 24:1–25:12

❏ Week 55

❏ Monday   Isaiah 26:1–27:13
❏ Tuesday   Isaiah 28:1–29:24
❏ Wednesday   Isaiah 30:1–31:9
❏ Thursday   Isaiah 32:1–20
❏ Friday   Isaiah 33:1–35:10
❏ Saturday   Isaiah 36:1–39:8

❏ Week 56

❏ Monday   Isaiah 40:1–41:29
❏ Tuesday   Isaiah 42:1–43:28
❏ Wednesday   Isaiah 44:1–45:25
❏ Thursday   Isaiah 46:1–47:15
❏ Friday   Isaiah 48:1–49:26
❏ Saturday   Isaiah 50:1–52:15

❏ Week 57

❏ Monday   Isaiah 53:1–12
❏ Tuesday   Isaiah 54:1–57:21
❏ Wednesday   Isaiah 58:1–59:21
❏ Thursday   Isaiah 60:1–62:12
❏ Friday   Isaiah 63:1–66:24
❏ Saturday   Jeremiah 1:1–2:37

❏ Week 58

❏ Monday   Jeremiah 3:1–4:31
❏ Tuesday   Jeremiah 5:1–6:30
❏ Wednesday   Jeremiah 7:1–8:22
❏ Thursday   Jeremiah 9:1–10:25
❏ Friday   Jeremiah 11:1–12:17
❏ Saturday   Jeremiah 13:1–14:22

❏ Week 59

❏ Monday   Jeremiah 15:1–17:27
❏ Tuesday   Jeremiah 18:1–19:15
❏ Wednesday   Jeremiah 20:1–22:30
❏ Thursday   Jeremiah 23:1–40
❏ Friday   Jeremiah 24:1–25:38
❏ Saturday   Jeremiah 26:1–28:17

❏ Week 60

❏ Monday   Jeremiah 29:1–32
❏ Tuesday   Jeremiah 30:1–32:44
❏ Wednesday   Jeremiah 33:1–26
❏ Thursday   Jeremiah 34:1–35:19
❏ Friday   Jeremiah 36:1–37:21
❏ Saturday   Jeremiah 38:1–40:16

❏ Week 61

❏ Monday   Jeremiah 41:1–43:13
❏ Tuesday   Jeremiah 44:1–45:5
❏ Wednesday   Jeremiah 46:1–49:39
❏ Thursday   Jeremiah 50:1–51:64
❏ Friday   Jeremiah 52:1–34
❏ Saturday   Lamentations 1:1–22

❏ Week 62

❏ Monday   Lamentations 2:1–3:66
❏ Tuesday   Lamentations 4:1–5:22
❏ Wednesday   Ezekiel 1:1–2:10
❏ Thursday   Ezekiel 3:1–5:17
❏ Friday   Ezekiel 6:1–7:27
❏ Saturday   Ezekiel 8:1–9:11

❏ Week 63

❏ Monday   Ezekiel 10:1–11:25

❏ Tuesday   Ezekiel 12:1–13:23
❏ Wednesday   Ezekiel 14:1–15:8
❏ Thursday   Ezekiel 16:1–17:24
❏ Friday   Ezekiel 18:1–19:14
❏ Saturday   Ezekiel 20:1–21:32

❏ Week 64

❏ Monday   Ezekiel 22:1–23:49
❏ Tuesday   Ezekiel 24:1–27
❏ Wednesday   Ezekiel 25:1–27:36
❏ Thursday   Ezekiel 28:1–26
❏ Friday   Ezekiel 29:1–32:32
❏ Saturday   Ezekiel 33:1–34:31

❏ Week 65

❏ Monday   Ezekiel 35:1–36:38
❏ Tuesday   Ezekiel 37:1–39:29
❏ Wednesday   Ezekiel 40:1–42:20
❏ Thursday   Ezekiel 43:1–27
❏ Friday   Ezekiel 44:1–31
❏ Saturday   Ezekiel 45:1–46:24

❏ Week 66

❏ Monday   Ezekiel 47:1–48:35
❏ Tuesday   Daniel 1:1–21
❏ Wednesday   Daniel 2:1–49
❏ Thursday   Daniel 3:1–4:37
❏ Friday   Daniel 5:1–31
❏ Saturday   Daniel 6:1–28

❏ Week 67

❏ Monday   Daniel 7:1–8:27
❏ Tuesday   Daniel 9:1–27
❏ Wednesday   Daniel 10:1–12:13

❏ Thursday	Hosea 1:1–2:23
❏ Friday	Hosea 3:1–4:19
❏ Saturday	Hosea 5:1–6:11

❏ Week 68

❏ Monday	Hosea 7:1–8:14
❏ Tuesday	Hosea 9:1–10:15
❏ Wednesday	Hosea 11:1–12:14
❏ Thursday	Hosea 13:1–16
❏ Friday	Hosea 14:1–9
❏ Saturday	Joel 1:1–20

❏ Week 69

❏ Monday	Joel 2:1–32
❏ Tuesday	Joel 3:1–21
❏ Wednesday	Amos 1:1–2:16
❏ Thursday	Amos 3:1–15
❏ Friday	Amos 4:1–5:27
❏ Saturday	Amos 6:1–14

❏ Week 70

❏ Monday	Amos 7:1–17
❏ Tuesday	Amos 8:1–14
❏ Wednesday	Amos 9:1–15
❏ Thursday	Obadiah 1–21
❏ Friday	Jonah 1:1–2:10
❏ Saturday	Jonah 3:1–4:11

❏ Week 71

❏ Monday	Micah 1:1–2:13
❏ Tuesday	Micah 3:1–4:13
❏ Wednesday	Micah 5:1–15
❏ Thursday	Micah 6:1–16
❏ Friday	Micah 7:1–20

❏ Saturday	Nahum 1:1–3:19

❏ Week 72

❏ Monday	Habakkuk 1:1–2:20
❏ Tuesday	Habakkuk 3:1–19
❏ Wednesday	Zephaniah 1:1–2:15
❏ Thursday	Zephaniah 3:1–20
❏ Friday	Haggai 1:1–2:23
❏ Saturday	Zechariah 1:1–2:13

❏ Week 73

❏ Monday	Zechariah 3:1–10
❏ Tuesday	Zechariah 4:1–14
❏ Wednesday	Zechariah 5:1–11
❏ Thursday	Zechariah 6:1–15
❏ Friday	Zechariah 7:1–14
❏ Saturday	Zechariah 8:1–23

❏ Week 74

❏ Monday	Zechariah 9:1–10:12
❏ Tuesday	Zechariah 11:1–12:14
❏ Wednesday	Zechariah 13:1–9
❏ Thursday	Zechariah 14:1–21
❏ Friday	Malachi 1:1–2:17
❏ Saturday	Malachi 3:1–4:6

❏ Week 75

❏ Monday	Matthew 1:1–2:23
❏ Tuesday	Matthew 3:1–4:25
❏ Wednesday	Matthew 5:1–7:29
❏ Thursday	Matthew 8:1–9:38
❏ Friday	Matthew 10:1–11:30
❏ Saturday	Matthew 12:1–13:58

❏ Week 76

❏ Monday   Matthew 14:1–15:39
❏ Tuesday   Matthew 16:1–17:27
❏ Wednesday   Matthew 18:1–19:30
❏ Thursday   Matthew 20:1–21:46
❏ Friday   Matthew 22:1–23:39
❏ Saturday   Matthew 24:1–25:46

❏ Week 77

❏ Monday   Matthew 26:1–27:66
❏ Tuesday   Matthew 28:1–20
❏ Wednesday   Mark 1:1–2:28
❏ Thursday   Mark 3:1–4:41
❏ Friday   Mark 5:1–6:56
❏ Saturday   Mark 7:1–8:38

❏ Week 78

❏ Monday   Mark 9:1–50
❏ Tuesday   Mark 10:1–52
❏ Wednesday   Mark 11:1–33
❏ Thursday   Mark 12:1–13:37
❏ Friday   Mark 14:1–72
❏ Saturday   Mark 15:1–47

❏ Week 79

❏ Monday   Mark 16:1–20
❏ Tuesday   Luke 1:1–80
❏ Wednesday   Luke 2:1–3:38
❏ Thursday   Luke 4:1–5:39
❏ Friday   Luke 6:1–49
❏ Saturday   Luke 7:1–8:56

❏ Week 80

❏ Monday   Luke 9:1–62

❏ Tuesday   Luke 10:1–42
❏ Wednesday   Luke 11:1–12:59
❏ Thursday   Luke 13:1–35
❏ Friday   Luke 14:1–35
❏ Saturday   Luke 15:1–16:31

❏ Week 81

❏ Monday   Luke 17:1–18:43
❏ Tuesday   Luke 19:1–20:47
❏ Wednesday   Luke 21:1–22:71
❏ Thursday   Luke 23:1–24:53
❏ Friday   John 1:1–2:25
❏ Saturday   John 3:1–36

❏ Week 82

❏ Monday   John 4:1–54
❏ Tuesday   John 5:1–6:71
❏ Wednesday   John 7:1–8:59
❏ Thursday   John 9:1–10:42
❏ Friday   John 11:1–12:50
❏ Saturday   John 13:1–14:31

❏ Week 83

❏ Monday   John 15:1–16:33
❏ Tuesday   John 17:1–26
❏ Wednesday   John 18:1–19:42
❏ Thursday   John 20:1–21:25
❏ Friday   Acts 1:1–26
❏ Saturday   Acts 2:1–47

❏ Week 84

❏ Monday   Acts 3:1–4:37
❏ Tuesday   Acts 5:1-42
❏ Wednesday   Acts 6:1–8:40

❏ Thursday   Acts 9:1–43
❏ Friday   Acts 10:1–11:30
❏ Saturday   Acts 12:1–25

❏ Week 85

❏ Monday   Acts 13:1–14:28
❏ Tuesday   Acts 15:1–35
❏ Wednesday   Acts 15:36–16:40
❏ Thursday   Acts 17:1–18:22
❏ Friday   Acts 18:23–21:16
❏ Saturday   Acts 21:17–23:35

❏ Week 86

❏ Monday   Acts 24:1–26:32
❏ Tuesday   Acts 27:1–28:31
❏ Wednesday   Romans 1:1–2:29
❏ Thursday   Romans 3:1–4:25
❏ Friday   Romans 5:1–21
❏ Saturday   Romans 6:1–23

❏ Week 87

❏ Monday   Romans 7:1–25
❏ Tuesday   Romans 8:1–39
❏ Wednesday   Romans 9:1–11:36
❏ Thursday   Romans 12:1–21
❏ Friday   Romans 13:1–14:23
❏ Saturday   Romans 15:1–16:27

❏ Week 88

❏ Monday   1 Corinthians 1:1–2:16
❏ Tuesday   1 Corinthians 3:1–4:21
❏ Wednesday   1 Corinthians 5:1–6:20
❏ Thursday   1 Corinthians 7:1–40
❏ Friday   1 Corinthians 8:1–9:27

❏ Saturday   1 Corinthians 10:1–33

❏ Week 89

❏ Monday   1 Corinthians 11:1–12:31
❏ Tuesday   1 Corinthians 13:1–14:40
❏ Wednesday   1 Corinthians 15:1–58
❏ Thursday   1 Corinthians 16:1–24
❏ Friday   2 Corinthians 1:1–2:17
❏ Saturday   2 Corinthians 3:1–4:18

❏ Week 90

❏ Monday   2 Corinthians 5:1–21
❏ Tuesday   2 Corinthians 6:1–7:16
❏ Wednesday   2 Corinthians 8:1–9:15
❏ Thursday   2 Corinthians 10:1–11:33
❏ Friday   2 Corinthians 12:1–13:14
❏ Saturday   Galatians 1:1–2:21

❏ Week 91

❏ Monday   Galatians 3:1–29
❏ Tuesday   Galatians 4:1–31
❏ Wednesday   Galatians 5:1–6:18
❏ Thursday   Ephesians 1:1–23
❏ Friday   Ephesians 2:1–22
❏ Saturday   Ephesians 3:1–21

❏ Week 92

❏ Monday   Ephesians 4:1–32
❏ Tuesday   Ephesians 5:1–6:24
❏ Wednesday   Philippians 1:1–30
❏ Thursday   Philippians 2:1–30
❏ Friday   Philippians 3:1–21
❏ Saturday   Philippians 4:1–23

❏ Week 93
❏ Monday   Colossians 1:1–29
❏ Tuesday   Colossians 2:1–23
❏ Wednesday   Colossians 3:1–4:18
❏ Thursday   1 Thessalonians 1:1–10
❏ Friday   1 Thessalonians 2:1–20
❏ Saturday   1 Thessalonians 3:1–13

❏ Week 94
❏ Monday   1 Thessalonians 4:1–18
❏ Tuesday   1 Thessalonians 5:1–28
❏ Wednesday   2 Thessalonians 1:1–12
❏ Thursday   2 Thessalonians 2:1–3:18
❏ Friday   1 Timothy 1:1–20
❏ Saturday   1 Timothy 2:1–15

❏ Week 95
❏ Monday   1 Timothy 3:1–16
❏ Tuesday   1 Timothy 4:1–16
❏ Wednesday   1 Timothy 5:1–25
❏ Thursday   1 Timothy 6:1–21
❏ Friday   2 Timothy 1:1–18
❏ Saturday   2 Timothy 2:1–26

❏ Week 96
❏ Monday   2 Timothy 3:1–4:22
❏ Tuesday   Titus 1:1–16
❏ Wednesday   Titus 2:1–15
❏ Thursday   Titus 3:1–15
❏ Friday   Philemon 1–25
❏ Saturday   Hebrews 1:1–14

❏ Week 97
❏ Monday   Hebrews 2:1–18
❏ Tuesday   Hebrews 3:1–19
❏ Wednesday   Hebrews 4:1–16
❏ Thursday   Hebrews 5:1–14
❏ Friday   Hebrews 6:1–20
❏ Saturday   Hebrews 7:1–28

❏ Week 98
❏ Monday   Hebrews 8:1–13
❏ Tuesday   Hebrews 9:1–28
❏ Wednesday   Hebrews 10:1–18
❏ Thursday   Hebrews 10:19–39
❏ Friday   Hebrews 11:1–40
❏ Saturday   Hebrews 12:1–29

❏ Week 99
❏ Monday   Hebrews 13:1–25
❏ Tuesday   James 1:1–27
❏ Wednesday   James 2:1–26
❏ Thursday   James 3:1–18
❏ Friday   James 4:1–17
❏ Saturday   James 5:1–20

❏ Week 100
❏ Monday   1 Peter 1:1–25
❏ Tuesday   1 Peter 2:1–25
❏ Wednesday   1 Peter 3:1–4:19
❏ Thursday   1 Peter 5:1–14
❏ Friday   2 Peter 1:1–2:22
❏ Saturday   2 Peter 3:1–18

❏ Week 101
❏ Monday   1 John 1:1–10
❏ Tuesday   1 John 2:1–29
❏ Wednesday   1 John 3:1–24

❑ Thursday   1 John 4:1–21
❑ Friday   1 John 5:1–21
❑ Saturday   2 John 1–13

❑ **Week 102**
❑ Monday   3 John 1–14
❑ Tuesday   Jude 1–25
❑ Wednesday   Revelation 1:1–20
❑ Thursday   Revelation 2:1–29
❑ Friday   Revelation 3:1–22
❑ Saturday   Revelation 4:1–5:14

❑ **Week 103**
❑ Monday   Revelation 6:1–8:5
❑ Tuesday   Revelation 8:6–9:21
❑ Wednesday   Revelation 10:1–11
❑ Thursday   Revelation 11:1–19
❑ Friday   Revelation 12:1–17
❑ Saturday   Revelation 13:1–18

❑ **Week 104**
❑ Monday   Revelation 14:1–20
❑ Tuesday   Revelation 15:1–8
❑ Wednesday   Revelation 16:1–21
❑ Thursday   Revelation 17:1–18:8
❑ Friday   Revelation 18:9–24
❑ Saturday   Revelation 19:1–21

❑ **Week 105**
❑ Monday   Revelation 20:1–15
❑ Tuesday   Revelation 21:1–27
❑ Wednesday   Revelation 22:1–21